A Miracle of Love

By R. L. Condran

Acknowledgements

This book is dedicated to my "Dad" for whom showed me that in order to love completely, sometimes you need to forgive those that mean the most to you even before they've known you've done it. It is up to them to forgive themselves for what they have done to you.

To my family and friends for their patience and understanding during my struggle and illness.

To my loving wife who allowed me the time to grow and complete this work. For being there when I needed her the most. I am eternally grateful for your love, understanding and companionship. You always said, "Go big or go home."

But mostly to God almighty, through whom all things are possible.

GOD SPEED YOUR LOVE TO ME.

First Printing June 2013

ISBN-13: 978-0615835549 (R. L.\Condran)

ISBN-10: 0615835546

"When the power of love overcomes the love of power, the world will know peace."

Jimi Hendrix

"The most beautiful thing we can experience is the mysterious. It is the source of all true art and all science. He to whom this emotion is a stranger, who can no longer pause to wonder and stand rapt in awe, is as good as dead: his eyes are closed."

Albert Einstein

"It matters not what road we take but rather what we become on the journey."

Daughter's fortune cookie

<u>Preface</u>

This is a love story unlike any you have ever seen or heard before or will again. It is not your typical can't go on without you story but one that goes as deep into the heart and soul of an individual as anyone could go. There is love and then there is true undeniable love. A love that looks past the flaws in each and every one of us and reaches for the good that remains. It is about the ultimate sacrifice to love and the measures a man might take to see that his life and love go on. It is through our legacy that we are not forgotten in time and by our life's accomplishments that all people remember what we gave of ourselves to better those around us and humankind. If this story doesn't grab your heart and make you feel like pumping a fist in the air as a salute to his unselfish sacrifice, then you need to examine the type of human you yourself are. Grab some tissues.

It will take you through several periods, past, present and future and some is true while some could be a fantasy…. or is it. That is up to the reader to decide because that is what life is really all about, making decisions. There's always another choice we could have made or might possibly be forced to make. It all begins with the moment we are conceived because even an unborn child can make a mark in your life. Sometimes it's deeper than a person shows on the outside but it eventually will show. All too often an unwanted child is aborted and along with it the secrets it held perhaps lost for all time. Maybe that secret is so important to human existence that it returns in another generation?

The beginning builds on the main character and reflects on his views, beliefs and qualities. Other people along his journey influence his decision making abilities and at times return later to help in his quest. It truly is a small world and we are all intertwined in some small way that makes the big picture or puzzle if you prefer looking at it that way. Inside each of us lies a task prewritten before our existence that will change another, alter an outcome or hinder someone from making the better choice. This is God's master plan and this is my view. Somebody else will view it differently and they have every human right to *choose to do so. It is essentially the dividing line between good and evil. Some try to ride the fence and you can only get hurt when you fall that way.*

The middle is how his choices, as hard as they were, helped to preserve and create an incredible human adventure along with his legacy and love. How a deadly secret <u>needed</u> to be kept a secret until the time was right to share with the whole world. The burden he felt every day knowing what was ahead and no way to tell about it until the end was unbearable at times but he pushed through. The trust he had to accept even though it was not his usual self. "Trust is earned and never just given unless you believe that person or persons has the same agenda, beliefs and desire for the end result." was his life's philosophy. It can be like playing Russian roulette with other people's lives instead of just your own if you make the wrong choice. When the correct decision is made a whole new world can open right before your eyes. And then there is the divine intervention of a miracle only God himself could have created.

The ending is inventive, magical, mind searching for truth and the cost for it. Ride along as everyone involved prepares for a journey not expected but unavoidably needed to survive. And just when you think it has ended, one last final monumental moment will leave you speechless, breathless and crying a good tear. Not all good guys finish last, but the best man does always win.

Enjoy reading. I know I enjoyed writing it.

The Beginning: Awakening

Everyone at one point in their lives wants to do something that everyone will remember for all times. It's human nature to be accepted socially and hopefully never forgotten in time. I had always had a profound belief that I too would someday have my moment in time and had often vocally expressed my desire to do something that could help impact man's existence in the universe. Without belief in ourselves our dreams would never stand a chance to come true. It took a great many years for me to believe and that's when the memories began. I never imagined or wished for what came after……

Have you ever had a dream so intense that it seemed real the moment you awoke but your mind knew that wasn't possible because it was still in that state of sleep confusion we experience when we first open our eyes? But what if an outside force coerced that mental mind state? Even implanted information it wanted you to have and recall later? Deja vu anyone? Your mind remembers an event that hadn't happened until your body passes back through that time window and you can visualize almost precise pieces of that moment without explanation? Now take it one step farther where another entity implants that image because they want your mind to work their doing at their desired time. To believe our species is alone in the vast universe and no other life could exist because God only created us is to say his power is limited. He does have the ability to create more and man has the power to subdue those beliefs if they so wish. It is what government has become but wasn't designed to do. Man's greed for power and the Devil's desire to destroy God's creation has brought mankind to a brink of human destruction. That is unless someone was empowered to do the unthinkable: End all governments and unite man as one. It would take nothing short of a miracle or vision of a potential idea that would free man from all wars. From gathering to destroy, to joining to build.

That was my dream when I was 12 in my parent's backyard camping out with my best friend, Hans, World peace for everyone. We were just lying on our backs looking up at the stars. It was 1975, war in Vietnam was ending and our local Army National Guard base was bringing in Vietnamese refugees. OPEC was still raising oil prices or as Dad would say," squeezing our butts dry." Unemployment was over 9% and Jimmy Hoffa was nowhere to be found. Gas prices were crippling at $.44 a gallon and Israel had survived another war. Why all the fighting and no one working towards World Peace? I remember looking at him and saying "I wish I had the power to stop all wars." His response was typical but absurdly accurate, "You're crazy! They'd try to stop you because war is money." At that moment a light appeared from over the second hill but neither of us had seen it crest the first. It was intensely bright and filled the whole lower valley area. After that we woke up the next morning, outside the tent we were in the night before. I vaguely recall my father yelling at us to get back inside the house. As I arose and kicked Hans in the leg I felt a strange lump from behind my right ear. Later in life he told me he too had that same strange lump but never told me he had also secretly made a wish.

We had both met in band, he played a great trombone and I was fairly good at my tuba. His wish was to be a famous trombone player one day. His wish came true soon after college and he still plays to this day for a big name Symphony. Little did either of us know back then, that our paths would meet again but in a much BIGGER way.

Chapter 1

In our early development years we are influenced by those around us the most, whether it is our parents, grand-parents and friends or neighbors, someone has done something we will always remember. I can think back to influential people like my band leader, pastor and our neighboring farmer who always seemed to be out in his fields working. Dad would say "that's a hardworking man like me so remember son to always work hard at whatever you do. A man will reap what he sows." Schoolwork was not one of those things I liked to do so my grades were not the best I could've done. I also lacked parents that were less than understanding and nonjudgmental so I was given every excuse under the sun for anything I asked. I recall one night asking them if I could have a girlfriend. To my dismay my mother's reply back was I didn't have any chest hairs, NO! Really? Chest hairs were a prerequisite for having a girlfriend? I was sunk by that thought because there was a girl who I really liked and had hoped to take to the school dance that week. We all know that is not a true statement because if it were, no Pro wrestler would have a girlfriend. I later realized this was a lie she whipped up to avoid answering a delicate question. She avoided an even bigger lie by not telling me for well over 40 years but that comes later in the story. I did have a few nice girls during the later years of High School and each taught me a new lesson about the female species. My last before graduating was most certainly my first love or so I thought. She made me feel good about whom I was and my parents even liked her! That relationship lasted the school year as I readied for life after high school. My grades just weren't high enough for the schools I had hoped to attend. That was the summer of nineteen eighty-one when life was simple.

So that led me on another path, instead of chef school, my hope at that time, it was into the U.S. Army. The recruiter was so good at convincing a young man like me to enlist, travel the world and yes I could become a chef while serving my country. Not all lies just stretching the truth a lot. Still it was an awesome learning experience where a majority of my character was molded into the man I'd become. Service teaches you to watch your comrades back, discipline, integrity and honesty along with much more. It's those bonds that never break over time and can help you later when you need it the most. If you're a good person, people never forget you but if you're bad to the bone, they'll wish they had never met you.

Basic training was both hard and fun. If you've ever been through it you know what I mean. Not only do you build body muscle, you build mind strength. It's not all KP duty washing pots and pans. A person can actually learn a lot about themselves during that time that they never knew before. How far you can be pushed to your limits, how mentally strong you can or can't be who your friends truly are and what kind of family backing you have. Family and friends may write just to make your day better hearing your name called out during mail call or it can be a lonely feeling when you get nothing at all. One of our roommates, who always seemed to be picked on, got nothing from anyone for the first 4 weeks. Hard not to feel someone's emptiness when they are in the same room as you, it brings out the human compassion if you are human at all. So I decided to ask the Drill Sergeant if there were a way I could include a letter that I'd write to Private "Jones", let's call him, and include it into the next mail call. He thought it was such a great idea and thoughtful of me that he made me the squad leader for the remaining weeks we were there. In his opinion it showed leadership qualities that reminded him of his Viet Nam days, which showed on his worn face. War will drain the life out of anyone it touches and doesn't care how it affects those around you. That first letter made heads turn when his name got called and raised his head up high with the grandest smile anyone can imagine. It was a contagious effect that in turn brought smiles to everyone. Even that old war hardened sergeant who had been spat on and ridiculed after returning from his third tour, to a war torn country he never wanted to go to, smiled. He patted me on the back later that day at chow and said, "as long as there are still good people like you, there's hope for mankind. Never lose that humanness and great things will happen for you." My earliest recall of someone telling me I could be great one day. That seemed to be a turning point for Private "Jones", whom later revealed to me he was about to give up and ask to go home. It takes strength and courage from deep within to admit to any one much less a stranger that you are at the edge of what you feel you can't take any more. It can also build your mental strength for what still lay ahead. A lot like building muscle mass only this type of strength is what you reach for when you've gone past that first breaking point and need a little extra push. The remainder of basic training became more like fun than a burden because we learned to adapt, overcome and help each other over the next big hurdle. After AIT and a brief visit home it was off to jump school where, wouldn't you know it, I met up with Private "Jones" again. This time he returned the favor and helped me.

Chapter 2

When you first arrive at jump school, you feel as though somebody made a mistake and sent you back to basics. Drill sergeants are always yelling and I could never figure how they didn't lose their voices. They actually seemed to get louder during the day if that was possible. If you happen to be unfortunate and make the top of their list, you will stay there, forever. Unless.... that's where "Jones" comes in.

I had developed a sort of cockiness from graduating and needed to be humbled down and I was at the right place for that. Almost immediately I became a target for their usage as how not to tick off the DS. Push-ups were a regular morning ritual but only helped my upper body. I was never in better shape than when I was coming out of basic training, jump school just helped chisel the toned physique some more. Week 5 was going along as usual when I hit a hole in the N.C. sand mounds and twisted the ankle bad. I had to be off of it for at least four days, doc's orders, before I could resume training. That put me in jeopardy with not making our official first jump. You miss that one and you're gone, no second chance. My buddy helped me by bringing my rigging to my bedside so I could practice folding my parachute in bed! He did this on his own time when he could have been sleeping or shining his shoes or a number of other miscellaneous items. He felt he owed me the same chance I had given him when he was ready to quit in basics. He wasn't going to let me fail or not have my chance. The day before the jump I was permitted to walk on the ankle if I could for a little while. It didn't feel bad but I knew it wasn't completely right. Your mind knows when your body's not jiving to the beat and lets you know with pain. First turn around and I could feel the tweak but held the pain from showing. I wanted my chance and nothing was taking it away from me, not even stubborn me. Yes, I can be stubborn as a mule at times especially if I feel I'm right about something. I felt I could leave this jump in my lord's hands and he'd watch over me. So the next morning we were up bright and early for a small breakfast then over to the airfield to load up. That's when the adrenaline pumps and briefly you forget your training. As I was getting in ahead of "Jones" I somehow missed the first step and came down hard on my already bad ankle. Carrying all the weight of the gear I wanted to support my step up with the good leg saving the bad one for the jump. Didn't quite work out the way I had planned but before I knew it I felt a pair of arms catching me and holding me up. My friend who wouldn't let me quit or fail had again been there to assist me in my time of need. The pain grew steady and more as the plane climbed to jump altitude. I had no idea how I was ever going to make this jump without completely breaking the ankle when I landed. There comes a point when even the strongest people need help and find the courage to say so. Or you can be tougher yet mentally and continue on to see where the road goes. You know the old expression "You made your bed now lay in it!" was my grandmother's favorite growing up in south central PA. Her words were ringing true that crisp morning as the call went out to harness up and prepare for the jump of a lifetime.

   Jumping off the jump tower was a piece of cake. You could see the ground below you and it wasn't far. As you walk towards the door of "a perfectly good airplane" as Dad would grumble, your senses begin to kick and the sounds amplify. You can feel along with the wind funneling in, each person's emotion in front of you electrifying the surroundings. As each step adds up, closing the distance between you and God's glory, your heart pounds faster. Then you're there and out the door beginning your descent through the heavens. As you gather yourself and begin to remember what you trained for and start instinctively doing each process memories appear like family and friends. Things you did as a child or dumber things as a young adult. You catch your thoughts and begin enjoying what is a marvelous view of our awesome world. Eyes pinpoint the landing area and then look around at what remains to be seen, the beauty of the land in its pristine state unharmed by man, unmolested for what may lie beneath. You double check your altitude, pull your chute too soon is as bad as pulling it too late. Descending to my right was "Jones" whom at this point even I was tired of calling him "Jones" so I asked him what his first name was. As the wind ruffled about us I thought I heard him say "JESUS!" which I wanted to clarify by saying, "WHAT!?" That's when I saw another jumper fly by us with his chute tangled around him. He had panicked and pulled too soon and the forces collapsed his chute around him and he was now in a death spiral. Before I could realize what I was now about to see, "Jones" nosedived straight for our falling comrade. Faster he went gathering speed trying desperately to catch the other jumper. With cat like reflexes he perfectly stopped his descent just before grabbing the helpless diver. He worked fast to release the bad chute then clamped himself onto the now unconscious private. Just in time of running out of altitude he pulled his chute as I was pulling mine above him. I silently said a prayer that they both would be ok and make it down to Jesus our Lord and savior. A good thing for "Jones" that not only was he in great condition but he was also a larger built man who could hold the weight of two. It must have seemed like forever to hit ground and roll but they made it. He had stepped up to the plate when it was his turn and delivered. I was almost to the ground when I saw him look up. With a thumbs up signal he said, "Jesus. My name is Jesus!" My landing was as soft as landing on a hill of cotton. My heart was pounding with emotions and adrenaline. That was a jump I'd remember all my life.

All those who saw what we termed "the miracle catch", gathered around to shake Jesus' hand, pat him on the back for his courage and bravery and share the feeling of the energy of that moment. I could only stop and think at that time what could have or would have happened had I not written that letter in basics that stopped Jesus from going home. We all know what MIGHT have taken place but because of my decision it stopped that chain of events. Private Jesus "Jones" was awarded at our graduating ceremonies special recognition for his acts that morning and I felt great just knowing I had a little to do with it.

A person doesn't always need to complete the whole task at hand to feel they were a part of the end result. Sometimes it's the unknown or unnoticed small parts that are more important.

Chapter 3

When you begin building character you also begin to develop confidence. So with the completion of jump school and basics I, to say the least, was feeling very good about who I was becoming. It wasn't the cockiness like at the start of jump school but a humble confidence. One that your body language says there's a man who is sure of himself, rather than my crap doesn't stink. This is the type of man who can lead by example or be led by design. God does work in mysterious ways and like a master artist or sculptor he will continuously mold you until you are the master piece he had planned. This can be a repeat process taking many, many years to perfect but after it's completed, like any great priceless gem IT will make multitudes stand and look in awe.

Heading to a foreign country is exhilarating and scary because you're not sure what it will bring but thrilled to be somewhere new. My first destination in early February 1982 was Berlin, Germany. Former centerpiece of Hitler's war machine, a capitol he'd later die in by Russian hands. It had been rebuilt since the end of WWII so I only saw pictures in museums of its devastation and the faces that were captured in time by the photographers. The look of uncertainty on each person was a horrible yet genuine look at what war leaves. From war <u>can</u> come good things but more is lost than gained and the people are the ones to suffer. A warlord still eats his daily meals with plenty to throw away but the child on the street searching for scraps to help feed his family may find nothing but gloom. That empty belly doesn't forget the pain deep inside from hunger and looks for divine help in that time of need. The man whose belly is stuffed never stops to thank anyone for his good fortune but the divine one never forgets this and takes note for future reference. War is only worthy if it means survival against annihilation. Ask any Jewish family how many of their ancestors perished in that Great War and often you'll get a tear of sorrow from remembrance before you see the changeover to a face that states "never again!" When you are faced with your own choice of destroy or be destroyed, what will you do? Can there be a THIRD option?

Stepping out of the plane you begin to relive what it might have been like during the Berlin blockade that started June 24, 1948 and went almost a full year. The massive numbers of planes that came in and out, the smells associated with refueling, the goods being unloaded and stored took an incredible amount of man power and supervision to maintain. The size of the airfield was enormous which every inch was needed to perform the task at hand. When our leaders back then, put their mind to achieving a joint goal, that was the greatness of America and I now stood center stage where it all happened. The energy I was absorbing sent me back to that night in my parent's yard and again the thought surfaced. Could World Peace actually be achievable? I am NOW standing quite possibly where Hitler stood to order his Luftwaffe to attack and start WWII, a war with but one overall intention, the systematic destruction of a culture and its people. Now it felt like the opposite end of the spectrum was happening but I was still unaware of who or when or even how. Then that voice echoed, "they'll never let you do it because war is money."

Eventually I regained a sense of reality to where I was and why I was there. Lucky for me because I almost ran over my new squad leader, who was there to pick me up from the airport. I must have looked like I was in a daze from seeing the surroundings for the first time as he snapped his fingers, as if he were a magician and I was his audience member. My bewildered look and tilting head signaled I was awake and he had my full attention enough that he introduced himself and why he was there. "Are you PFC Conrad?" as if he couldn't tell from my name tag? "Yes Corporal I am." was my response back. "Great then, follow me so we can beat the traffic out of here." I saw no need to rush but he was the leader and I was now the follower so away we went. You would think he'd offer some sort of hand with my bags but never did. The weight wasn't too much for someone who had been through the physical training I had recently endured so I managed. I figure we walked close to a mile before arriving at the jeep and he never said a word. He never glanced back to see if I was still there, like he had eyes in the back of his head and could tell without looking. I must have surprised him when he eventually turned around and I was only two steps behind. Finally the silence was broken when he snickered, "If you follow that well you should make a great leader someday."

Another reference to my increasing leadership ability.

The trip through downtown was like being guided by a local tourist enthusiast but at least he was talking now. As we passed the rebuilt church, the Kaiser Wilhelm Memorial Church, the only building that wasn't totally destroyed in the massive air bombing of Berlin, a light shined through one of the magnificent stained glasses. Instead of that blinding light you experience from being directly plastered by an intense beam, it was a soothing, calming soft glow that appeared to be directed only at me. A sort of divine spotlight shall we say that made me feel at ease in this big city. Whenever I've felt terribly down in life, I've recalled that special moment and how it made me feel inside and everything just seems to get better.

The Corporal looked over to say something I presumed about another landmark, when he suddenly jerked the wheel as he realized he had been tranced by the image that shown on me. I hadn't even noticed it until he muttered one word, "cross" and pointed at my shirt. There within the radiant beam was a cross symbol that stood out. Had it had any real heat to it, I would've been branded like cattle on the Double D ranch. Immediately he stopped alongside the road to try and get a picture but as quickly as it was there it had left when the sun went behind the clouds. He asked what faith I was and expressed that he was Catholic and very proud of it. I had been raised a Christian of Protestant faith which I told him. How oddly curious this was because the church is of Protestant faith and he firmly believed it meant something and was going to call home to find out what he could from his local bishop who was great friends of his family. We waited for a short while and the sun returned but the cross never reappeared. A short moment in time caught only by our eyes but still undeniable that it happened. I never took it for anything more than that but he never gave up on his search for an explanation. It was something he just had to have an answer for, much like a child who continuously asks the same question until they are satisfied with an answer you hadn't given before.

We went past other historical landmarks like the Brandenburg Gate, the Reichstag and of course the Berlin Wall itself. Nothing seemed to compare to our time at the church but Berlin was still a beautiful city nonetheless. So much culture and history inside that city, that it's hard to believe an ugly part of humanity came from there. The angels must have rejoiced the moment it all stopped and the healing could begin.

Finally we made it to the barracks which at this point I was glad to see 'cause I needed a bathroom break and nap. I got my much earned break but the nap would wait, it was down to meet my new Mess Sergeant. Master Sergeant Brooks was a shorter than me stocky built gentleman from Louisiana, New Orleans area I thought I was once told, who had a smile that was like a cross between a grin and an I got my eyes on you expression. He had heard I was due to arrive and they needed someone to represent our mess facility in the "Cook of the Month" competition later that week. Yes, I was given less than a week to prepare and had always tried to do my best at anything I asserted myself into. This was not my choice to compete, it was my duty to my new company and all eyes would be on me to represent us well. And win!

So after getting settled in and a short nap I began my crash training on what would be required and expected at the competition. For three straight days I studied and studied more. They had my cook whites brand new and pressed, my shoes shined like mirrors and my appearance in tip top shape. I looked like a soldier straight out of basic training but had the seasoning of a veteran with confidence. I didn't let them down or myself and answered every question correctly and performed each task I was asked to do in a timely manner. I aced my first "Cook of the Month" and walked away with my head held high. That began a string of six straight months our mess hall won. At the end of the year they held a "Cook of the Year" event. I would miss it and being able to compete because we were on maneuvers. Later I unexpectedly received an invitation to partake in the award due to an Air Force Sergeant being transferred back to the U.S. and being the only monthly winner who scored a perfect score. I always thought my mess sergeant had a hand in it to because I couldn't compete while being on training maneuvers. He never denied or confirmed my suspicions but I always felt grateful. Here was a man that I never met before coming to Berlin but was confident enough to go to bat for me knowing I wouldn't let him down.

The reward was very special because we were given the opportunity to cook alongside some of the greatest chefs in Europe at the time. What we were taught in those four weeks was more than some learn in a lifetime. How to make exotic foreign dishes to roses on wedding cakes to breads of different cultures even how to make ice sculptures! If it was food related we seemed to touch base on it someway or somehow. This all happened months before I was due to go back state side for my next duty assignment which was going to be in the Washington, D.C. area. This was great knowledge to take back and I'd try to keep it fresh in my mind. I was psyched to be heading to our nation's capital area, a lot of chances to advance there, IF you play your cards right.

About three weeks before doing my out-processing a soldier, who was just transferred to our unit, came strolling through the chow line which I was working. We both stopped and looked long and deep at each other's face, like we knew the other but just couldn't explain how. Then the light went on in my head, it was the jumper from school who Jesus had caught. Apparently it still didn't register with him mostly because everything happened so fast that day for him. He really hadn't remembered me from the jump but did after being told the whole story behind why Jesus was there that day. Just because I hadn't been the one to catch him didn't mean I didn't play a role in it. He had hoped one day he could thank me in his gratifying way for the small thing I did that not many knew for without it happening he would not have survived. Amazing how one simple gesture can make a huge ripple that in return causes another huge ripple and so on. I told him who I was and where we met previously. Now his lights were on and the eyes teared up. Around the corner behind the line he came charging arms held wide like we were brothers who haven't seen the other for years. A gripping hug from such a small framed guy but as thankful as any I had ever been given before. No one near us said a word because they all were waiting for an explanation. By now I had achieved the rank of Specialist 4 equivalent to a corporal which was the rank of Corporal Cox, the guy who was now hugging me.

From around the other side came Master Sergeant Brooks and had only one word to say, "Aaah hmmmm?",like he was trying to clear his throat which broke Cox's hold on me. "I'm sure there's a good story to this Specialist Conrad. Right?!?" were the next words he spoke.

Before I could reply Corporal Cox broke the suspense of the moment and resoundly told the story of how "I saved his life." which no one had ever heard before this. Again it drew silent as everyone was waiting for me to justify the tale they had just heard. With a single, "Yaup." and nod of my head I confirmed what they had just been told. A story it was but a true story, the kind that you never forget, a round of pats on my back from my fellow warriors because we all get pumped up from acts of heroism even if it wasn't us who performed that act. It just gets the adrenaline running.

"I knew there was something special about you Conrad..." came from the deep voice of Sergeant Brooks. "...even after being told about your cross when you arrived here." he added.

"What cross?" asked Cox.

"He had the Cross from Kaiser Wilhelm Church shine on his chest when he was first touring Berlin a while ago. It was a big story too back then." was Brooks' reply.

Cox went completely white when he listened to Brooks. He too was a Catholic and his grandmother's best friend was a Jewish prisoner held in one of the darkest concentration camps in all of Europe, Auschwitz. Here was a devils workshop that sent well over a million lives to their demise all by a mad man from the city we now stood in. Her friend often spoke of how the faithful would pray and wish for their redeemer to come and rescue them from this hell hole. Finally the soldiers did come but they were not the one they had wished for. They still await the redeemer to right their wrong. Along with that wish came a story from a small child, a girl who watched her parents be taken away and never return or be seen again. She prayed and wished for one special person to come and rescue all of those worthy of being rescued and take them far away from the evil of this place. A wish can be powerful especially if it comes from an innocent child with purity of heart. God does hear all of our wishes but it is those that are of true heart he admires the most and graciously gives a chance. The girl child had a dream vision late that night and this is what she was told by the angel who visited her dream.

"A man will return to the city from which the wrong was ordered but will unknowingly be of another faith. A cross will appear upon him in an unusual way from the faith he now serves. He will be from the country that frees you and your other captives. He will look like he comes from this terrible country but is a descendant from yours. He will not know for many years his true identity until the lord so orders it to be acknowledged. He will undergo a spiritual awakening and discovery of himself after which he will be shown how to prepare the people for the End of Times. He will address all the nations of the world that their path leads to destruction unless they hear God's warning which he will bring. Their obscure vision will lead to a multitude of deaths like never seen before. The Pope will blame the events on his blasphemies of God and he will be sought out but not found. The righteous of the true church will protect him because they believe what they have heard because it is also written, but was never given to man. Man learns about the deceit but all too late. An enormous planet never seen in the heavens before will create many troubles for those on Earth. Unexplainable events, by top leaders in their fields of expertise, will cause hunger, pestilence and destruction. Finally only a few shall remain to inherit what remains of this planet and to rebuild according to God's laws not Man's. The man will lead all who remain into a peaceful time. He will be like no other man before because his blood comes from the sacred chalice. "

If you stop and tell a room full of people a story like this I bet you all jaws will drop and you'll hear total silence like we did that day. Out of nowhere came the voice of the Corporal who picked me up from the airport saying, "I'm NOT taking him back or anywhere!" which drew chuckles from around the room.
"I highly doubt I'm the one in the story." I offered back. "That doesn't sound anything like me."

"That's still not changing my mind. Have your new buddy take you. He doesn't seem fazed by the legend or you." laughed the corporal.

"I'd gladly do that for him if I'm allowed." Cox submitted.

"Let's not fight over our Messiah." added Sergeant Brooks, which he then called for us to all get back to work.

I told Cox where to meet me later so we could catch up on times and he joyfully agreed.

The base Canteen was an easy spot to find and we could get whatever we wanted to drink since I had no idea if he did drink at all, liquor that is. Shortly after 8pm I caught him walking in and looking around for me which I had already chosen a spot away from the speakers so we could hear each other speak. I waved him over just as the other corporal was standing to ask him something. It didn't appear to be a heated discussion but was definitely an intense one. They both walked over after a few minutes and sat down with me. The peculiar look on Cox's face was totally different than the one I had seen earlier or of that fateful day at jump school.

"Corporal Gabby here just told me another tale he was enlightened to by his Bishop from home. Seems the legend grows more interesting." started Cox. "He spoke with him shortly after you arrived here in Berlin and told him what happened at the church. He found it very amusing until a fellow bishop conveyed the original tale of the girl. Gabby never told anyone until he heard me speak of my grandmother's friend today. Seems we have something in common with our matching stories." He ended.

"I just told Cox what my Bishop knew and added a part he hadn't mentioned but also knew from the story. The angel told the girl the next German soldier to enter would bear the name of the Messiah she sought. The next morning a lean built young soldier entered to take her for her meal. On their way she asked him his name. He responded it was none of her business and to remain silent so she did and heard his name being shouted by his commandant. His name was..." just then a loud siren blasted. It was the base alert signal for all to report for duty. It usually meant the Soviets were moving a brigade of troops and we were brought to an alert readiness state, a cold war game of chess, to see who would flinch first. Almost as soon as we exited the canteen you could sense something was not right. There was smoke everywhere and overhead lights from helicopters circling the compound. Someone shouted out, "This is not an exercise or drill! We are under attack!" Within seconds the familiar sound of an RPG could be detected and then the flash of it hitting its mark. Not soon after another added to the confusion as it left its trail of smoke heading for its destination. I could see fellow soldiers hustling to their stations to gather equipment and ammo to return fire. Some made it just inside as the second blast scattered debris and bodies. Not hearing any new RPG's being sent I made my attempt to help those lying on the ground. A sense of being in someone's crosshairs sends chills down your spine and you act accordingly. That is unless someone has already begun their move to get you out of harm's way. I felt Gabby's body crashing into mine just as the bullets began to fly. Others had now joined us outside with their weapons in hand and began to repel the attackers. The helicopters were now able to target the enemy forces and fired a direct hit launching the vehicle high into the air. What remained of their small group quickly dropped their weapons and ran for the woods from where they came. A few distant rounds could be heard as pursuit commenced to apprehend the aggressors. After an "all clear" was given I turned to see just who had tackled me. My blood chilled as I looked back and saw Gabby now gurgling blood from his mouth as a result of a direct shot into his abdomen area. The hole was large and the exit hole even larger. He took a large caliber round that should've hit me but he sacrificed himself. Immediately after seeing how badly hit he was I yelled for a "MEDIC!!!" As I took my outer shirt off to cover his wound he tried to speak. I told him to save his strength but he insisted on trying to finish what he started to say inside the canteen. "Please have Cox finish telling you…" was all he could manage before he passed out. Medics rushed in and pushed me aside as I looked down at my hands now bloodied from a man who came to my aid. There was nothing I could do to repay him back but I vowed at that moment I would if ever a day came that I could.

"Are you OK Conrad?" came the voice of Cox his hand on my shoulder. I now took the time to look myself over and determine I was not hit. As I looked up to assure him I was, I saw he too had been hit in the upper chest area from the red blood stain seeping from his shirt. In all the excitement he never knew he had been shot. Another medic now saw what I was pointing at as Cox fell to the ground. They grabbed both wounded soldiers and headed indoors. Working with all the knowledge they had, they attempted to stop Gabby's blood loss and seal Cox's wound before an ambulance came. Somewhere along the way to the hospital they lost Gabby but not before he muttered one last word.

Chapter 4

"Hold on Gabby! Hold on buddy! Almost there!" shouted Cox. "Say that again what you told us. I need to confirm your story." Now only blocks away he was slipping fast but Gabby tried one last time.

"Adelstein." was all he could get out but was enough for Cox to hear. As they pulled into the Emergency Room area of the hospital Cox could feel himself beginning to fade. Somehow he had to relay the message back to me but couldn't find a secure way as he drifted off as they pulled him from the ambulance. Gabby was now gone as they removed his lifeless body next. His mission in life was complete. He had done what was asked of him and now had earned his right to eternal life. We never know when our time will end, it is what we accomplish in our time that matters the most.

Cox was going in and out of consciousness as he lost more blood and the doctors worked franticly on his wound. It was very close to a main artery which made it that much more difficult. One cut the wrong way and he'd bleed out there on the table. The other problem was finding blood that was usable because of his rare blood type. Also back in the early part of the eighties, AIDS was becoming a worldwide epidemic and still not completely understood. This made using blood more difficult for fear of it being contaminated. He needed blood badly but with no family member close by his options were running out. The call went out for anyone with B+ to donate if they weren't sick.

Back at the base we had begun to clean up after the assault. I had been taken to the base infirmary to be checked over due to all the blood on me. I had a few scratches which I figured were from being tackled to the ground. All I could do was keep looking at my hands and wondering how the guys were doing at the hospital. After getting the medic to release me finally, I headed for the mess hall to see Sergeant Brooks. He was on the phone talking in a hushed tone when I entered his office. I stood at attention which he waved off with a quick hand gesture and a single finger up suggesting to me to stand fast. A few nods and an occasional "yes sir" later and he was off the phone. His look was not satisfying as I could read the wrinkled forehead and its message.

"Corporal Gabby didn't make it. They lost him on the way there. Cox needs blood and they are looking for donors. You wouldn't have B+ blood by chance now would you?" inquired Brooks.

"Actually I am B+ Sergeant. Here are my dog tags to prove it." As I showed him them, the blood from Gabby could be seen in spots.

"Get yourself cleaned up fast and I'll get you over there ASAP! We need to move like ten minutes ago soldier!" commanded Brooks.

"Yes Sergeant!" I yelled as I turned to leave.

"Lord help him." I heard come from Brooks as I left. Then came "Lord help us all."

I could sense the urgency so I began undressing as I ran up the stairs to my room. I was almost completely bare as I entered the room which surprised my roommates. I only had one thing on my mind and that was getting to the hospital to help Cox who needed my direct help this time.

"Are you ok?" most of the guys asked, wondering why I was disrobed. They must have thought I was losing my mind or over reacting to the day's events.

"Yes but another soldier needs my help. Someone help me get clean clothes so I can shower and get to the hospital." I asked gently. Each one assisted me like I was the CEO of a big business and they were my servants. No one asked why or if they could do more as though they were reading my thoughts. Everyone was still shaken from the attack and trying their best to contain their emotion until the floor Sergeant came barging in and made us all jump nearly out of our skins.

"Conrad let's go! You can finish dressing on your way there. They need you now and fast. Cox has slipped into a coma." he could barely say as he was now out of breath from running the flight of stairs.

"Geez Sarge, think you should exercise more?" came a voice from the back of the room. A few chuckled under their own breath but he was better at hearing than running.

"You're all correct and we'll ALL start with a five mile run, tomorrow morning. So rest up ladies, ah I mean MEN! Who's laughing now?" as he turned and left out his own deep sinister boohaha type chuckle.

"Awe just great and I was going to see my favorite girl tomorrow. Now I won't have any energy left for her. Thanks whoever riled up the Sarge." toned in Carmichael.

"Don't worry she'll be busy with her other John's!" slapped back Jaminski as I grabbed the remainder of my gear and headed down the hall. With a semi-salute back to them I thanked them for their assistance.

Outside awaited a Jeep with Sergeant Brooks behind the wheel. As I hopped in with my gear he gave that snickering smile and eyes that suggested I better buckle up for this was another ride I was going to remember in Berlin. My head snapped back as he hit the gas and released the clutch at the same time. This jeep meant business and so did he. I could barely grab clothes through the turns to keep dressing. I really felt like laughing because it reminded me of when I was a kid riding snowmobiles with Hans, my best friend back then. We rode as hard and as fast as we could pushing the other to try and outdo the other. Once he went so fast into a snow drift that it sent him sailing, right on his back as the sled kept going! We laughed all the way home and I conceded by not trying the same jump.

As we made our way into the Hospital grounds Sergeant Brooks asked me the oddest question. "Have any idea who those attackers were?"

My puzzled look didn't answer him so I shook my head and replied "Not a clue. Should I know?"

"Well Army Intelligence believes they were a faction from the Middle East with intent to cause terrorism." in a not so sure tone. "A few were captured and are being interrogated now. One mentioned something to do with the one who bares the cross but wouldn't add anything more. You were the first person I thought about after what happened in the mess today."

"But I don't wear a cross just my dog tags. Some wear jewelry just not me Sergeant." I calmly added.

"I know that Specialist but the situation remains the same. They are still looking for this person and have vowed not to stop until they have him. HIM not her they specifically stated." in a more sure tone Brooks submitted. "Now let's go see if YOU can help save Cox."

Chapter 5

Pushing open the Emergency Room doors with authority, Brooks yelled out for anyone who could assist us with directions to Corporal Cox. The closest nurse summoned us to follow her which I had no trouble doing 'cause she was an attractive woman. She walked with a confidence that was more than just military training, she was secure with who she was and it showed. I caught a smiling glance back one time and returned the smile before I realized why she was smiling. "Better close that barn door soldier before the bull gets out." She flirtatiously batted her eyes.

"Sorry ma'am I was trying to dress on our way over here and missed a few things it looks like." I grinned back red faced now. "How is Cox doing?"

"Don't really know just knew to be looking for someone coming in to donate blood. Are you his brother?" she inquisitively inquired still looking down to see if the barn door was closed.

Before I could answer, Brooks tapped me on the shoulder and quickly sent, "We are all brothers in arms. He is here to help."

"Doesn't matter to me Sergeant if he is or isn't. Just matters that he has acceptable blood we can use. It would benefit his brother if he's a match." now the nurse's kindness seemed to diminish. She appeared to be offended by the reply from Sergeant Brooks.

One of the unexplained abilities I seem to have is detecting mood changes or attitudes of people or their true feelings some try to hide. While some feel it's better to hold in your emotions, I can feel that holding and could never understand why. With her I could detect being hurt by not being told the truth even though it really didn't matter to her either way. What mattered was he felt it wasn't any of her business yet in some ways it could be. Here we were taking her time away from someone who may have needed her assistance with another patient or updating charts or even getting a break SHE needed. No, she had every right to feel unappreciated by Brooks but I made her feel the other way.

"Nurse Kelley?" I asked.

"Yes Specialist?" she warmed.

"I'm very good friends with Corporal Cox and we've known each other since jump school." I fibbed a little. "He would be doing the same for me if things were reversed. If you could help your friend, you'd do the same thing, right?"

Now she felt appreciated and useful to which she admiringly added, "I'd do anything for you if you were my friend so yes, you're correct."

Moments later we arrived at the room where Corporal Cox lay motionless. Monitors and tubes were connected everywhere and he was covered in blankets and sheets. Another nurse sat in a chair next to him and stood up as we entered. Cox's doctor was at the X-ray screen looking at his films just inside the door to our left. Sergeant Brooks went to him and provided our information so he knew who we were and why we were there while the nurses spoke amongst themselves. To me it seemed odd that he wasn't in a room more accustomed for a patient of his degree of injury. I noticed how nurse Kelley kept looking back over her shoulder with that warm smile and her nurse friend would giggle silently covering her mouth hoping no one could hear or see her childish manners. They saw before I did the other two in the room heading over to me and became more professional in their attitudes.

"Specialist Conrad this is Doctor Marshall. He will go over what is needed of you. I'll be back later to get you. Don't leave here until I come to get you. Understood soldier?" barked Brooks.

"Yes Sergeant, completely understood." I confirmed. He turned like a top and out the door he went without ever saying another word. Again the nurse felt his coldness but simultaneously showed her gentleness with her glowing smile at me.

"Specialist Conrad, your friend Cox needs a quick transfusion of blood. We need to check yours before we can proceed with the direct transfusion. Please have a seat here and one of the nurses will take care of you." And I knew which one I wanted.

"Can I make a request for one so they don't fight over me?" I chuckled as I asked.

"Certainly you may if you wish but I'd suggest Nurse Kelley because she has, shall we say, more experience." eyes up smile from the Doc.

"Great that's who I had in mind." And over she came due to the doctors flexing finger.

"Yes Doctor?" she asked like she didn't know why she was called over.

"Specialist Conrad has asked that you perform his blood work as I suggested you would be the better choice." he nonchalantly ranted as though she owed him.

"Very well then, I'll make sure to do a good job." she winked as an approval towards me.

"Ok I'll be right back in a few minutes. I need to check on some other things. We'll leave you two so you can get to work." The Doctor pointed to the other nurse to go with him and they disappeared down the hallway.

"Ok I need you to remove your shirt and lie down on the bed over there." Nurse Kelley now in command firmly said.

As I did as she asked, I had to pass by my fellow soldier who still lied unresponsive on his bed. Again in life I saw him unaware of what was taking place around him only this time I held his fate in my hands. If I couldn't help, there was no "Jesus" to catch his fall and nobody was lined up after me. I placed my shirt on the chair next to the bed and lied down. Nurse Kelley who was already waiting with syringe in hand now looked like a true professional. She placed the items on the tray next to the bed, took a swab and cleaned my arm area where she planned to take the blood. Next she wrapped the strap tenderly around my upper arm and tapped my vein to which she complimented"nice veins." I wanted to say the same but not about her veins but held that inside just offering a smile back. You always know what comes next but the quick prick somehow always catches me off guard. That smoothly she was that I never felt the needle enter or the blood beginning to fill the vial.

"Wow you are good." I gratefully stated. "Been a nurse long?"

"Oh about 4 years now so I have some experience at doing this." she calmly went. "How long have you been a soldier?"

"Oh about 3 years now." I recalled.

"So how long have you been in Berlin?" she inquired.

"About two years now. I'm getting ready to head back state side in a few weeks." I continued.

"Oh poop." she sighed as I began to wonder if something went wrong. "I always meet the nice ones too late. I guess you have a girl too?"

"No, no girl on my arm or in my heart. I'm waiting for the right one. I'm sure you understand that being a beautiful woman yourself." I sent to her to see her reaction.

"Well I just ended a yearlong relationship with a total jerk. Why do guys always get jealous after you meet them but never show it before?" she instinctively asked.

"Not all guys are like that. I feel jealousy is a wasted emotion due to insecurity with oneself. Some guys get caught up with being provoked into being jealous by the women they are with because some women WANT you to be that way. It's like they feed off of making you crazy over them and then that's not love, that's a control factor." I philosophically said.

A tear began to well up in her eyes as she heard words she never knew a man could speak, truth. She was finished taking the blood and closing off my new needle mark when the good doctor returned. Quickly bandaging my arm and helping me sit back up as he came over she handed him the freshly filled vial.

"So was she as good as I said she was?" he began.

"Actually she was better than you made her out to be. I never felt the needle and she's a great conversationalist. Glad I had the time to find out first hand. Thanks Doc." I graciously thanked him.

"Well next we check this blood to make sure it's ok and then we can do the transfusion. As I said it will be a direct transfusion which means we will direct your blood straight into Corporal Cox. It can be an intense moment so we want to be sure you're ok with it as much as we need to check your blood. Are you sure you want to do this?" Doctor Marshall asked genuinely.

I could see Nurse Kelley almost confirming with her head nod as I answered firmly and soundly "Yes, I'm sure." I then started to bow my head in prayer for everyone involved for God's guidance and helping hand as I noticed something I hadn't seen before. As I looked closer over to Cox's hands it seemed odd and I couldn't distinguish what exactly I was seeing. I could feel the doctor's pat on my back and him saying what a great thing I was doing but couldn't take my eyes off of Cox's left hand.

"We'll be back in a few minutes after we are done checking your blood to start the transfusion. Sit back and relax for a while. You'll need your strength." And then the doctor left with Nurse Kelley. A soft offering wave from her to assure me everything was going to be ok.

After they were out of sight I went over to Cox's left side. I reached out to hold his still hand and continue my inquiry into what I saw. As I opened his clenched fist, the first thing I saw was what appeared to be symbols, symbols written in blood, his own blood! But I was looking at them upside down so I turned his hand more so I could make out what he apparently had wrote. I gasped as I read what I now saw but couldn't understand what it meant.

Chapter 6

"Adels? What is that about and what does it mean?" I murmured. Obviously he was the one who did this but why and for what reason? I heard voices in the hall so I went back over to the bed I was standing at and there I saw more alcohol swabs on the tray. I looked to see who it was but only saw two interns walking down the hall towards where the doctor had went. Nobody was in the area so I opened the packets and grabbed Cox's hand to begin cleaning off the letters. His hands were rough and other than the blood he used to write the letters were fairly clean. He definitely had hands of a soldier. I quickly finished erasing the remainder of his hidden message when I noticed on his right hand was another symbol. This one wasn't in blood but instead a tattoo of a Jewish Star of David on his thumb area. "Now that's odd because I remember him saying he was Catholic?" I tried to understand the conflicting information. Now my mind was in motion like a deciphering tool on a mission. How did all this connect and how was Cox associated with it? I had to know. I gathered all the used alcohol swabs and discarded them in a container across the room hoping no one would discover them at least not until later. I hurried back over to the bed and sat down on the chair where my shirt was draped. My heart was racing and I needed to calm down before the good doctor and nurse returned. I began thinking about my grandmother and how she loved making cookies for me when I was a child just before we'd go over to see her mother.

Great-grandmother Oberholtzer was the oldest person I knew and the home she lived in was not far from our home. She'd always have a great big smile when she'd see us driving up to the building. She sat at her window everyday waiting for anyone to come and visit so this particular day we were her shining outlet. We never made the same cookies but somehow she knew like a physic what we brought her. She wasn't like others at the home that had a restricted diet, she could eat anything and she loved her cookies!

"So I detect someone made me Chocolate Chip cookies but with white chocolate?" she predetermined.

"Yes great-grandmother, again you knew. Do you have a way of seeing us while we are baking them?" I childishly asked.

"God lets us see everything we need to see when we need to see it the most. He directs our eyes to places we may have never looked before. It is up to us to look and understand what he's showing us." she winsomely proclaimed.

"Does he give us special glasses like yours too?" I asked seriously.

"He gives us many things and tools to complete our life's tasks but only when we are ready to handle them and properly use them." Great-grandmother concluded and began choosing which cookie was going to be her first eaten that beautiful day.

Grandmother sat with her for a long time talking about family and friends just so she could catch up on news and enjoy what we had brought her. She offered others who could partake in our baked goods a sample but most just said thank you and walked away. After about an hour she decided we had been there long enough and needed to head back home. We never stayed as long as I thought we should have but the time was always relaxing and calming so I try to go back to those moments when I need to gather my composure. Great-grandma always ended our visit with her signature kiss. The overly wet with stubble lip smooch that you really only miss after someone like her is gone. I missed those kisses after she passed more than I realized.

"So how's my Specialist doing?" came a familiar voice while walking in the door which startled me at first. "A little jumpy are we?" said Nurse Kelley.

"Just wondered off in thought and never heard you come in. I guess you could say you caught me off guard but not from your beauty." I allowed her the pleasure.

"My, my you do have a golden tongue don't you now? Well your blood is fine so we can proceed with the transfusion. If only I can be half as lucky as your friend then today will be a good day." she smiled.

"Well then we shall see after you are done. Maybe?" I offered.

"We'll see there soldier. First let's see if you can deal with the task at hand." as the doctor walked in.

"Sorry to interrupt you two but we need to get things moving here. Specialist Conrad please lay back down on the bed and Nurse Kelley will begin to prep you. I will start on Cox and we should meet in the middle, I hope." he jokingly tried his humor.

As they began their work, I worried that either one would notice the used swabs in the trash or the smell of the alcohol that lingered in the air. Figuring they were both accustomed to the odor I quickly dismissed the thought. Nurse Kelley was being very professional now with the doctor in the room so I just gave her one of my good old boy smiles. For the first time I noticed a faint paleness on her ring finger like a ring had been there at one time. She must have been serious enough about the "jerk" to agree to marry him I proposed in my head. Such a nice appearing person to have another one make her lose her feelings, he most certainly must have been terrible. His loss if she was the type of woman I thought she might be but with me leaving soon it just wasn't something I'd have enough time to find out for myself. Long distance relationships are hard to maintain and even worse to trust unless you've had time to develop that trust. So she was just another pretty face in the crowd for me.

"How are we doing there Nurse?" Doctor Marshall asked unprofessionally.

"He's ready for you to complete the transfusion Doctor." she said with disgust at his demeaning unprofessionalism.

"Ok now Specialist you'll feel a sharper pinch because the needle is larger for more blood flow. Ready and here we go."

The doctor was right and it was nowhere near as smooth as hers before. I could feel the blood beginning its journey but chose not to follow it. It wasn't that I feared passing out from the blood, it was because I had made a choice and was now honoring it by helping someone I just knew would do the same for me if I needed him to. I had felt a calling to do what was deemed a necessity and there was no stopping it now.

"So how are you feeling?" asked the concerned doctor. "Any discomfort, dizziness, lightheaded or nausea?"

"No I'm ok right now sir." I replied back.

"Good, we wouldn't want you to roll off the bed or start getting delusional on us, would we Nurse?" again being unprofessional.

"No doctor, you are the only one here allowed to be delusional." she said with a half cocky smile.

Now the light bulb went on and I quickly began putting the pieces together with these little clues. I certainly wasn't going to feed this fire with any questions after being connected by these two bickering ex-lovebirds to a man that deserved better attention.

"Let's not start things here in front of the patients Nurse Kelley. It wouldn't be professional." Like he knew what that was.

"Oh sure Charlie, now you want to be the big little doctor." She chirped holding her two fingers slightly apart.

I just closed my eyes and pretended to be out so it must have worked because the doctor saw this and shook me slightly to ensure I was still there with them.

"Don't pass out on me now we are almost finished. We can't take all your blood now, right?" again he tried his humor.

I offered one eye open and simply said, "Not funny Doc. Not funny at all." To which he didn't find amusing but Nurse Kelley enjoyed. Somebody had stood their ground and put him in his perspective place other than her. Now I was being the really good guy not just another guy.

Corporal Cox began to move slightly now as a result of the life giving blood transfusion. They already had him strapped to his bed so they weren't showing much concern over his changing condition until I informed them. Immediately the doctor changed his demeanor and began telling Cox who he was and where he was at. What had just taken place and who was there with him. As soon as he heard my name he turned his head ever so gently to glance and gave a nod of thanks to which I understood. He then used his eyes to look down towards his hands to which again I understood but couldn't just say it because of our other visitors in the room. I could only offer a swift wink back and hoped he was coherent enough to comprehend. The result was a thumb up with his right hand.

"I believe your brother is saying he's thankful for your humanity in his time of need Specialist Conrad." spoke a smiling Nurse Kelley. She now showed more fondness and the signals were clear. Perhaps if the opportunity arose I'd ask to take her to dinner before leaving this beautiful city. It certainly wouldn't hurt and she sure could enjoy a night out on the town with someone who wasn't a "jerk".

"I do believe you're correct ma'am and hopefully he's not the only one." Now I was getting a light headedness from the giving of blood. I would need some fluids to replenish my level before leaving.

They both worked together now to complete the process of unjoining us. The doctor requested that I allow them to take another pint for backup. I graciously submitted knowing it would lower my own blood level but also figured it would give me more time to see Nurse Kelley, I hoped. They used my existing tube to run an IV of fluids and I just laid there watching them work on Cox, getting him ready for his next trip to repair more of his wound. I gave him a thumbs up back and said, "Good luck buddy, see you back at base." And off they went.

Now I was all alone in the room hooked up to this IV and nowhere I could go. The absence of blood sent my head spinning after they left so grabbed for the nurse's bell to get somebodies attention. Back came the first nurse who was with Cox when we got there and she was all smiles. "How can I help you, specialist?" she asked.

"I felt a little dizzy and wanted to let anyone know. Can I have a drink of water or something to wet my mouth please?" I asked.

"Sure thing honey we have juice also if you'd like?" she added.

"Only if the juice has something good in it ma'am, if you know what I mean." I tried to joke. She didn't seem amused by my comment.

"We don't allow alcohol here." back she came. "But I seem to smell some in here? Did you have some on you?"

Oh no! SHE smells the alcohol swabs. I thought quickly searching for an answer that would alleviate her inquiry. "No ma'am I'm not a drinker, I was just joking." I tried to offer.

A cleaning crew now began to filter in to begin getting the room ready for its next use. I sighed some when I watched one of the guys remove the bag from its trash bin that held the swabs. Away it was going and no evidence to what I had done.

The nurse grinned like she didn't believe me but retreated out the door to fetch me my drink. Good nurse go do your job, I chuckled to myself for what I was able to get away with. Cox's secret is still his and mine if I could figure its meaning.

Meanwhile upstairs on the next floor, Cox was being rolled into the surgery room as the doctor's prepped for their task. The crew on the floor began cleaning Cox some more when one opened his right hand and noticed something odd. He called for the lead nurse and around the side of the table she went to see. In the palm of his hand were the letters:

$$T\mathcal{E}l$$

Chapter 7

As Nurse Kelley sat in the observing room watching over the procedure she heard the others begin to talk about what was inside this silent soldier's hand. She pressed the intercom button to ask what was happening, as the doctor walked in from the scrub room. He heard her voice and looked up as if to say not your business and told the others to just continue cleaning it off, it was nothing, so they did as they were told. He walked over to review the X-rays once more, turned back to the table and asked for the first instrument. Away they began to repair my fallen comrade.

Nurse Kelley wasn't accepting the push off from her past companion so she waited for him to conclude the surgery. After knowing everything that could be done was done, he exited the room where he found Kelley awaiting with a disgusted look.

"How could you say that was nothing after what happened to those soldiers today? It could have something to do with the attack! Or didn't you think about somebody other than you again?" she almost screamed.

"Calm down young lady I know you're hurt by our breakup but this is no way to react to something that simple. It was just gibberish in his hand I thought." Doctor Marshall fired back.

"And that gibberish was what exactly?" she demanded to know.

"It appeared to be three letters together, a" t", an "e" and an" l", if you must know." he rashly scolded back. "Now how about getting back to work and where you SHOULD be!" he finished and away he walked.

What an insensitive individual I allowed myself to be used by she thought as she made her way to the elevators. Never again will a man mistreat me like he did, NEVER! Her mind was in motion and she knew where she was going back to work at, finding me with her news. As meaningless as it seemed to one person, to another it could mean much.

I was all but finished with my fluid IV and drink when in walked Sergeant Brooks who had been notified I was going to be soon done. It was always nice to see his smirking smile as I had often felt he was like a father figure to all of us in the Mess Hall.

"So how did everything go soldier?" he began. "Any word on Cox's condition yet?"

"No Sergeant. Nothing yet, I was hoping you had some news." I said tiredly.

"Well we can check after they are finished here with you. You did a great duty Conrad. You make me proud of knowing you." almost sounding choked up.

In rushed Nurse Kelley and I felt like I was turning white when she quickly left us know that "Cox was doing better but not out of the woods yet. His next 24 hours will be his most critical." The bullet had done more damage than the X-rays could show but they managed to stop all the bleeding. He just needed time to heal.

"Thank you for the report Nurse." said Brooks.

"Yes thank you Nurse Kelley." I smiled now beginning to feel less dizzy.

"Can I speak with you alone sometime Specialist Conrad?" she asked concerned.

Here was my chance that I was hoping for to ask her out. "How about going to dinner tomorrow night? If you have off that is." I asked cross fingered.

I could immediately tell it was startling news that caught her off guard but then that warm smile came out and she shook her head yes. "Yes, I would like that." She went over to a table and wrote down her home number on a piece of paper, came back and placed it in my hand along with a soft stroke of my head. She leaned forward to kiss the side of my head and whispered into my ear, "I have something more to share with you."

I grinned like any man would and could only manage, "Thank you." My groin was beginning to ache in wonder of what else she had to share but I also knew I was never that type of guy. A woman should always be treated like a woman and that was my only intention with her. I certainly was not going to ruin a new friendship for a one night stand. As the nurse finished my fresh bandage and informed me I was done, I began to think of the night we had just planned ahead. We exchanged last glances and I gave a gentleman's wave a due. Out the door Brooks and I went.

"So you were busier than I thought it seems, eh there Specialist?" Brooks chuckled.

"Just serving my country, Sergeant!" I said with my own deep chuckle.

"And you serve her well young man! Yes you are an honorable man to wear that uniform." he said with a huge smile like a proud new papa.

As we marched in unison down the hall behind us at the doorway stood Nurse Kelley watching. "I must relay my news to him about his friend." she thought. Then a smile crossed her face as she too began to have thoughts of their evening ahead.

Outside as we strolled to the Jeep Sergeant Brooks noticed two well-dressed Middle Eastern looking men sitting in a car just outside the gates. As I got in he asked as quietly as he could if I had seen them and not to look over. I did as he commanded and replied, "To the backside of the gates."

"Yes, that's the two I saw also. Notice anything else about them?" he continued.

"Yes, a Star of David plate on the front of their car." I couldn't help but think of the one I had seen earlier on Cox's hand. This was going to be a long ride back to base I felt.

Chapter 8

As we approached the exit gate I could tell Sergeant Brooks was getting fidgety. His hands were adjusting to the wheel like a race car driver would do for a better grip. At the gate he notified the guards to contact A.I. and the MP's that we suspected unwanted company, especially after the recent events. They confirmed his instructions and opened the gate to allow us to pass. He glanced over at me and laughed when he saw I had already buckled up and was ready for our presumed rollercoaster ride. We nodded at each other and away we went.

Entering into the Autobahn he could see our new companions were closing in and with us being in an Army Jeep had no way to out run them. So the only other options were to use the other vehicles on the road as blockers or try to run them off the road if they got too close. His driving was precise and better than I had known. We weaved in and out of the flowing parade of European motors but still our pursuers gained. It became more and more apparent that we were headed for a close encounter. "Where are those idiots when you need them?" growled Brooks.

"Who Sergeant, our backup or theirs?" as I saw yet another auto had joined in the chase.

He had been so busy concentrating on traffic and the first car he never saw the second one join in the pursuit. He began to slow down. Up ahead the traffic was thickening and we could only hope for our troops to assist soon. The original two men had now pulled to within a half a cars length on our left as the new members closed in on the right. We were like trapped rats in a closing maze and no one to help us. Brooks saw a sign for the next exit coming up quickly and chose to go for it in one swift move. All the way across the traffic and never braking once he aimed for the off ramp and barely made it. We had miraculously lost the first pair but the second ones had been in position to easily move and exit with us. Their momentum caught us in the rear as they slammed into the Jeeps backend. Our heads jerked and Brooks held on to the wheel with all his might. Mine and his fate were firmly in his hands as these two were not giving up on catching us. Sergeant Brooks was beginning to take this rouse personally and it showed on his forehead. "You want to get rough sonny? Let's do it my way then." He yelled back at them. A fast jerk of the wheel left with an applying of the brakes simultaneously and they were now alongside of us. I could now describe the driver in detail as I sat looking over at him. An olive skinned middle aged man with dark hair and a thick mustache well dressed with a surprised look from Brooks' move. "Keep your hands and feet in at all times." Brooks went on like a circus ride operator. Again he threw the wheel to the right this time into the side of the car. If the window had been open, I could have slapped the driver, we were that close. I saw a flash of light from inside the car coming off the gun the passenger had pulled from his inside coat pocket. I yelled, "Gun!!!" and Brooks hit the brakes hard but pulled right again catching the assailants car in the left rear side turning it sideways. Their auto careened out of control and rolled and flipped over and over. We were barely able to maintain control of the Jeep but Brooks proved to be the better driver. We stopped just short of the wreckage and jumped out of our victor Jeep.

Brooks smiles his usual grin way and says to me, "That's what they get for messing with a good ole boy ex-bootlegger driver from the south!" Yes, he had shown his ability to outdrive the other guy but the game wasn't over yet. We ran over to the upside down heap and opened the driver's door but no one was inside! They had managed to exit on the passenger side without us seeing. Sirens could be heard in the air so we rejoined our Jeep until they arrived.

Army Intelligence is not as intellectual as they want you to think but somehow they still do their job. The first officer to join us on-site proved that by asking, "Who caused the demolition derby here?" He was a short Irish sounding smug that wore an aged suit, awful aftershave and a two dollar haircut. From his look I figured he was an undercover officer like from my favorite show, Baretta.

"Well, Sir, that would be the drivers of the other car." Brooks offered back.

Not being amused by his answer he looked directly at me and asked if that were the case. Surely he didn't expect me to offer another explanation so I confirmed what Sergeant Brooks had already stated. "So where is the other driver?" he questioned sternly.

"He and his partner exited the side and must have went into the woods, Sir!" I barked back.

"So you lost them? Can you at least describe them to us?" now asking disappointedly.

"We didn't lose anyone Sir! And Conrad got a good look at both of them." Brooks challenged back.

"I don't see either one so please explain. If they are not here then they are lost. Right?"

"No Sir! We never pursued them! That would be YOUR job. Right?" Brooks snickered.

"Sergeant I KNOW my job and we will see to it that it gets done." A crackling radio from his side broke in with muffled chatter. "This is Officer Maloney, repeat that last transmission!"

He adjusted the knobs and received better signal now. "We have found two that matched the description from the other car." the voice from the other end updated. "You are NOT going to believe WHO they are and WHAT organization they are from, Sir."

"Well I don't have time for guessing games whoever this is! I have two more to catch because someone let them run!" he blasted. "Now who are they!?!"

"Sorry Sir! They are MOSSAD, Sir!" in an awkward tone.

"Mossad? What the earth are they doing chasing two of OUR soldiers?" Maloney asked under his breathe. "OK, tell them we have questions and they better have good answers. They are to be escorted back to A.I. for questioning."

"Mossad? Sergeant Brooks what is Mossad?" my curiosity spiked.

"That is of no concern to you Specialist!" yelled Maloney. His composure was declining and my nerves had had enough from today. I snapped without thinking.

"Hey! They were chasing us! WE were attacked earlier today at our base AND I just came from saving a fellow soldiers life, I hope. Somebody better give me a straight answer because I'm tired and want to get some rest!" my eyes bulging. When someone gets under my skin I tend to unload and it doesn't matter if they are higher ranking especially if they are causing it.

"So you need some sleepy time soldier? I think your night has just begun." as he signaled for an MP to place us in their car and drive us back to A.I. for more of his interrogation. He was tougher than he looked but knew there were answers he wasn't going to get out here. He looked towards the woods wondering to himself what MOSSAD was doing here in Berlin AND why? The solution was out there and he was going to be the one to find it.

"Sorry Sergeant Brooks, I didn't mean for us to lengthen our night with my outburst but that guy just irked me!" I said.

"And that is what he wanted to do. They are trained to get those types of responses and if they don't get them they suspect more could be hidden." Brooks replied.

With a puzzled look I replied, "Then why take us in for questioning?"

"To protect us more than ask questions. Also to see the reaction they get from the two MOSSAD agents, would be my guess." with his guessing eyes went Brooks.

Yes! That seemed perfectly obvious but Brooks knew more about these things than did I. He had proven to be a wise mentor in the past I will follow his lead on this too. "Then I shall do my best to keep my mouth closed and my eyes and ears open, Sergeant Brooks." I proclaimed with confidence.

Entering into the compound that housed Army Intelligence felt like a return visit to the hospital. Mazes of concrete, wire and gates were in place to keep people out and in. Making our way to the building and its vast parking lot I saw the original auto from the hospital with the two agents standing alongside of it. Walking up to them was Officer Maloney with an extended hand of friendship. I nudged Brooks who was also looking and just nodded as if to say, "See what I mean." They were being dealt with utmost respect as customary with all law enforcement but almost too much I thought. These men were pursuing us along with their cohorts and now are being treated like family but not ours. This made me even more furious inside and wanting answers of my own. A long night I had been promised and a long night they were going to get until I had my fill. One man had died, one was fighting for his life and I unknowingly was about to begin the fight of my life.

Chapter 9

Getting out of our transport I noticed our new friends were watching our every move. We certainly were not going anywhere and had no intentions to. I was glad we were heading inside. It felt warm and appreciated after the ride in the open Jeep and a heater not working in the car. A good thing though because coupled with exhaustion and a drain of blood from earlier my body was ready to drop on the closest couch so the cold kept me awake. I would have to fight off the warmth if I wanted what I came here for.

The object of the game is to divide and obtain all the useful information you can achieve from the person or persons that are being questioned. Our scenario allowed multiple angles with two of them equaling the two of us. Sergeant Brooks would be taken to his own personal room and mine would be further away. This permits a sense of loneliness that the interrogators can use to their advantage. If you understand their methods you can use them to your tactical benefit too. My mentor had mentioned this during our time in the Mess Hall as he recalled his captive days in Viet Nam. He enlightened all of us just in case we happened to fall victim to our own demise. Being a prisoner or treated like one has many mental effects that can last for years, sometimes never going away. You have to think in reverse but answer your captors convincingly enough that they believe your story. The truth is easier to remember than a lie but if you want your foe to play his cards then you have to out bluff them and make up your tale as you go. Actors refer to it as adlibbing, spies or enemies call it mind twisting.

We had just enough time to plan our strategy during our ride and it was simple enough so we could both remember. Sergeant Brooks would use his aged knowledge to seek why the MOSSAD were following us. I would pretend to know nothing and was just at the wrong place, wrong time. I knew this was easy to do but my knowledge of Cox's hidden message made my nerves short. This wasn't going to be as easy as we planned I feared.

Heading into the semi-dark room the smell of ammonia faintly scented the air. Did the previous interrogators use it to awaken the last one here or did they do this to make me think it? My mind was tired and already working in overtime. I had to control myself. The seat was as hard as concrete but they had soft padded chairs? Why wasn't I given the nice cushioned one and this criminal take the rock hard seat? And why were all the eyes in the room focused on me? I wasn't even driving. I just gave blood and a lot of it. Head's spinning can't think straight or see well. What is happening to me?

"Are you OK soldier?" asked the first gentleman. "Do you need a glass of water or anything to drink?"

"I think he's getting sick from the changes of cold to hot. We need to ask him questions now." The Israeli agent suggested. "I don't have all night."

Well, all night he might be here my mind thought. "Who is he to be asking ME questions!?!" I asked as I slammed my fist on the table. "He's not even American!"

"Settle down Specialist Conrad." Maloney said. "He is assisting us in our investigation of today's events."

"He doesn't know?" asked the Israeli curiously.

I don't know what? Wait! They are using us opposite of our planned tactic! I'm the one who needs to find out why MOSSAD was here! OK let's play ball. My eyes refocused on my prey and my mind sharpened.

"No he hasn't been debriefed yet but since you let the cat out we may as well start it now." with a look of disgust. "Specialist Conrad these are MOSSAD agents Saif Kabak and his partner Aviv Maciar. They were brought in after the earlier attack for intel gathering. The group that perpetrated the assault is a known terrorist organization that goes by the name Al Atta. They, we believe, were trying to stop a flow of information from someone in your compound that knew of their activity in Eastern Europe and extends to the Middle East. MOSSAD would like that information too so they can close down their camps, assaults and other suspicious activity before innocent civilians get killed or injured. Have you ever heard of this group?"

I had never heard of anything like this story before and that's exactly what I thought they were trying to feed me. B.S.! "Do you really expect me to believe that hogwash of a tale?" I laughed.

"This is not funny to my people Mr. Conrad!" screamed Saif. "They live in terror each and every day because of people like Al Atta. It is my duty to protect them just as it is yours to protect your countries people! We are soldiers to a hidden war. They are cowards who fight for pathetic reasons and for those who believe that God has sent them to rebel. He asked a simple question now answer him." looking sternly straight faced.

"I have NO idea who any of these people or groups are and have never heard of them before today. Why don't you ask your other two partners that tried to wreck us out on the Autobahn? Maybe they have the answers you want?" I returned his stern look.

"Funny you should mention them? How do you know they were our partners?" Saif looking puzzled.

"Because they joined you in following us, that's how!" I said confidently.

"Well they weren't our partners MR. CONRAD! And we were trying to keep them FROM catching you two! Lucky for you two your Sergeant knows how to drive because that's all that saved you." furiously he went on. "They were AL ATTA!"

I WAS STUNNED! My look and inability to speak for the moment assured Saif that his words were getting through. Now he wanted to know what I knew and I saw it coming. I had to keep secret what I saw at the hospital until I could be certain he was worthy of this information. I didn't know what it meant and I didn't trust someone I had just met much less an agent of MOSSAD. *Senses, regain your senses! Think idiot! Why are they asking me? What more do I know?*

"So Mr. Conrad tell us about your day and please, don't leave anything out." he said as he sat down in front of me.

Over on the other end of the building, Sergeant Brooks sat watching the monitor closely as their interrogation of his understudy continued. He could tell our plan was working but in reverse order and pursed his lips so as not to snicker. "How long are they going to keep me here?" he asked his guardian watchdog.

"As long as we need to, don't worry, your time is soon. He's going to break I can tell." he said with a small smile.

Yes, he too could tell I couldn't last much longer fore he had seen it in his captive days in "Nam. A person can only take so much before cracking. He had to take the pressure off of me before it got that far. "Hey tell your boss I know more than he does and can help." This should buy some time he thought.

"OK you tell me what you know and I'll pass it on." The guard said.

"No! I only speak to the head man and only now or I'll shut up!" Brooks beckoned.

Over to the speaker box went the unfazed guard where he pressed the call button and waited for the answer. On the other end he could hear the proceedings from the other room and a voice "Hello?"

"Yeah, tell Maloney that the other one has something to say but will only speak now." with a slight chuckle in his tone.

"Ah sir, for you." as he held the phone directed at Maloney.

"This better be worth my while or someone's going to regret wasting my time." he said with a scowling look. "Yeah what is it?"

"The Sergeant says he knows more than your guy and wants to talk but will only speak with you now. Your call sir." as he clears his voice.

"OK hold tight for five and call me back. Let's see what he offers next."

"Yes sir, acknowledged." And then hangs the phone back on the receiver. "Have a seat, he'll talk to you next."

If your holder is of much lower ranking stature and shows his fear of the boss because he wants to impress him or is looking for that promotion, you can usually tell by his demeanor. Ask the right questions and you'll get a sense of where he is on the ladder. Notice the obvious along with the unseen to gather your own intel. Does he wear a ring? Cologne? What type of clothes? Is his haircut? Is he shaved? It also helps to have great hearing so when Brooks heard five over the phone immediately he knew something was happening in five so he needed to work fast. Ah, no ring or scent of cologne, cheap suit, a two day growth but hair is combed. No wife or girlfriend I'll bet, boss works him hard so he can't shave but combs for neatness so he's trying to impress someone. OK, my turn.

"So, haven't I seen you downtown near the red-light district hanging on that tall blonde that wears the fake furs all the time? She must cost you a bundle. How often do you see her?" Brooks probed.

"That wasn't me you saw, ah, must have been another man." He said fumbling for words.

"Oh sure, you have a doppleganger, right? No that was YOU! I knew it when I first saw you." Brooks kept nudging. He knew he had hit on something, now it's time to press.

"Keep quiet or you'll be singing a different tune when Maloney gets here." As he turned away to keep from being hassled more.

"Well that attitude won't get you anywhere in this organization. I warned you I wouldn't talk so have it your way. Now my lips are locked." Acting like he was twisting a key and throwing it away.

"Real mature Sergeant. What's next, stomping your feet?" he amused himself.

Nothing came from Brooks' mouth. He wouldn't even look at him. He could sense the pupil was being schooled by the teacher and was growing impatient. He crossed his arms and raised his head higher. This infuriated his captor more until he said, "So what if that was me there. I'm off duty when I go there for some much needed relief shall we say. I have no wife or girl so no conscience to deal with in the morning."

BINGO! He had already figured that much but he confirmed it! Now time to go for the jugular. "So would the boss mind if SHE were a spy too? And you were giving her information while you slept?" Now his mouth was silent and the eyes were scanning for realism to his story. Brooks was too smart at this game and had learned from some of the best in 'Nam. He had his guy on the ropes and made one last request, "Now get your boss on the phone and tell him we talk." He said as softly but confidently as he could without losing his cool.

The phone rang again in my torture chamber as I had begun to mumble about hidden words. I stopped as I slammed the chair leg into my foot to regain consciousness, a tactic Sergeant Brooks had taught me.
"Yeah now what?" the answerer went. "Didn't he say five minutes?"
It obviously seemed like less but was closer to five than they had known. Maloney looked over and again showed disgust with the interruption just as he was getting somewhere. "This guy will be in Siberia in the morning if it's not good. Maloney here. Now what?"
"He has something to say directly to you this time." Hesitantly went the guard.
"You told me that the last time." Maloney grew angrier.
"This time he'll do it over the phone." The reply went back. "Here he is."
"Yes Sergeant Brooks getting tired of waiting your turn?" he grinned.
"Let's stop wasting our night. I KNOW what you're after and I HAVE it." Brooks stopped.
"And how do I know your story isn't just a story? Trying to stop me from questioning your soldier?" His face grew looser with a laughter building. "Did you just say Marmaduke?" The room chuckled with him, all but the Israeli agent who turned with precision and looked at Maloney with ice in his eyes.
"Ask him to say it again." Saif pursued.
"Please repeat that but wait I'll put you on speaker this time." Still laughing.
"MARDUK! I said. Not Marmaduke you idiot!" Brooks yelled.
The Israeli jumped from his seat and ran out of the room heading straight for Brooks' location with Maloney in tow. "Take me to him NOW!"

Chapter 10

My grandfather would always tell me, if you want to grab someone's attention, do something out of the ordinary. If you want to keep their attention, tell them something they think no one knows about. This was one of my stories I had told Sergeant Brooks when we first met and were working in the kitchen. It was one of his favorites of mine and now seemed like a great time to use it. Now the focus was on him and he had moments to figure what he was going to add to keep their diligence. His brother-in-law was an observer at a secret government location and earlier that year they had found through their huge telescope a new planet system entering the sector they were watching. This system was not normal so it grabbed their interest and was monitored. What made it irregular were the wobble of the middle planet and the closeness of the other four. It appeared to look like a cross. Ancient cultures had spoken of a planetary system resembling a cross, just before their destruction! Now every brain, scientist, historian and higher up was enlightened to its existence. Within weeks it had been determined this was top priority with a Top Secret classification on a need to know basis. Brooks only knew because his bro was a loose lipped bragger of sorts and felt he had one up on good ole Sarge. They had often squabbled in the past about Communism taking over and Sarge saying he'd never let it happen on his watch. He really had no idea what it meant but caught somebodies ears and they were coming fast. It sounded like a parade of loafers as they entered the room where he stood still cross armed.

Saif was barely breaking a gasp and immediately bellowed, "What do you know of Marduk?" his eyes blazing into Sergeant Brooks.

"I know its location and how far away it is." Brooks said as he sat back down on his comfortable chair. Neither of which he was lying about but it was a start.

"Wait. What do you mean ITS location?" Saif sensed he was being played. "And which location are you referring to?"

Brooks' eyes opened wider fore he too sensed the game being administered but wasn't going to be played. Time to reel this fish in and see how big it is he thought. "You tell me why you're really here and I'll disclose the Top Secret info I have. Deal or no deal?" They locked eyes to see who would blink first but Sarge was an old pro at this and had nowhere to go.

"NO! We go back and question his Specialist some more and get what he was about to tell us. Then we come back for him. Let him sweat as we finish off his accomplice." Saif wanted control of the situation and wasn't letting an old fool play him as he suspected. We'll see who is better at playing chicken, a game he grew to love from his time in the U.S. for training. He looked back over his shoulder and said to Maloney, "What were the last words his soldier said to us? Something about hidden words?"

"Yes I do believe that is what he mentioned before we got drugged away with lies." Maloney knew to play along.

Last chance Sarge pondered. Got to play the ace now, "Is Nibiru a lie also?"

Now Saif grabbed his own chair and sat beside Brooks. "Tell me what you know you old fool! People have died because of him!"

When the old fool realized both were talking about two differing topics he knew his choice was bigger than he imagined. Somehow the planetary alignment and the man Saif was after had a puzzling fit but how? It was certainly time to come clean or at least explain exactly what he knew. He couldn't expose his source though and get his brother-in-law deep in trouble most likely losing his job. So that was his next planned step. Trade his knowledge for allowing his Top level informant to remain secret.

"I will tell you everything I know on the subject but my source is to remain anonymous. Is that clear?" he said firmly.

"Why hide your outside accomplice?" Saif inquired.

"Because this person is more valuable at the top, not the bottom. Plus they could get me more critical intel on the inside. Want to keep looking from the outside in?" a rather astute claim Brooks was making.

Looking unclear of Brooks' intentions, Saif felt it was more important to hear what he knew and go from there. "OK, continue telling me your intel. I'd like to hear it."

"I don't know a man whose name is Marduk or Nibiru. It is a closely watched planetary system that entered into a sector that was being monitored. The names came from ancient text describing a system of powerful destruction. Many times before, it has been theorized, it came close to Earth. Each time an event has occurred that changed the face of our planet. If it were to pass our planet now the effect would be what they classify as an ELE."

"ELE? What exactly is an ELE?" toned in Maloney.

"An Extinction Level Event." Saif quickly answered with disbelief in his voice. "That is why he chose Marduk for his name. He hopes to eliminate all Jews unlike Hitler was able to do. My God what will he do?"

"OK your turn Saif, who is this Marduk? And why is he concerned over us?" Brooks now asked.

"An old story from my ancestor's days of captivity in Hitler's hell holes spoke of a redeemer who would escort in a time of peace but only after the great tribulation. It was a little girl's wish for her to see her parents again. An angel came to her that night and told her the story of our redeemer. We have continued to watch for his signs and so has Marduk. I can only speculate why he is searching here but I would guess your soldier has a tie into this." Saif assumed.

"But Specialist Conrad is not Jewish, Saif. How could he be a part of this fairy tale?" Brooks went on.

"I never said it was him, did I?" Saif now looked stern-faced. "So Mr. Brooks tell me about your ancestor's history? You appear to be of Muslim descent? Yes?"

"There is record of a Muslim heritage yes but so what? Does that MAKE me Muslim? And it is Sergeant Brooks not Mr. Brooks." He angrily corrected.

"Please accept my apology; I never intended to offend you and your heritage. Our cultures have always collided as they will again in the future I'm certain." and Saif pursued it no further, for now. He thought to himself, "He became very agitated at my observation. Why? Is he hiding more and is he cleverly trying to hold it in? I'll have some of the other agents watch over him for a few days. This is not concluded, yet." and just smiled as he stood up to offer a hand of truce.

Sergeant Brooks did not like this Israeli agent but went along with the gesture and shook his hand firmly while looking him straight in the eyes. Yes, *game on*, he conjured up in his mind. I know there is more to your story than you are telling. Give me time and I'll find out what it is.

Chapter 11

As the pair walked down the hall together comparing notes, Maloney felt isolated from the proceedings that were taking part in HIS building. He had lost control but only for a short moment he believed. By watching Saif and Brooks marvel over their stories he had learned some valuable information. As they approached the room where Specialist Conrad sat regaining his senses, he asked "Do either of you have an idea who Marduk was trying to get to when they attacked?"

"I would assume a possibility would be the man in the next room." Saif said as he turned back to continue his conversation.

"But you said in my room it wasn't him." Brooks added.

"No, I said, I never said it was him. You both must have assumed it was him." Here he stopped just outside of the room. "I can only follow the clues as you will also Mr. Maloney. May one of us find the answer before it's too late for all of us."

I could detect voices in the hall, muffled but close. I knew Sergeant Brooks was one of them and felt a relief that perhaps our night was soon coming to an end. I was able to gather myself although my big toe was thumping from the smashing I had given it earlier. First to enter the room was the Israeli followed by Brooks then Maloney with his henchmen.

"Mr. Conrad, if I may call you that?" asked Saif. A nod from me allowed it after noticing Sergeant Brooks' wink. "Tell me of your ancestry if you know it?"

An odd question after the former lines I was succumbed too but I answered. "My father's side is German, my mother's is Irish-German so I've been told. Why do you ask?"

"Do you know any last names other than yours, of course." Saif never answered my question.

"My great-grand mother was an Oberholtzer. My mother's was Teahl and my father's mother was Daub." Again I wanted to ask why but waited.

"Has anyone ever mentioned an Israeli connection?" Saif continued.

"No. I've never heard anything like that." I said quickly but certainly sure of my answer.

"Then it must not have been him gentlemen." concluded Saif looking back at them. "I do believe we have taken enough of their time tonight and can let them go." directing his words to Maloney.

"Very well then, these two will show you out and an escort will take you back to your barracks." Maloney finished with a sweeping hand towards his men. "Oh and don't try to leave the country. We will probably have more questions for you."

"Then they better come fast because I'm due to head back state side in a few weeks and I'm going." I divulged.

Testy little guy Saif thought as Maloney answered "You'll go if we say you can go." stabbing back with his eyes.

Sergeant Brooks attached onto my arm and semi-pushed me towards the door. As we passed the two questionnaires, Saif arose and made one last comment "See you again soon." with a glint in his eye.

All I could think about on our way out was that last look. *"See you again soon." What does that mean?* Sergeant Brooks never said a word until we arrived at the outer doors.

"Good night gentlemen." he spoke with little care in his voice. He too was tired of the day's events and wanted some rest to which he was thankful he didn't have to drive. "Let's go my apprentice. Let's go home and get some sleep."

The barracks were just a temporary home for me. To me home was always Lebanon, Pennsylvania, the home of Lebanon Baloney, the George Washington Tavern and my Alma Mater, Northern Lebanon. There I was taught more than schooling. I learned who true friends are and how working as a unit with our band can produce success. The leader of our great marching band was widely known during that time and a privilege to be under his tutelage, a mentor with a soft voice but firm conviction to perfection. He would rather see a person try their hardest and fail then fail without trying. He was a great leader.

My drifting in thought was brought back to reality as we got closer to the base. By now it was pitch dark morning and there were very few street lights. It had an eerie silence that was broken by a lone barking dog in the distance. Looking over at Sarge, I couldn't tell if he was actually asleep or just resting his eyes. He had a remarkable way of sitting cross-armed and eyes shut that no one could distinguish if he were sleeping or acting. His voice confirmed he wasn't doing either.

"So when we get back I've got two questions to ask and then to sleep we go. OK soldier?" he asked opening just one eye.

"Sure thing Sergeant Brooks. Ask anything you want." I smiled knowing his questions were for my best interest.

The faint aroma of gunpowder and burnt shards of wood lingered in the crisp morning air as we entered our home away from home. The ride back had been an uneventful one and we were all glad for it. The two thugs that drove us gave us Officer Maloney's card with his direct number with instructions if we remembered anything from tonight that we hadn't already discussed to contact him. As we watched them drive off I slowly turned to Sarge and asked "What two questions do you have?" curiously eager to know.

In his no nonsense way of being direct he answered "First, what were you guys doing together last night?"

"I met Corporal Cox at the Canteen where we were joined by Gabby. We were just catching up on old times." I paused, waiting for the last one.

"And what was the comment about a hidden word back at A.I.?" now looking me in the eyes.

I knew if there was anyone I could trust it was Sergeant Brooks BUT at this point without knowing Cox's intent and who the message was intended for exactly, it was better to wait and not give away my ace. "That was to satisfy their curiosity. I knew nothing and bluffed like you taught me to do." not sure if he was going to buy it either.

With a smile like a proud teacher of his student's accomplishment and a pat on the back, I knew he had taken my story. I hoped I wouldn't need to tell him differently. When you're not sure who's playing on which side, you're better to play it alone until you know. We shook hands, said our pleasantries and went our separate ways.

Checking my watch as I went in I knew it would be late evening back home and I still had one unanswered question of my own. An uncertainty had arisen from within after hearing Saif asking about my heritage. Was I not told a part of my ancestry? Only one person would know and I needed to find out. A call record is kept for those who wish to phone home. This allows equal time for all the soldiers and helps if you haven't talked to anyone in a while. That was my case as I knew it was just weeks until I'd see my family again but I had to ascertain a burning urgency to speak to my mother, the one person who knew our background more than anyone. I spoke with the desk sergeant and arranged a time for the next evening. That would also help me leave my planned date with Nurse Kelley early.

My thoughts reflected back to earlier in the evening and her warming smile and it made me feel at ease. She was very special I knew it, just as my father must felt have years before about my mother. "It's time for a good day's sleep." I whispered heading for my room.

Chapter 12

Reveille always sounds off too early but today I had off so I just covered my head with the pillow and ignored the tooting. My roommates had to report for duty so that allowed me to take full advantage of having a quiet room to myself. Simple luxuries are sometimes forgotten until you want them. This was a reward for my extended duties and I was happy to accept. I dozed off but during my sleep had one of those dreams you automatically recall when you wake up. There were the usual familiar faces and then some new ones like Cox, Nurse Kelley and Saif. It is thought that our dreams reflect future events. Our mind is the most powerful object in the universe. Learn to decipher what it is attempting to convey and your world becomes two-folded. Almost an insight to a revelation before it occurs giving its viewer an advantage. In this particular dream I could see Kelley showing me something she had written, agent Saif showing up at the restaurant and Cox fading away. Nothing made sense, but the vision of the restaurant I had had before and knew where the place was located. I never recalled seeing a fireplace at it from past visits but in my dream there was one and we were seated right next to it. It had a beautiful cozy setting with warmth and sensuality, the perfect spot to show this lady how a real man could treat a real lady. Saif's appearance was disturbing and I was unsure of its intended meaning. Did he have me followed? Cox's fading was the worse and I knew it meant something bad. A former acquaintance was into dream interpretation and she had shown me a few books on the subject matter. I hoped her teachings were inconclusive because if someone disappears in your dream it often means they've left your world, as in died. Then just as the dream was ending my mother came into the picture. Her last words were "I have something to tell you." and it ended there.

Jumping up to get the blood flowing more, my head became light again and immediately sent me back down on the bed. It felt like a hangover but I hadn't drunk in months. I was tired of the nauseating feeling of the drinking binges and decided to give them a rest. And I was glad I had because I could run faster, concentrate better and had more money in my pockets. No, drinking was not for me and had a control over me that I had never given to anyone or anything before. I lay for a short while and began to imaginarily plan my date night. I always liked to be prepared and the Army was the reason for that. I already knew where we were going and hoped she had never been there before. The time was preset but flexible so that gave us some time to talk and at least get to know the other a little better. Starting to feel my head coming around, I decide it was time to get a shower and find something to eat.

After my refreshing cleansing and application of clean clothes I began to look like a soldier again. Now to fill my stomach and I knew just where to go and who I wanted to see. The Mess Hall is only operational to the other troops during meal times or to get a drink if they need, I needed more and had privilege to enter even when I wasn't on duty. The next meal time items were already being prepared and their aromas filled the late morning air. There are always items from the previous meal sitting out to cool and awaiting to be put away so my options were fair to good this day. A little of this and a little of that, a few potatoes some toast and my plate was appearing to portray a feasting. Sergeant Brooks had not come in yet so I warmed my meal on the nearest grill, placed it back on my plate and walked to the closest table near his office. It tasted appetizing and my palate tingled with enjoyment of food then up from behind approached Sergeant Brooks like a slithering snake who was spying on his prey.

"Good morning Specialist Conrad!" in his jarring early morning tone. "Get some good sleep did you?" to satisfy his curiousness.

Jumping from his verbal assault on my sensitive nerves, I sprang to my feet and replied, "Yes Sergeant. Very good sleep and now a warm meal." to which I added my own snickering grin in an attempt to impersonate his. It was a terrible try but he laughed.

"At ease soldier. You'll grow old fast if you keep that up. Grab your stuff and we'll eat in my office, just let me grab a few things." and over to the remaining items he strolled. I admired how he always presented himself appearing to have just walked out of the dressing room even if it were twenty hours before. A tidy man who ran an even tidier ship as was evident when he barked commands for anyone to "get this food put away, now!" sending more than one cook scrambling to adhere to his request. He turned around with his trademark smile and nodded towards his office. We met almost simultaneously as he opened the door and motioned for me to enter first. I started to feel this was not going to be just a breakfast we were sharing together. "Have a seat my good man." and around the desk he went to sit in his.

Curious to know why he was in so early but hesitant to ask, I patiently waited for his next opening. He had to have been up for some time to be here this early because he lived off base. I had been there once over the course of my time in Berlin and it was a great pad as we all referred to it. Living alone has its advantages and disadvantages but Sarge enjoyed the seclusion. He had no car of his own and used the Army vehicles they gave him but the Jeep was damaged so that meant he used the bus to come in or another mode of travel. He was most certainly as hungry as I was when I first began to eat and never stopped. He finished before I did and when he looked up, he had noticed the same. "Guess I was famished?" he asked almost as though he was looking for an approval.

"We had a long night Sergeant Brooks, I too was extremely hungry." signaling my understanding. "What brings you in so early then? Just wanted something to eat?" to which I was sure he had some food of his own at his bachelor pad.

"Just came in to do my job soldier." but I knew there was more. "And to talk with you."

Ah ha! I knew it! "Talk? About what Sarge?" he hated that use of the word and seldom permitted anyone to get away with calling him that without his speech that "Sarge" is a dog's name not his title. I watched as he shook his finger at me but never said a word, just smiled.

"There was a topic mentioned last night that you almost broke during their questioning. Is that true? Haven't I taught you better?" Sergeant Brooks asked endearingly.

Sheepishly admitting to my almost failure I lowered my head and nodded to confirm the first part but added, "I smashed my big toe in order to stop myself, so yes sir, you have taught me well. My mind was strong going in but it was like something in the air made me lose control?"

My mentor looked puzzled at me and my comment. He began to ponder silently had I been unwittingly drugged? "Were you alone at any time in that room?"

Thinking back in time as best I could, I did recall when I first went it, I was by myself. The odor in the room smelled odd. "Yes, when they first took me to my room I was alone and an odor I remember smelling."

"What did it smell like?" now sitting forward in his chair pressed across the table in anticipation.

"It had a sweet yet burnt faintness to it like beans?" Growing up in the middle of Pennsylvania you often pass through Hershey and the smell of cocoa beans roasting in the air. It is a smell you never forget once you've enjoyed the experience. There are some aromas in life that you truly wish could be bottled and then there are others you hope you never encounter again. This was one I never wanted to run into ever again. "Does that help you any?"

"I think they may have drugged you and you would not have known it. How did you feel this morning when you awoke?" Brooks asked wide-eyed.

Recalling the hung-over feeling I began to see what Sarge was hinting at. "My head felt like it did months ago when I would come to work with a hangover. I'm sure you remember those days? Don't you?" He had stood by my side and continued to believe that I was a better man than what the alcohol had been turning me into.

"Yes, and you have come a long way since then. I'm very glad you took control and didn't let it take control." he spoke with appease.

"So what do we do about them and your suspicions of them drugging me?" I knew he'd already be thinking the same thing.

"I guess time will tell and we'll play this one by ear. You know they'll be back? Right?" anticipating our follow up visit.

"I was already certain of it after Saif's last comment of "See you again soon." remember?" I pointed back to the night before.

"Yes, I did remember, so I'm troubled with his intentions. It is my duty to protect ALL my soldiers. I've lost one and don't want to lose another." his guardian father like inclination speaking.

"I'll be fine Sergeant Brooks. I've got God watching over me, remember?" and we both softly chuckled.

"So what plans do you have for yourself today? Going on that date still? She sure was a pretty lady." moving his eyebrows up and down.

"Oh gosh! I haven't called for reservations yet! Or her! Where is my head today?" as Sarge laughed at my high-schoolish like rant.

"Here you can use my phone. Do you even know where you're going or how to reach her?" he instinctively asked.

"Oh yeah, I'm taking her to the <u>Heising</u> and I've got her number right here in my pocket." as I dug it out with confidence. First call would be to the restaurant. I loved French cuisine and the restaurant had a great reputation as THE place to go for finer dining. An impressive choice for any first date but it helped to also know the Chef as he was one of my teachers during my cooking excursion. Bernhard was direct from Paris and his style was unsurpassed as were his signature dishes. As I began to dial the number, reflections back to our days working together turned my state of panic into a smile of ease.

His wife answered in her French flair but in German. "Guten tag. Heising."

I knew some German from my time there but I also knew she didn't speak much so when I answered in English she delighted in a chance to exercise hers. "Hello

Mrs. Heising, this is Specialist Conrad. I was one of your husband's students. I'd like to make a reservation for this evening. Do you have an opening?"

She recognized the name as soon as she heard it and waved over her husband. He could tell from her smile that she was speaking to someone she knew or so he thought. "Yes Specialist Conrad, Bernhard and I would love to see you again tonight." she said loud enough for him to hear who she was conversing with and now he was signaling for her to hand over the phone. "Here's Bernhard now. See you tonight." and the phone changed hands.

"Hello my American son. It has been a while since we last saw you. You have pretty date, Ya?" he knew I often brought women of higher caliber to his place. I liked to date but just never found the person I felt complete with and kept searching but never used them. A one night stand guy I was not and never wanted to be so I chose to be friends and that meant more in the long run. Respect is more valuable than the satisfaction of sleeping with a multitude of women.

"Yes my friend and German father," always made him feel appreciated being called that, "I have one last special date this time. I'd like to make it extra special for both of us. I'll be leaving your beautiful city soon so this may be my last time ever there." A cold chill of reality set in as I realized my words were never truer and sadness came over me. So much I had learned here and my time was shortening with every tick.

"Oh no, we will miss you but hopefully it won't be the last time. I have just the perfect setting for you and your friend. She will love it as will you I'm sure. How about 7 o'clock tonight? Sound good?" he tried not to show emotion.

"That would be perfect my old friend. See you tonight and tell momma I'll have her favorite." He knew what I was referencing to and smiled as he hung up the phone.

"Momma, save for him our newest setting. He has a gift for you so let's make it memorable." a tear began to fill his eye.

"OK one down, one to go." I said to Sergeant Brooks. I could see the admiration in his glaze. "This should be easier. She was an affable type of woman and that should make for a pleasant evening." I stated as I dialed her number. One ring, two rings, three rings...

"Hello?" a man's voice spoke on the phone.

Startled by it being a masculine answerer I hesitated then asked, "Is Miss Kelley there?" unsure if I had been given the wrong number.

A short pause and then the male speaker inquired "And this is who?"

"I'm sorry I should have properly introduced myself, I'm Specialist Conrad and we met last night at the Hospital. Do I have the wrong number?" trying to be as polite as my mother had raised me to be. Again a short pause. Odd and I just shrugged my shoulders at Sarge like I wasn't positive I knew I had the right place.

"Hello this is Amanda Kelley, who is this?" her warm voice revived my affirmation I had dialed the number correctly.

"It's Specialist Conrad from the Hospital. We met last night? Remember?" I tried to assure her I wasn't some stranger although we almost were.

A muffled "You fool." sounded over the line and then she was back on. "I told my one roommate that I was expecting a call but Derik, the one who answered, worked a double last night and never got her message so he didn't know who you were. Sorry about that miscommunication but he's harmless, more like a watchful big brother."

I could tell by her tone she was glad to have heard back from me. I was anxious to tell her where I had planned our date but hopeful she had not been there before. "So are we still on for this evening? I have a very special place picked for our relaxing evening together." I asked with gentleness.

"Absolutely! I've been waiting to hear back from you. What took you so long to call." giggling as she spoke. "I must sound like a teenage girl going out on her first date. I'm just happy, that's all. Please forgive my chattiness. So where are we going?"

Thinking she must be a swimmer to hold her breath so long, I laughed mildly and asked "Have you ever been to Heising?" The phone I heard hit the floor on her end and made a loud crack on mine enough that I held the receiver away from my ear. Sergeant Brooks laughed louder then covered his mouth to conceal his presence just in case she heard him. "Hello? Everything all right there?" I detected the phone being picked back up and still could hear her giggling, more now.

"Is that the nicest French restaurant in Berlin you are referring to?" regaining her professionalism.

"Yes, that's what they tell me." I didn't want to spoil the surprise that I knew the Chef so I pretended like I had never been there either.

"If that's where we are going, I can't wait to go. Charlie would never take me there saying it was too rich for his pocket. What would he know if we'd actually never go? I've always wanted to try it at least once so thank you from the bottom of my heart. You really are one special guy. I'm glad we met." her thoughts never letting her forget she had another reason to reunite with me later. "Got to let him know what they found on his friends hand." went her conscience.

"Ok great! I'll pick you up at 6:30 sharp our reservations are for 7 o'clock. I'd like to get there a little early if you don't mind?" I probed with delicateness.

"Early is fine with me, I'd just like to see the place. I can't believe we are going there." she raved.

"Well if you don't tell me where to pick you up I'll be going by myself. Your address is?" and wrote it down as she gave it to me. "I know the area so I'll see you later." smiling as big as a proud new papa.

"Yes you will you Special IST." she punctuated. "Yes you will." and this time placed the phone back on the base without dropping it.

"That went well I thought, she seemed more than pleased with my choice of restaurant. I guess I should decide what to wear, don't want to look too shabby." and we both laughed for he had seen how well a dresser I was.

Chapter 13

I already had planned which clothes I was going to wear but needed to check them because I hated wrinkly clothes. A neat freak not exactly but looking tidy I believed was a show of personal pride. Presenting one's self commands a certain respect from others and often shows by the way they treat you. Now that my outfit was ready next it was over to the PX for Mrs. Heising's gift. She loved the Hershey's kisses and would put them in her candy dish at home telling her friends that visited they were direct from Hershey, PA and I brought them. Not all a lie 'fore they were shipped in and I did take them to her. When I went home for Christmas one year, I actually brought back one of the king sized bars, the 10lb. bar! She went absolutely crazy and showed everyone! They had married later in life so children were never planned. I had become a sort of adopted son and enjoyed the family feeling away from home. My own parents were never very loving, so this foreign love was cherished. I spotted an unordinary figurine on my way to the registers and stopped to look. Immediately a smile crossed my face and I just knew it would make an unforgettable token of appreciation to Amanda for her help. It was a child dressed like a nurse holding a heart with a signage below that read, "Your heart is in good hands." The clerk carefully wrapped it in fine paper and placed it in a box. When I got back to the room I wrote on the top in marker a simple "Thank you." I checked the time and saw it was only going on 2 o'clock and laid down for a short nap. Knowing my roommates would soon begin to filter in I waited just so someone would see to it that I didn't sleep long. Private Kelsey busted in not long after and he was the most reliable so I told him what I had planned and when to wake me. He accepted the responsibility graciously as he looked up to me as much as I looked up to Sergeant Brooks. Now that the night's plans were rolling it was time to relax.

Around about 5 o'clock I felt the tugging on my arm and a voice yelling "Get up soldier!" I jumped to my feet as I had that morning but this time felt no ill effects. Kelsey stood laughing at his impersonation of Sergeant Brooks and made an almost perfect face like his. We laughed together after I realized it was him and not Brooks.

"You better hope he never catches you do that impression of him." I told Kelsey.

"Oh he won't. Now I have my date to get ready for also." and away out the door he went.

I grabbed my showering items and headed for the bathroom. Good, no one here. I can grab the best one. A tune started going through my head and I sang out loud but softly, it was Spandua Ballet's <u>True</u>. It must have been a fair attempt because it drew an outside audience that clapped when I concluded. I hadn't realized just how far a person's voice carried from inside the showers. I tried to out wait them but time was of essence so back out I went to my room. A few still remained and bowed as I walked by leaving me to order them to carry on. All in good nature and much needed before embarking on my date. As I dressed and looked over my appearance, my confidence soared. I was pleased with the man I saw reflecting in the mirror and hoped Amanda would be as equally delighted. All that remained was to grab my gifts and head out. I made one final stop at the on duty desk to verify my time slot for the call home. It remained there so I proceeded down the stairs to find a cab.

I never liked taking taxis for I always felt they would take you the long way unless you knew the local area. Being a soldier left an open target for any of them to take advantage. It was also expected of you to take the next one in line so if you timed it just right, you could get a driver that didn't smell like he'd been living inside the cab for weeks that was if you were acquainted with the regulars. I spotted someone who I previously rode with but he was second in line so I pretended to tie my shoe so the fellow soldier walking behind passed me and got the first one.

"Ah ha I got this one." he chirped as he jumped inside but I saw his expression as they drove away. His frown from the human aroma confirmed my reward and I waved with a smile as he looked back. He'd remember to never grab this cab, ever again.

"So where are we going tonight." my hired escort asked in almost perfect English as I entered.

"Two stops please first I need to go here." handing him Amanda's address. "Do you know this place?" responsively asking.

"Oh yes sir. And the second?" he waited.

"Heising restaurant. Reservations are for 7 o'clock so we should have plenty of time." I said with a smile.

"Very nice place. I took my wife there for our anniversary. You'll love it." not knowing I'd been there many times before.

"Yes I hope we do." I envisioned as we pulled away from the base. Holding both the box and the candy between my legs so I could balance my body with both arms as we made our way through the streets of Berlin I thought about what I had to ask my mother later that night. Was there more to my heritage than she had told me or couldn't? Quickly I dismissed the idea and returned my attention to the driver.

"We will be there soon. Only a few more clicks." referring to his meter. "Will you need to get out or is she meeting you outside?"

"I will need to find her if she's not outside so I do not know." I understood why he was asking as many GI's in the past had jumped out without paying. "Don't worry I need you more than trying to stiff you on a fare. Here, take twenty marks to keep the taxi running." I could see that was more than half the fare showing and figured he wasn't leaving a potential big tipper. The neighborhood looked exquisite where he was slowing. "She lives here." I thought, apparently out loud.

My driver confirmed with a shaking of his head and saying "This is the address you gave me."

Opening the door of the cab was like going through a time portal into the past. The buildings I had never seen while in Berlin and they were breathtaking from their exteriors. I could only imagine what treasures lie within, then, I saw the precious treasure I had come for. She had been waiting just inside the foyer for me to arrive. When she noticed me getting out of the taxi she couldn't wait any longer or risk the chance of me not finding her. I was marveling at the beauty of the architectural designs when I saw her appear. My heart pounded harder and then skipped a beat as I watched this lady graciously walking to greet me on the walkway meeting her in the middle. Our eyes couldn't look away from each other and we talked all the way back to the taxi. Even our chauffer for the evening smiled from seeing the emotion we emitted. Love is truly grand when it's shared with the right one. I opened the door and held her hand as she got in and then I followed. The boxes were sitting on the seat where I had left them and she grinned cautiously.

"Are these for me?" she curiously asked.

"Only one, the other is for my other love in Berlin." I answered back.

"Another woman? I didn't know I had to compete for your affection but I will if I need to." she giggled like earlier.

Our driver had slowed his pace. I figured he wanted to keep us in his vision so he could admire her beauty a little longer plus he knew he had time. We were both caught off guard when she yelled "Move it buster, I want to meet this other woman tonight." then she turned and batted her eyes at me. "Hope I wasn't too hard on him."

I relished the idea that this woman was able to speak out and let known her feelings. The others before her were dainty, prim and proper or manlier than I was at times so her ability to play both roles was invigorating. "He probably gets that at home so he's used to it by now." we laughed together. "I find it stimulating that a woman can be so diverse yet be a lady." our eyes still fixed and hypnotized by the others. I could feel this was going to be a great final night with the family.

Smiling still after his lashing, the driver cleared his throat and announced we were there as we stopped in front. The twenty marks proved to be more than enough for the fare but I wanted him to return if at all possible so I gave him another twenty with instructions of when to be back. He was more than willing to accommodate my request and continuously said "Thank you. Thank you." even after I got out to get Amanda's door.

"Please allow me to get your door my lady." I said with a Bogart style voice. The night air was chilly but tolerable. As I opened the door and watched the golden legs reveal themselves, I could detect inside patrons were looking on. As she stood to join me outside the cab she also viewed the audience we had drawn. Their attention fixed on the pair of well-dressed young people as high society will often do to see who the new money is.

"Why do they always stare?" I was uncertain what her next words would be.

"They stare because you are more radiant than their dessert and they are jealous." I placed a small soft peck on her check to add comfort for her and a visual to others that she came here with me and would be leaving with me also. "Remember, jealousy is..."

"...a wasted emotion." she had recalled. "You are right so let them gawk all they want."

I turned back around to our cab lucky he hadn't left yet but he saw the boxes in the back. He was now holding them in his hands out his window, "Looking for these, sir?" I nodded a yes and he handed them over. "Have a nice time and I'll see you back here at 10 o'clock. Yes?" wanting to confirm his instructions.

"Yes my friend, 10 o'clock and I'll have something special for you to take home, I promise." and waved him off.

Juggling the boxes, my dates arm and the door became tricky but someone had been waiting just inside. "Come inside to momma." she commanded. "We'll get you nice and warm." Amanda half smiled not sure if what she had just heard was true.

"She's your mother?" an honest question considering the comment. "What other surprises do you have for me?"

"I'll explain at the table but no, she's not my real mother. She's more like an adopted mother figure." trying to offer an explanation on our way to our table. "Momma, did you do some work in here since I last visited?"

"Yes my son and you'll like what we have planned." she giggled similar to Amanda's.

A small amount of renovation can add dimension to a room and beauty. As 'momma' stepped to the side and showed us to our table, there stood a magnificent new fireplace burning with fresh embers and a subtle glow. It was picture perfect and I showed my affection for her dedication with a warm embrace. "This is perfect for a memorable last night with you. Thank you and Bernhard." a tear now showing in my eye. "Here, these are for you." and handed her the box of delectables she loved. She opened them there, as was customary for her and pulled from within a single kiss, unwrapped it and then savoring the moment closed her eyes as she placed it in her mouth. A smile and another tear filled my face. Amanda must have noticed the surfacing emotions and lovingly stroked my back with her hand. Women love an emotional man, someone who's not afraid to show it.

"Please sit down." and momma scurried back to the kitchen with her prize.

"Nice lady. I like her already." Amanda commented as I pulled her chair out and then helped her back in. "Did she teach you your manners?"

"No, that was my real father who taught me those. I just worked to make them better." now taking my seat at the table. "He tried hard to be a role model and from that I learned what real true love is."

"Hmmm, this should sound good. Tell me, what is real true love?" Amanda tenderly asked.

I sat back a little to prepare what I had already spoken many times before. It's always interesting to see the reaction you have before you start and then the one you get when you're finished. I guarantee you it's never the same. "It is more than just two people meeting and having emotional feelings. It is more than spending a lifetime with someone you know you'd do it again with. It's more than giving of yourself to that special someone. It is in a sense to be willing enough to sacrifice your life and love to ensure the other can live but trying to find a way so both can live." The admiration in her eyes said it all and I touched her hands that lay shaking on the table. "It would be a love for humankind like Jesus had and dying for it but knowing you are not divine. It does not have boundaries or clauses or stipulations, it has full trust. It is unconditional. That is what real true love is to me."

She sat silently for a few more moments, still holding my hands, still looking deep into my eyes. Finally a waiter came over to our table to break up the silence.

"Ah, compliments of de haus." he said in his hard German accent. A nice bottle of 1982 Chateau Latour Grand Vin was presented for our palates. Since I had stopped drinking months before and did not want to offend our sommelier, I asked Amanda if she was a wine aficionado and wanted to try our gift.

"Certainly I'll do the honors. I haven't had a great bottle since my sister's rehearsal dinner back home. My father loves wine with dinner, lunch…. Heck anytime I suppose!" she explained with a soft mocking laughter not her usual giggle. "He tried to teach all of us how to distinguish a good bottle from an average bottle and he had some of the best while traveling all over the world."

Relaxing back in the new comfortable chairs I watched this amazingly cultured delicate woman's smile as the sommelier poured a sample for her evaluation. Almost child-like with an appreciation for life's finer qualities she began by holding the glass in front of her to view its color and clarity. The fireplace added to the ambience. "A nice dark Carmine red with a hint of amber on the sides." She assessed as she began to swirl the wine to awaken its aroma. "A balance of blackberries, cassis, cedar, a hint of coffee, licorice and walnuts, very nice aroma." Next preparing to sip a small amount a quick wink of excitement showing she was enjoying this appurtenance bestowed on her. "The taste is silky smooth and continues to evolve as I allow it to caress every part of my mouth." She finished by closing her eyes fashionably like momma savoring her moment. "Thank you for allowing me the privilege most guys would never surrender." while showing her gratitude with an under the table leg rub. "I must find a way to reciprocate the favor." the wine now beginning to show its warming effect on her blushing cheeks.

She is going to make being a gentleman harder if she keeps this up much longer my mind attempted to rationalize. She was certainly enjoying her first experience at Heising and no one would supersede this moment. The sommelier smiled showing his gratitude of her discerning ability and rewarded her with a glass full of the prize. As he turned and began pouring mine, I noticed the label on the bottle for the very first time. The depicted picture was of an apparent Lion on top of a building, an odd choice for being a French wine I thought. "Monsieur, can you tell me about the label? What is its meaning?" I curiously asked.

From behind me, Bernhard appeared and our waiter handed the bottle over to him. Dressed in his full chef attire and smelling like wonderful dishes that were being assembled in the kitchen he proceeded past me to place a small kiss upon Amanda's cheek. "Hello and welcome to my home dear. I hope you have enjoyed the wine I chose for you?"

"Yes, very much, my father would love this being an aficionado." Amanda said with gratitude.

"So my son, she is more beautiful than your momma and all my artwork. Sehr gut!" he proclaimed as I stood to give him a hug. "So sorry to hear you are leaving. We will miss you much." a somber tone in his voice.

"And I will miss you also, my friend." an attempt to break smoothly from feeling like family and more like a friend. "I will cherish all my life the cooking lessons and life's lessons you have endowed me with and carry you and momma both in my heart." ending with a longer firmer embrace. Trying to regain my composure I quickly changed the topic back to the bottle. "I asked our sommelier about the wine label before your visit to our table. Can you interpret it's symbolism for us?" knowing he studied in France.

"Ah yes, the Chateau Latour." now seeming to drift off in thought. "It is where I met my beautiful wife, your momma." he was reminiscing. "So, you asked about the label. They have used that label design since the early part of this century. The building was built as a watch tower during the 100 years' war. The lion portrays fierceness and a protector of his house. The original tower was totally destroyed by the King of France's forces during the Battle of Castillon and much later rebuilt. But, the most interesting part they tell you on the tour is that it was rebuilt from the original edifice. So, that which can be destroyed can be rebuilt if the Lionhearted so desires. You like that story, Adel?"

"A who?" quickly asked Amanda.

"Your date my dear. Didn't he tell you his name is Adel? Why are you so shy of such a grand name my son?" Bernhard quipped.

It was an unusual name and I was often razzed when growing up. My mother picked it from a baseball hat full of suggestive names was the story I was told which later I found was untrue. She would only say she'd tell me how I got that name in good time, an expression from the Dutch influence in Pa. My loving grandmother was the honest one to share the part truth with me and hounded her to confess the rest. I was still awaiting the explanation she held deep within.

"I am not ashamed or shy and my name is Del, that is what I prefer and you know that." scolding Bernhard for his tattling.

"Well gentlemen, I find the name Adel very masculine and sexy in its own way." my date quickly interrupted.

Both Bernhard and I looked at her and started laughing with delight.

Not sure if we were laughing at her she grabbed the bottle and poured a refresher into her glass. This being her first noticing of the label we had been discussing she looked white as though she had seen an effigy.

"Are you OK Amanda?" I instinctively asked unsure if she was affected by the wine.

"Ah, Del, did you look closely at the lion's head? It looks like your face on it." She continued to look puzzled. "How can your likeness be part of an image decades old?"

"What? Let me see that again." Incredibly she was right! The likeness was uncanny, like looking into a mirror. "I have no idea other than to say coincidence?"

"Well I must be going back to the kitchen, Del. I will see you again before you go?" Bernhard asked.

"Yes, we'll stop at the door to let you know if dinner was good or bad. Just kidding, I know it will be great. I hope momma saved you some of those treats." He did his about face and I chuckled at his hurry shuffled back to the kitchen. I turned back to my date that was busy digging through her small clutch purse. I anticipated she was hunting for her lipstick but instead she produced a torn piece of paper that was folded but appeared to have writing on it.

Amanda looked dead at me and in a soft whispering like tone said, "I have been waiting all night for us to have some time to ourselves. When your friend went up for surgery I went along so I could speak with Dr. Marshall. While they prepped him the head nurse saw this written in blood on the palm of his hand. Does it mean anything to you?"

I took the paper from her hand as though I were caressing her hand. She giggled from the touch. I opened the shred and looked over it but made no sense of its meaning. She saw it was upside down and reached with her soft hand to motion for me to turn it around. Now I saw what she had intended me to see. The three letters she had written, a 't', an 'e' and an 'i' meant nothing to me. Scratching my head I peered back at her and shrugged. "They don't mean anything to me. Are you sure that's what she saw?"

"That is what I was told. I never saw the markings or letters. Dr. Marshall was shall we say persuaded into telling." grinning at her own cunningness.

I looked again at the letters and then the flash from the morning's dream happened. A trance effect ensued as the visions became reality. Combining the letters I had seen written in Cox's left hand with these new letters began to produce another fuller word but still I drew a blank.

ade / sτει

Then from the corner of the room I saw a flash rushing towards me, it was Saif and his associate. As he closed in panic began to set in, then fury. He was not here for the food and must have had me followed. What questions would he have now? Couldn't he have waited until after my dinner date? Instinctively I crushed the wad of paper into my hand to conceal it.

"Good evening Mr. Conrad we meet again. Sorry to interrupt your dinner with such a pleasant looking lady."

"Hello Saif, this is my date Amanda. Saif is MOSSAD my dear so don't worry, he'll protect us. Isn't that correct, agent?" in a mockery tone.

"Protect us from what, Del?" she nervously asked.

"There are many bad men in the world Miss?" digging for a last name to complete hers.

"Nurse Kelley actually." she boldly stated.

"So you know each other from the Hospital? How curious...do you also know Sergeant Brooks?"

"What is with all these questions Saif? You know there is still protocol to follow. If you want to speak with me contact Officer Maloney." growing more furious by his presence.

"You are right, Del was it? We shall speak again in the morning." extending his hand as a token of friendship.

Oh no! The paper is in my hand! What if he sees it? His suspicions will explode! Acting as though the cool night air had made me want to sneeze I stood and pretended to do so while changing the hand that held the note. Saif must have been a germaphobe and dropped his hand. I felt glee rather than being offended by his actions and sat back down.

 "I shall take no more of your evening and I'll see you in the morning Del." he snickered as he turned to walk away. He pulled his partner closer before they left and said something to him in what I thought was ancient tongue. Here was my best chance to rid my hand of the evidence I held just in case he decided to come back. As I tossed it perfectly into the fire his head circled back and he saw the paper find its mark and ignite. What it was, was no more. Only a few knew what secret it held.

Chapter 14

Saif had caught a glimpse of my hand in motion before he watched the fire consume whatever it was I had thrown into it. Again in the same dialect he spoke to his man only a little louder, he wanted me to hear what he said. He was glaring deep into my eyes as he spoke and I returned his glare, like two bulls heading straight into one another.

Amanda tenderly laid her hand on my arm and asked "What did he say?"

"Watch them."

"And how do you know that's what he said?"

"I don't know but somehow, somewhere, I've heard that expression before." I shuddered from the chill of the thought.

The moment was interrupted by our waiter bringing the start of our meal that only Bernhard could have envisioned. We were never asked what we would like he just knew what would be perfect for us. Everything they brought was delicious and Amanda delighted with each new item. But the mood of the night was ruined by our earlier encounter. Although she tried to act like nothing had happened, Amanda could see the despair on my face. We managed to make it through dinner and headed for the kitchen door to pay our respects for a job well done.

They only had a few items remaining to make so Bernhard left his Sous Chef in charge and grabbed momma by her hand and said "Let's go somewhere quieter." and started to lead all of us upstairs. Momma reached for her box of kisses and then I remembered the box for Amanda I had left on the table.

"I'll be right back."

"You can use ours upstairs." Bernhard must have thought I was heading to the 'toiletten'.

"I don't need one of those I forgot something at our table."

"Oh! OK. I'll go with you. You ladies go ahead and we'll be up shortly."

"What did you forget, Del?" Amanda asked.

I smiled back and replied, "You'll see." going our separate ways.

As momma opened the door to their upstairs pad the décor changed from the elegance of the restaurant to a more manageable modern style. She had once explained to me she only liked the upscale look for 'poppas' needs and they stayed downstairs. This was her home and the kitchen was his.

"Your home and restaurant are both lovely, Mrs. Heising." Amanda showing her gratitude of their hospitality.

"Oh please call me momma too. Everyone calls me momma."

"OK."

"So how long have you two known each other? He hasn't come here in a long time. You've been keeping him busy?" with an old persons smile.

"No I'd say the Army has been keeping him busy. We just met."

"What?!?" momma let out.

"What is all the yelling about momma?" Bernhard asked as we entered.

"She tells me they just met and he hasn't been here to see me for so long? Why Adel? I thought she was why and a good reason too." momma visibly upset.

"I had been having some troubles momma and here is not a good time to talk about them." I gave as my excuse.

"But you are leaving soon and we will never talk again." she predicted.

"Nonsense you foolish old lady." growled Bernhard. "He'll come back again, someday. I know it in my heart."

"Nothing is so bad that you can't tell them, can you Del?" Amanda lovingly asked.

I was more ashamed of the drinking than I was of telling them that was the reason. So I took a deep breath and proceeded to explain hoping for their understanding and knowing they were all correct. There may not be another moment to express your feelings and my date had been amazing with her openness so I too needed to be honest. After I finished we all stood together in the middle of the living room holding and hugging. I had faced myself and the support I needed was always there. We sat and talked for a short while more and I saw the time was getting close for our cab driver to return. I peered out the window to see who was outside and in a car sat Saif's hand-picked follower.

"We still have company my dear but I have a plan."

The driver showed just as scheduled and with a big smile. He wasn't missing this tipper and was thankful for being selected for the return ride home. He honked twice but we were already at the bottom of the steps. I walked with Amanda out of the restaurant and went directly to his door window. Handing him a fifty mark bill I instructed him to keep quiet and listen. He nodded in approval.

"I want you to drive my date back to her home. I will act like I've gotten in and then close the door but I am not going with you. I'll crawl back behind the next car so you'll need to watch in your mirror. Once I'm there then you can leave." I opened the back door for Amanda to get in and once she had slid into her spot I started my acting job. First actually sitting partially on the seat, I handed her the box I still held in my hand. "This is a small gift of appreciation for the wonderful night we had yesterday but mostly tonight. You are an amazing woman and I wish we had more time to get to know each other. I will always remember you and your warmness." I could no longer resist the desire to lovingly kiss her and gazed deep and hard into her eyes. Reaching with my hands I held her face with them and passionately kissed her goodbye. Tears filled her vision and down towards the sidewalk I moved as I closed the door to my little piece of heaven. Scurrying back to the next car, the driver had watched as instructed and once safely behind I gave him the thumbs up signal and he drove off. I could only wait to see if the bait had been taken. Moments that seemed like forever elapsed and the sound of the motor coming to life was my cue that the follower was doing as he had been told.

In the doorway stood momma and Bernhard, unseen by the man in the car. After he drove away, they opened the door to alert me the coast was clear.
"I hated to let her go on her own but after last night's fiasco, I wasn't having her anywhere near. I cherish that you are helping me and hope you don't have any repercussions." I said to them as we began to walk towards their car.
"Poppa, you take him home. I'll stay here to close up." and she gave him a fast smooch then went back inside.

His Mercedes may have been an older one but it was meticulously kept. In we jumped to make our get away. "I'll have some heat for us in a bit. Your lady friend is very nice. We both like her and hope you can find a way to keep with her." he smiled widely.
The warmth I held in my heart from our lone kiss was enough to keep me comfortable in any cold. "I'll feel better after you have me back at the base and no longer in your car. As for my lady friend, that is in God's hands but I wish we could too."
The remainder of the ride was silent as neither of us knew what to say. Our time was coming to an end and the sorrow showed on his face. Like a parent sending their child off to college, he was sending his far, far away not knowing if he'd ever see me again.

The base entrance was always well lit for security measures. He parked the car just outside the gates but allowed the motor to run. The heat was comforting on this chilly evening making it that much harder to exit. The tears began to well up in his old eyes. This would be more difficult than when I left my Pennsylvania home many months before. My own father sobbed but my mother was unemotional. She had a cold heart from her past and it was taken out on me. Bernhard shook my hand then could not hold back his emotions any longer and held me tight. This was the kind of loving embrace I expected from my parents and gently hugged him back.

"You take care of yourself and don't forget to write us when you can. Momma would like that." and then tried to smile through his tears.

"I will Poppa. And I'll send kisses every Christmas." my feelings now flowing too. "It's time for me to go." Exiting the car my thoughts transferred to Amanda and wondering how her trip home went. Did she open my gift yet and what she thought of it. I focused back on my friend as I closed his car door and felt the same awful feeling I had when I watched Amanda leave. This was the end and we were going our separate ways. I waved as he drove off and he watched me fade into the night from his rearview mirror. Beginning to feel the warmth subside, I made my way back inside the compound and headed for my barracks.

Amanda could read what I had written on the box top but even though she was anxious to find what lie inside, she chose not to open it in the taxi. Instead she reminisced about the wonderful evening I had given her but mostly the incredible kiss. She had always dreamed of being kissed that way but after many years of frustrating relationships, she began to believe it was just a fantasy that she'd never experience. I had proven that wrong in one tiny moment of time. The driver was more talkative than the earlier ride but she wasn't, she just smiled. Finally she was back home. She thanked the driver and wished him a good night. Carefully she opened her door fearful she might drop her package. Safe inside she went to the kitchen to start a teapot of water. The wine was slowly wearing off so she decided a nice cup of tea would be a great way to end the night. Now that the water was on she sat at the table where she had left her box. She untied the ribbon that wrapped around the sides and pulled the tissue paper apart to reveal the figurine. She cried as she read the writing on the placard the child nurse held, "Your heart is in good hands." As the teapot began to whistle, she thought out loud to herself, "Yes, it was in good hands." and then a knock at the front door startled her. Who could it be at this time of night? Maybe it was me? She rushed to the door forgetting the teapot, her heart fluttering in hopes it was me. "Oh it's you, what do you want?" she said to her visitor. Before she could move, a hand covered her mouth with a cloth. It smelled terrible and her conscious began to fade.

The desk Sergeant was snoring loudly as I walked up to the counter. I tapped just loud enough to awaken him but not make him jump. "Yes Specialist. What can I do for you tonight?" he mumbled.

"I have a call time scheduled. Can I make it now?" I asked.

He checked over the log book and verified my time and told me which booth was mine. The phone booths were private but not very comfortable. The seat was hard wood and I always figured it was so guys wouldn't hang on the phone long. Most callers were smart and brought along a pillow to sit on. I didn't take the time to get one from my room. I hadn't planned on a long call. The switchboard operator placed my call through and I waited for the answer. "Hello." a deep voice answered.

"Dad, it's Del. Is mom home?"

"Yes she just sat down. Hold on." then I could hear him say, "It's your son."

"Is everything OK over there?" the first time I had heard concern in her voice.

"Yes mother. I called to ask you a few questions." silence filled the phone.

"About what Del? We saw the news cast about the attack. Are you sure you're alright?" she hesitantly asked.

"Yes mother I'm fine. I called to ask you about my heritage for one. And about us." I knew my parents had split when I was real young but got back together after many years. Dad was a good type of fighter. He fought to keep their love together. She was a runner and had more partners than a law firm. That was the most I ever knew or they would share.

"Our heritage you already know son. We've been over that many times." she briefly stops. "Can't we discuss these things when you get home in a few weeks?" she always looked to find a way out of answering these types of questions. I was probably better off asking in person because you can see someone's facial expressions when you ask about certain topics.

"Just answer me one, please? Is there any Jewish background?" I waited for her reply.

A brief pause then, "No I don't recall any on our side. Why would you ask something like that?"

"Oh, there are just some strange things happening here. I'll see you soon. Tell dad I said I love him. Good night." I could tell from her reply she wasn't being truthful as usual but I wasn't pushing the issue, for now.

"Good bye son, see you when you get home." and then the sound of their end hanging up. "He knows something or he wouldn't be asking, Jon. Should we tell him when he gets home or wait?"

"How do you know?"

"A mother has that instinct. It's how he asked, not why."

"Then let's find out what he knows first. Then we'll decide." and back to reading his paper dad went. In his mind the thought forced through, "I knew this day would come but now?" A ruffle of the paper washed away the contemplation.

Exiting the booth after finishing my call my mind again thought about Amanda. It was interrupted by another soldier who had been patiently waiting for a chance to call home. Since mine didn't take long the time was open for him. "Are you done?" he asked.

"Sure, it's all yours." and proceeded to the desk Sergeant. "Any word on Cox?" I asked him.

"Who?"

"The soldier injured in the attack. Corporal Cox?" I again asked. "Any news on his condition?"

"Oh, that one. No word that I've heard." as he put his feet back on the desk to relax.

"Thanks, you've been a big help." sarcastically I said then headed for my room.

I could hear music coming from our room while walking down the hall. "Kelsey must be back, he always plays his music too loud." I thought to myself. A blast of "Beat It" by Michael Jackson greeted me as I walked in before I realized he was dancing with his ass hanging in the wind. You can imagine the scene I viewed, a southern white boy grinding his hips while imitating a gifted artist. He had just showered and was getting ready for date number two. Only the towel draped over his shoulders stood between birthday suit and redemption. I could never stand to look at other men in the nude it just wasn't my forte, so I flicked the light switch off and on to grab his attention. It worked and he wrapped the cloth around his bare loins. "You really should turn that down before someone complains." I scorned but laughed afterwards.

"Sorry Specialist, it's my favorite song right now." he laughed along with me. "So how was your date?"

In one word I summed it up, "Memorable." and sighed.

"Too bad you're leaving soon. Can I have her number?" he tried to make me laugh.

"Don't you have enough women already?"

"Hey one more to the stable can't hurt. Could it?"

Trying to be as nice as possible I informed him, "She's not that type of woman. She's a one of a kind, the kind I've been waiting to find."

"Oh well, I'll just have to do with the four I have now." Kelsey bragged.

And I thought silently, "That's why I'm not that type of guy."

Chapter 15

Amanda lied motionless on the floor from the chloroform just inside the door when Derik entered. Her auburn hair was soaked from sweating from the effects. Immediately Derik knew she was in distress. He checked her vitals. Shallow breathing, faint pulse and her pupils were dilated. This was not good. The place was in shambles so he had a hard time finding the phone. He needed to call for an ambulance and quickly. She began to mumble but he couldn't take the valuable time to stop and listen. *Where is the damn phone!?! There in the corner, I found it.* Grabbing it off the floor, he hung the receiver back on then up to his ear. What? No tone? The cord had been pulled from the wall. He hunched over her again and looked into her beautiful blue-green eyes as he had done many times before, "Hold on! I'm going for help!"

Again she tried to speak, "Tell him...."

"Tell him what? Who?" he exclaimed.

"Del. Tell him I love him." and she collapsed.

Standing to run next door, he asked himself, *"Who is Del?"* then said as he went out the door, "I'll be right back."

Pounding as hard as he could on Mrs. Keiner's door, Derik's heart raced. *Who could have done this to her? And why?* She was like a kid sister to him and he had helped her through her breakup with Dr. Marshall. He held a love for her as much as his own sister and would do anything for either one. Finally Mrs. Keiner opened her door.

"Was ist los?" she asked in her strong German accent appearing to have been awoken from her sleep.

"Telephon bitte." he asked repeating it over and over again. Finally she escorted him to her phone sensing it was urgent.

He called the hospital. "Come on, come on, come on." holding back the panic trying to set in. "Yes, this is Derik Conway. Yes, that Derik Conway the nurse. I need an ambulance sent to my address immediately. Nurse Kelley is hurt and her vitals are weak. Please hurry!" the nurse who answered had just finished working with Derik on his second shift. She knew they weren't too far away but time was critical.

"We'll have someone there within 10 minutes." she assured him.

"Thank you." he hung up the phone then turned back to Mrs. Keiner. "Danke schon." and back over to his house he went.

Sergeant Brooks had just settled back on his easy chair when his phone rang. "Why couldn't you call when I was standing." he said truculently. He hated people who called late. Most times it was a wrong number anyways. He picked up the phone reluctantly. "Hello." he grumbled.

"Good evening Sergeant Brooks. This is Officer Maloney. Am I disturbing you?"

He wished he could say yes but didn't. "No sir not at all. And to what do I owe for this late night call?"

"I am with agent Saif. It seems that we have a small problem. He spoke with your Specialist earlier this evening and feels he is not being honest. Can you bring him to A.I. in the morning? We have more questions for him."

"What time?" hoping not too early.

"Let's say ten a.m., that will give you some time to sleep in." and he lowly chuckled.

He thinks that's funny, I'm not laughing. "OK we'll see you then." Hanging up the phone he huffed, "Now what did that kid do?"

"How much longer will it be? It's been ten minutes already." Derik worried. "Come on Amanda you've got to hold on." her signs of life were weaker now and she wasn't responding to anything he said to her. In the distant darkness he could now hear the sirens of the help coming. He held her hand in his and said a silent prayer. "God be with her."

"Yes, this is Sergeant Brooks. I need to speak with Specialist Conrad in room 204." he directed the desk sergeant.

"I'll get him for you. Should I tell him why?" he asked.

"No, I'll tell him when you get him on the damn phone!" Sarge was getting tired and it showed in his demeanor.

Slam went the phone on the desk. Down the hall the desk sergeant stormed. *Yell at me will he, I hope he's out.* He could hear the music now, turned down to an acceptable level. He knocked twice then opened the door. "Is Specialist Conrad here?"

Standing behind my locker door, he hadn't noticed I was in for the night. "Yes I'm right here." closing the door.

"You have a call from Sergeant Brooks and he sounds pissed."

"At me? What would he be pissed at me for?" I queried following the sergeant out the door. "He really sounded ticked?"

"Yeah and I'm sure I didn't make it any better by slamming the phone down." he boasted.

Great I get to have my ear buzzed for something you did, idiot. To the phone we went. "Yes Sergeant Brooks this is..."

"Yeah I know your voice. What happened to you tonight? I just got a call from A.I. and they want you back in tomorrow morning for more questions. Did you have a run in with that Israeli agent?"

"Yes, the arrogant ass showed up at the restaurant we went to, can you imagine?" I was pissed myself now just thinking about it.

"Well we have to be there at ten so I'll be there in the morning to check the Mess and fetch you. Meet me in the Mess, early. I want the whole story." He did sound pissed I thought.

"OK I'll be there. Have a good night, what's left." and hung up. "Sergeant, can I use the phone again to make another call? I'll need to go and get the number from my room."

"That's fine with me since no one is using them now. Make it fast, I want to relax again."

Sure thing, lazy man, I'll hurry so you can sleep while you guard us. Not! "Thanks, I appreciate it."

"Finally, you guys made it. She's up here. Follow me." Derik had gone to the street so the ambulance wouldn't miss the house. Now he led them to his stricken friend. "Last I checked she had no vitals and I don't know what's wrong with her. I found her on the floor when I got home."

"We'll take it from here sir. Please give us room to work." the first paramedic said. Speaking now to his partner, "I have no pulse or respiratory signs."

"I'm hooking up pads now. We should have a read in a few." the second signaling he was almost finished. "Flat liner hit her with the paddles."

"OK, clear! Nothing, hitting her again. Clear!"

Derik began to sob. "Please keep trying. Get her to the hospital if you need to but don't stop."

They knew who she was from working together in the ER. Confirming with a head nod, they loaded her onto the gurney while continuing to work on her. Their look of despair sent chills through Derik. This wasn't what he had hoped for when he called.

I hurried back to the phone booths with Amanda's number. I had hoped she wouldn't get mad at me for calling so late. The number was busy. I hung up and tried the number again to assure myself I had dialed it correctly. Still busy, I'll just have to try again in the morning, I told myself.

Even though Derik was exhausted from working a double, he felt the need to go along in the ambulance. He had locked up the house before leaving and attached a note to the door. It simply read "Stay out! Call Derik at the hospital!" He knew this was now a crime scene and investigators would be combing it for evidence. His father was a detective in Chicago and once wished Derik would consider joining the force. Derik wanted nothing to do with law enforcement after watching how it affected his dad but he still respected the work they did. "The person or people who did this better hope I don't get them first." he told Amanda while stroking her hair.

"Did you reach her?" Kelsey asked when I returned.
"No, it was busy." looking perplexed.
He had finished dressing and was on his way for his second date. "Get some sleep and I'll see you in the morning. I think I'll stay overnight with this one." and laughed as we shook hands.
"Yeah, I'll do that and you have fun, you dog!"
Across town Dr. Marshall stood nervously in front of the Middle Eastern man. He had eyes that were as black as the night sky and a soul as cold as the North Sea. "I tell you I looked everywhere and couldn't find anything." as he begged.
"Too bad for you." the man said unfazed. Pointing the silencer equipped .45 at the doctor's midriff, he fired two rounds. The doctor fell to his knees holding his bloodied stomach. Another final shot to the head ended his pain.

There were still no signs of life coming from Amanda as the ambulance pulled into the ER. A rush of doctors joined the paramedics as they unloaded her. "Into room number one!" shouted the first one.
A shot of adrenaline was administered straight into her heart. They waited for its effects. It had been well over fifteen minutes since they began working on her. There was nothing from the shot. "Sorry Derik, we have to call it. It's been too long. She's gone." as the lead doctor offered his condolence.
Derik dropped to the floor. Extending his arms upward to the ceiling his fist clenched he cried out, "No! No! No!"

Chapter 16

Morning reveille sounded the start of the new day. The halls were busy with soldiers heading to their post. I was heading for the Mess and decided I'd try to call Amanda's number one more time. It was busy yet again. *Oh well, someone forgot to hang the phone up. I've got to eat before I meet Sarge.*

The line was short which was good for me. I hadn't eaten much of my dinner last night. I was more interested in listening to my date talk about the food and her family. *Wow! I was such a lucky guy to have met her when I did*, my mind deduced. A slap on the back brought me back to an awareness of my surroundings. It was Sergeant Brooks and he didn't look like he was in a good mood. "Good morning Sergeant." I snapped to attention.

"At ease soldier, in my office, now." he scowled.

"Umm with my breakfast or without it, Sergeant?" I had hoped the first option.

"Bring it along."

I looked at the cook serving on line and signaled him to add more eggs. I had a gut feeling it was going to be a long morning.

Walking into his office for the second time in two days drew looks and murmurs from my associates. "Close the door." he indicated with his hand also. He was on the phone listening but not speaking. "Yes, this is Sergeant Brooks, may I have Officer Maloney, please." Now his gaze fastened on me, his upper lip drawn tight. "I have him here with me now. Should I bring him? OK we'll be leaving in a few."

What, we are leaving now? It's not nearly ten. I started stuffing food into my mouth knowing when Sarge said move, you moved.

"Slow down soldier before you choke. Besides, I haven't talked with you yet. How was your date last night?"

Attempting to clear my mouth with some juice so I could speak clearly, I smiled in reflection of my recollection of the night. "It was perfect, except for the small annoyance from agent Saif. Why do you ask?"

"Oh, I just spent the last four hours explaining why a call went from my office to your date's home number yesterday, that's all."

That explains why he looks so drained. Why did he need to explain? I waited for his next words.

"Well finish up so we can get this over with and I can get some sleep."

I lost my appetite but gained a sense there was more that he wasn't telling me. It reminded me of the conversation I had with my mother. There is always that hesitation in her story as was with his. "Ok, I'm ready. I'm not hungry anymore."

I told him how my date went on our way over to A.I. How he would have been proud of my stealth in fooling the follower. That I hated to let her go but looked forward to seeing her one more time before I left. About my call home when I got back and Private Kelsey dancing in his birthday suit, to which he laughed for the first time that morning. It dissipated when we pulled up to the gates. Through the maze again and to the main building he drove us.

Saif and Maloney stood at the window of Maloney's office watching as the pair parked. "Do you think he did it?" Maloney asked Saif.

"That's what we are about to find out." is all he said and headed for the front doors.

"*Arrogant ass. Why are they all like that?*" Maloney pondered as he wrestled his coat off the chair and followed.

Saif and Maloney met us as we came through the door. "Thank you for coming so fast. I know it's earlier than we planned." Maloney smiled with his hand out as a gesture of friendship. Saif just stared at me as he had the night before, coldly. Neither Sergeant Brooks nor I offered to shake. Sarge had a good reason, I just didn't like him. "This way gentlemen. I'm sure you know which room by now, right Sergeant?" and continued to smile.

Sergeant Brooks gave him his own half cocky smile and a "Heh, heh." back to which I chuckled while covering my face with my hand.

This time the room had no odor as I sniffed around. "So why am I here now? I have someone I'd like to call and a friend to visit in the hospital." getting right to the point.

"We ask the questions, you answer them. Understood?" Maloney jumped at me. This time he was taking charge, he convinced himself "Now where were you between 10 and 11 last night?" and his questions began.

"Derik you should go home and get some rest now. They called to say they had finished their investigation and you can return. She'd want you to go if she were still here." the nurse on duty informed him.

"Still here? Well she's not and her killer is still out there. How do you expect me to sleep when all I can see is her lying on the floor?" he was pissed and tired. "Sorry I didn't mean to blow up on you, she, she was like a sister to me and now she's gone. You're right I need some sleep. Can you call me a cab or have someone drive me home?" his attitude adjusting.

"Sure thing bud, we'll get you home." and she called for a cab.

"So his alibi is solid. He was not only on the phone miles away but he also has a few eye witnesses to confirm being in the barracks. He couldn't have done either one." Sergeant Brooks obstinately concluded. "Can we go now?"

"Wait! I couldn't have done what?!?" my curiosity getting the better of me. "What is this all about and I don't care if you're asking YOUR questions, I have my own now."

"Either you two tell him or I will. It's your choice." Sarge added looking stern.

"Very well then, there were two murders committed last night that required our attention because they both were military personnel. Dr. Marshall was the first victim. He was brutally shot, three times." Maloney waited for a response. *That's odd. No reaction, no remorse? I still believe he has something to do with this.*

Waiting to hear his continuation I watched Sergeant Brooks bow his head into his hands. "Just tell him damn it!" he exclaimed through his hands.

Knowing he couldn't hold the truth any longer he said the next person's name without any feeling. "The other was Nurse Amanda Kelley."

A tsunami of emotions swallowed me whole. I felt weighted down to the chair but slid off of it onto the floor wanting to get as far away from the words I had just heard as I could. I wanted to scream out and release my inner feelings. I wanted to jump the first person I thought was responsible and I was looking dead at him, Saif. His glare back was of sadness, for he had seen such sorrow in his homeland. He recognized the genuine look of pain and not guilt. He actually began to feel his own sorrow for me because he saw the joy in my eyes the night before and now the sullen heavy heart. It was never easy to watch anyone lose a family member. It was harder to watch a new love lost.

"We will catch who did this, I assure you Mr. Conrad, but I know it wasn't you." Saif offered his insight. "You must have loved her greatly?"

Attempting to gather what senses I could and reply back, my grandfather's words played in my head. He was a very whimsical man with few words but when he spoke, those words were never truer. He would rarely say, "True love knows true love and never forgets."

"Yes, Saif, for having only known her a short time, I'd say she was special indeed." *A one of a kind.* "If you don't get them, I will. Even if it takes the rest of my life, I'll get whoever did it." *God help me please get whoever did it!*

In a warehouse less than a mile away listening into the proceedings at A.I. with the help of their inside man, Marduk sat impassive. "This little man is nothing but a fly on my nose, a nuisance. I want him killed. Immediately! If he discovers who he really is.....the world will change. Al Atta will be nothing!"

"Sergeant Brooks, how could you not tell me? You knew we were together last night and then I included you into my feelings for her but you never let on she was already gone? I thought you were my friend?" broken hearted I asked.
  "We had to know for certain you had nothing to do with the murders. Face it, you were with her last, you knew the truth about her and the doctor, so they thought it was a love triangle gone bad. That was until they searched the house." he stopped. "It wasn't so much what they found. It was what they found that killed her. They pieced the two together for her death. It only left the doctor's demise in question. That's where they thought you came in at. He killed her you caught him and then took him far away to kill him. A simple closed case for them."
  "Only one problem, I apparently wasn't the last to see her alive and the same for the doctor, which that means the real killer or killers are still running around. Are they looking for me too now?"
  "That we do not know and I don't want to find out and neither should you. They have moved your stateside transfer. You leave in a week and start out-processing tomorrow. You are also restricted to the base except for essential needs with your paper work. Is that understood soldier!?!" he wasn't budging.
  "Yes Sergeant! I'm heading home with questions and no answers. My heart is shattered and my friend is on the other side of the fence. I feel all alone in life, again." I walked out to the new Jeep my head held low with anguish and slouched into my seat. The once proud soldier I was was brought to his knees and needed a way to rise back up from this affliction. I spoke not a word the whole way back to the base. I was concocting my plan. I had made up my mind I was getting some answers before I left and it was starting with tonight.

  A ring on Maloney's private line drew the attention of Saif, who stood peering out the window. He'd been watching Sarge consul me all the way out to the Jeep. *More bad news on the case?* He thought.
  "I don't have that answer for you at this time. I will have to get back to you when I know more. I am trying my best, please give me time." Maloney conversed with whoever was on the other end. Seeing Saif observing he offered to him, "Damn Statesmen! They want to know everything before I have the answers." but looking ill shaken from whomever it was he was speaking to. "Goodbye to you to."

"I have my own work to do on this case. I shall see you later?" Saif asked like he wasn't sure he'd ever see him again.

"Yes, yes. Later today let's meet and compare any new news. Shall we say dinner time?"

"Anywhere but fancy, last night was enough for my taste buds. Something simple with a lot of people just let me know when you have decided. You have my contact number." They shook hands and parted.

"Try to get some rest before tomorrow Conrad. OK?" Sergeant Brooks pleaded. "You'll have a long day with all you'll need to do. It'll be longer if you're tired."

Still trying to digest the fact that Amanda was gone, I slowly lifted my head and replied, "Sure thing Sergeant Brooks. Now you go home and get some much needed sleep too."

He could still see the disappointment in my gaze. "Hey, my friend, you are not alone in this matter. I have your back, partner." and with that he left.

As I watched his jeep head out the gate, Kelsey was just returning from his night out. "Hey, Specialist Conrad! Heading out to see your new lassie?" He never noticed my somber look until I turned to face him. "Wow! Did Sarge give you an ass chewin'?"

"No Private, he didn't but he might if he catches me doing what I plan to do next. Can you help me?"

"Sure I'll help. What do you need?" and we started for the barracks.

"First, let's get you changed so you look like a soldier again. Then what I'm going to ask you to do next could get you in a lot of trouble, if we get caught. You still up for it?" and in to the building we went.

Chapter 17

Saif was great at smelling a fox in the hen house and he knew Maloney was acting too incredulous. His partner for the last ten years, Aviv, was more reliable than his own brother. Either would lay down their life to protect the other and he always felt safest when they worked together. "Aviv, I need you to do two things before tonight's meeting with Maloney. Find out who he was talking to if you can. OK?"

"Sure Saif and the other?"

"Find out where Mr. Conrad is going when he gets back to the states that I will definitely need to know. Shalom my friend."

"Shalom Saif."

"As many times as you've helped me since I came to Berlin, this is the least I can do. This will be a piece of cake. I'm great at pretending to be asleep even when I am!"

Huh? What? "Just remember if anyone comes looking for me to act like you are me asleep in bed. Good thing our uniforms fit each other. Make sure they can see my nametag but cover your face with my hat." patting him on his back for encouragement.

"Hey I outrank you now." smiling. "Sorry, not funny. That really sucks about your girl. Go get her killer."

"You look good sweetheart." attempting to lighten up. "Thanks for doing this, I owe you."

"I don't know what happened between the doctor and the nurse, I wasn't there. I only told him to retrieve the information he gave her not kill her. Hell, he probably didn't know the chloroform would have the effect it did or he wouldn't have used it. I didn't know it could make someone have a heart attack but he should have. Why did you need to kill him too? Now there's a lose end that needs closed. What do you expect me to do with your mess?" Maloney urged.

"We will clean up our mess that is what we do best. You only need to worry about your problem. Now, where is the American soldier going when he gets back to the states?" the voice on the other end quizzed.

"Hey Kelsey, is Conrad in his room? Sergeant Brooks is on the line and is asking." the new desk sergeant asked.

Trying to do my best imitation of my switcher I gave a quick reply. "Yes, he's sleeping sergeant." and continued on my way. *Whew! That was close!*

"Yeah Sarge, he's sleeping from what Kelsey said. Should I wake him?"

"No, no just make sure he doesn't leave and does sleep. He starts out processing tomorrow. Have a good day, oh, and by the way, my title is Sergeant!" slamming the phone. "Damn fools when will they learn!"

My plan was basic and simple just like Sergeant Brooks taught us, K.I.S.S., keep it simple stupid. First head to Amanda's house to hopefully find a roommate to talk with, next over to the hospital to check on Cox then back to the barracks all before night fall. Any taxi would do and the first one was perfect, my good friend from the night before. "Hello again, you're up early. Do you remember me from last night with the pretty lady?" I instinctively asked.

"How could I forget such a lovely lady and generous man, did you make it home ok?"

"Yes, my friend took me back here to the barracks. How was your ride to her house?" curious to find out if there were any problems.

"Ah, she smiled all the way home and not because of me, no, she smiled at that box you gave her. She had a look of love in her eyes. I know, I see in my wife's face every time I come home." He gloated. "So where to or don't I need to ask?" eye brows going up and down.

"Do you remember the address?"

"Of course I do, it was just last night and she was my last fare."

"Then please, take me there and don't be slow." doing my own imitation of his eye brow movements. "So she was all smiles, I'm glad I made a difference." *She died happy so I should give thanks to God for the time we did have together, but why did he take her this way? She didn't deserve that.*

The ride was less of a blur during the day so I could enjoy the view I missed from last night. The city is one of rebuilt beauty and shows pride in the good that can come from evil. All too often society doesn't learn enough from their past mistakes and repeats them far worse. Some good had to come from my one night love's untimely death.

"Here we are again sir." the driver was jubilant with his memory. "Should I wait?"

Unsure if anyone was home I paused to answer, "Let me see if someone is there first. If I wave you can go, if I walk back please wait and thank you again." It was more than odd this time knowing the person I wanted to see would not be walking out to greet me but the memory of her the night before rushed over me and I was unprepared for the emotion. I dropped to one knee and prayed for the strength. The taxi driver was watching and jumped out to see if I was ok and from hearing the door open I knew I had few seconds to act. "I'm ok just tying my shoe." He seemed to buy it and got back in for the moment. I continued on the walk to the front door. I could now see a young man standing at one of the windows talking but couldn't distinguish who he was talking to. I'd take my chances and let the driver go. I turned back to him and waved him goodbye and he returned the gesture from inside. I envisioned Amanda possibly doing the same thing just before she walked into the presumed safety of her home. *I should have been here with her, she'd still be alive. Or would we both be dead? Stop thinking like that and get back to why you're here!* I was never able to see her front door due to the darkness. In the daylight it was magnificent and huge. Hard to imagine her being able to open such a large wood door for such a small framed woman. I knocked and cleared my throat just before it opened. It was the young man I saw inside. "Sorry to bother you but I was looking for someone who could help me with Amanda's, ah…" I didn't know what words to say.

"And who are you? All the investigators left a few hours ago. Do you mean her death?" he was hardened by his colleagues passing.

"I'm Specialist Conrad. I was her date last night."

"You bastard! Did you kill her!?!" he shouted out as he lunged towards me.

With cat like reflexes from all the years of training I repelled his advance with a side sweeping block sending him into the stone wall outside the door. His nose erupted with blood as it cracked from the hardness of the rock. He stood holding his hemorrhaging ego and wounded pride. "Stop, just stop, I didn't have anything to do with her death!" still in stance waiting for his next assault. I sensed another pair of eyes in the area and turned to the doorway where the other roommate watched in horror.

"Derik stop, you're injured. Come inside so I can clean you up. "all the while glaring back at me. "I'm Ashley Webb, Amanda's other roommate. Who are you again?"

"Specialist Conrad, I took Amanda to dinner last night." forgetting I had Kelsey's shirt on.

"Then why does your nametag say Kelsey?"

Good eyes for being a blonde. "Long story but I needed to borrow my roommates." figuring she'd done the same with clothes before. "I apologize for his nose but he did jump at me first. May I please come in? I'd like to ask a few questions about what happened here last night." preparing to beg if I needed to.

"Well if she felt comfortable enough to go out on a date with you, then I suppose a little time won't hurt. Besides, I have Kung Fu Derik to protect me, isn't that right?" now laughing at his chivalry. "Do you mind showing me your ID to prove you are who you are or is that a longer story?"

Got to admit she is careful. Guess that's what Amanda liked about these two, they were protective and caring. Qualities hard to find in most people with the way the world is nowadays. "Here you go, Ashley was it?" smiling like in the picture.

"Good memory, please come in, Adel? Bet that's the longest story of them all." now strolling into the kitchen after handing my ID back. "Would you care for some tea? We were just about to make some before your knock."

"Yes, that would be appreciated, whatever kind you're making is fine with me."

"That's good because we only have one kind, cheap." she humored herself. "Let me finish cleaning up your handy work and we'll be back to chat about Amanda. I'm sure Derik and I have some questions of our own and you won't mind answering them, will you?"

Sure why not, everybody has questions these days. "No problem at all answering anything." sheepishly smiling back.

While they were gone, I couldn't help but notice the nurse figurine I had given Amanda sitting on the table. I walked over to revisit it and attempted to visualize her opening the box perhaps in the chair where it now sat near. The curvature of her face in the subtle glow of the light, her delicate fingers untying the ribbon, her posture as she sat cross-legged and most of all the warmest smile I had ever seen. The tears that I had held inside now forced their way out and I broke down sobbing.

The pair of nurses returned from their bathroom to find me crouched on the floor. Ashley had heard me crying as they got closer to the kitchen and now huddled alongside me. "It's OK, let it out." holding my head motherly- like while shaking hers at Derik in an "I don't know what's wrong with him." fashion. Her compassion was comforting but couldn't replace the embrace I remembered from Amanda. Feeling more like a fool now than the steadfast soldier from the front door, I strived to regain my composure.

"Thanks, thank you for your help and understanding." I appealed as I stood. "Shall we talk now?"

She guided me to a chair and started the water for the tea. Derik still had a look of uncertainty in his swollen face but with a slight hint of reasoning. He too felt the compassion I must have had for his adopted sister and began to liken me some. "So, Adel, please tell us how the date went. Did she enjoy herself?" Ashley asked.

"She, sorry to use this terminology, was in heaven. It was a dream come true for her and I'm happy I had the chance to give it to her. My other self-adopted parents who own the restaurant we went to just absolutely adored her. She was a big hit with them and they saw a look in my eyes they've never seen before, total enjoyment of being with someone special. If I had to say it, I'd say I was falling in love with her all in one momentous night and she was feeling the same."

"Then why weren't you here with her if you were so "in love"? Maybe she'd still be here with us." Derik angrily interrupted.

"Oh stop Derik! He had nothing to do with her murder. The cops already told us they had the person who did it in custody." Ashley yelled.

"Wait, what?!? They told you they have her murderer? They lied to both of you then. It was Dr. Marshall. At least that's what they told me when they questioned me."

"And why did they question you?" Derik piercing his gaze deep into my soul, as he looked for any dishonesty to my story.

"Look Derik, I empathize your feelings and had I known what was about to happen I would have never left her. I honestly believed I was taking her out of harms' way not driving her directly into its path. If I could go back in time and change things I would be the first. They thought I was the one who killed Dr. Marshall but it was proven I couldn't have done it. That is why they questioned me and why I'm here to ask you two for anything that can help me find the true mastermind behind all of this." I was hoping they'd join in my quest.

"DILLIGAF!" Derik screamed in rage.

What did he just call me? I'll push that nose in further if he says it again! "Are we going to keep this up all day? 'Cause I don't have that much time." I was now growing impatient.

"DILLIGAF is an expression we use in the ER. It means..."

"Do I look like I give a fuck?" Derik finished at which point I acted like I was going after his nose again and he jumped back. "Stay away from my nose. I can't breathe so as it is, I don't need you hitting it."

OK we have established who the Alpha male here is, now let's get to business. "I'll stop if you stop being a putz. Deal?" I slammed back.

"You both will stop acting like children." the teapot whistling signaling for attention. "Do you take cream and sugar with your tea Adel?" she politely asked.

"It's just Del, please call me Del. I hate my name, Adel, about as much as someone named Ronald being called Ronnie by his family all the time. And just sugar for me please."

He's very polite and well mannered. How ironic she finds a nice man and then loses him. God I'll miss her. "Here you go Del. If you need it sweeter, I'll stick my finger in it." giggling softly.

"Thank you Ashley. Your giggle makes me think of hers, it was so innocent and child-like for a beautiful woman." holding back the tears.

"Hey where's mine? Don't I get any?" Derik chimed in.

"It's on the stove, you're legs aren't broke, just your nose." she sarcastically fired back. "So, Del, you were saying about the evil doctor Marshall being the killer. Do you think it's true?"

"I honestly don't know but if A.I. is investigating it and they say he's the man then I'd have to believe it to be true. I mean, who else could it have been? Derik here?" laughing as I pointed at him.

"That wasn't funny, Adel. I loved her more than you ever could have in one night." being serious through his pain. "What do you know about love?"

"True love knows true love and never..."

"...forgets." Derik interrupted again. "How do you know that saying? My grandfather would always say that same thing."

He likes to interrupt a lot, must run in his family. "Was your grandfather in the big war?"

"Yes."

"Was he on a ship or in the Army?" I searched.

"Airborne with the Army actually, the 101st ..."

"...the Screaming Eagles, Rendezvous with destiny." I finished this time but then instinctively we stood together and manly yelled...

"Currahee!" sending Ashley wondering as we chest bumped. Finally a common territory we could relate to.

"So tell me how did your grandfather come to know my grandfather's saying?" I asked Derik.

"There was a guy from his unit that saved him when they fought together during the "Battle of the Bulge." An enemy sniper had my papa pinned down and this guy ran across the street to draw the snipers attention. He took a hit in the leg but kept going. It gave my papa enough time to fall back to another corner where together they managed to take out the sniper with a bazooka shot. They became best friends after that and he would always use that saying when they talked about the women they loved back home."

"Was this guy's name Cyrus by any chance?" I asked gleaming with pride.

"Ah, yeah, it was. Oh my God! Your papa was Cyrus?" he now caught on. "I wouldn't be here now if it wasn't for his bravery that day. So how is he doing these days?"

"He passed away in my senior year from a heart attack. I would spend hours just talking with him about the war and his memories. Grandma would just shake her head and start knitting or cooking or doing whatever 'cause she knew it would be awhile until he finished. When he died, it was the first time I had ever seen my father cry, I mean really cry. I try to honor him every day by being the best soldier I can be. I know he's watching so I want him to be proud."

Ashley sat admiring the story while savoring her tea and relishing the stoppage of fighting. "Hey Derik, didn't you tell me Amanda had asked you to forward a message to a Del? He's got to be the only Del in miles and he was the one she was with so tell him. I'm sure it would make him feel much better."

"She asked you to pass me a message? How, how could she and when?" trying to comprehend.

Sorrow beginning to rebuild in his eyes, he managed to disclose the terrible events from the previous night reliving them as he spoke. "She was lying on the floor at the door when I got home. When I knelt down to tell her I had to use the phone next door but would be back, she said, "Tell him..." choking back the tears of remembrance, "Tell him I love him." and then she collapsed."

This time we all comforted each other with a group embrace.

Chapter 18

"Oh thank God you're home. Any word on Chelsea, dear?" Maloney's wife pressed for answers.

"No Olivia but we are still looking. I'll find her, I have to. I must go out later to meet a colleague for more information. Will you be alright here alone or should I have someone come over?" his mind in a thousand places.

"I need you to find our daughter and get her back from those madmen, that's what I need, William. How did they ever get her in the first place? These things are not supposed to happen when you're a cop. Are they?" her emotions were fragile.

"They had her before they contacted me. There must be someone working with them from the inside but I can't figure who. This had to have been planned for quite some time. That worries me most because if they knew certain things before all the events of the last few days, how much more do they know?" his eyes filled with a grim fear for the worst.

"What should worry you the most is what I'll do to you if you don't get our daughter back before something worse happens to her." she stared straight into his face. She presses her body to his and holds him in desperation. "Find her."

"I can't be staying much longer. I still want to go to the hospital to see my friend who was shot in the attack. *I also need to avoid being caught outside the base.* Thanks for the tea and your time. You should be appreciative of the time you two had with her, it was more than I had." trying not to deaden the friendship I had just made.

"Hey Derik, don't we need to take some clothes over to the hospital for Amanda's trip home?" Ashley summoned. "Del could go with you."

"Yes we have to do that sometime, why not now? It's not like I haven't slept in two days." he groaned.

"Oh alright, I'll go with him. He'd be better company than you right now anyways. We'll go, just let me grab her clothes and my keys." smiling like she had other plans. "Can you at least call us a cab, Derik?" she politely asked on her way to her room.

"Damned woman, you'd think we were married some days." staring up the hall in the direction she went.

"I heard that. Honey." echoed down the hallway. I chuckled but he didn't find it humorous.

While he placed the call for the taxi, I began to help clean up from our tea party. I hadn't noticed when we were sitting but the box that contained the figurine was pushed off to the far side of the table behind a napkin holder. The lid had been closed so the "Thank you" was visible but there was more writing on it now. I ambled to that side of the table to see what it said. Underneath my message she had wrote "You're welcome." with a smiley in pen. That was a symbol to me that she liked what I had given her. Tears began to build again as I pictured her smiling while writing her message. Did she intend to give it back to me? And when would she have time? Perhaps when I went to visit my "brother" in the hospital? Answers I'd never know now.

"You gave her the box?" Derik asked now back from calling for the cab. "You're a very emotional type of guy I can see."

"Yes and yes, I've always been able to show affection. Don't know where it comes from because my dad I've seldom seen shed a tear and my mother is a sister to the wicked witch of the west." We both laughed at that analogy.

"The figurine, do you want it back?" he hesitated to ask.

"No, that was hers, she should keep it. You can send it home with her other belongings. I'll just write a quick note to explain it so her parents can understand its true meaning. I know if the situation were reversed, I'd feel better knowing someone cared enough about my daughter to had made her last night one of the best in her life. They deserve to know that much. Wouldn't you say so too?"

Shaking his head in an acknowledging fashion he placed his hand on my shoulder and offered these words for comfort, "I've known her for two years now and I can honestly say I never saw her light up more than yesterday when she self-agonized over what to wear. If guys could get her to go out she'd just throw anything on and that was it. It was not that way for your date, you were something special to her and she wanted to look extra nice. So don't beat yourself up over what has happened, it was God's will and that is the hardest to understand at times like these. Use the pain to focus but use the love she saw as inspiration and you'll reach your goal. That is what her family needs most and what would make her smile in Heaven."

He was absolutely right. That small talk showed me the big picture and direction I needed to travel. "Thanks Derik, you were a good "brother" to her and a greater friend. The best person was with her when she needed someone the most last night. May that comfort you for the remainder of your life. I guess God saw a need for my grandfather to save yours when he needed it so you could be here with her. He does work in mysterious ways, doesn't he?"

"Yes Del, yes he does." and we gave each other a manly hug. "Currahee."
"Currahee."

"So are you two finished exchanging tales of testosterone? He did say he needed to go soon." Ashley now standing behind us holding the dress and ensemble in her arms.

"Yes it's getting late and I must be going if I'm to keep my schedule. Derik, it's been a pleasure meeting and talking with you. Don't forget to tell your papa we met and stay in contact. I'll give Ashley my home address and she can get it back to you." and with a hand shake we left, Ashley leading the way.

"You know this was her other choice of what she couldn't decide to wear until I talked her into wearing the light blue outfit. I thought that one matched her eyes and she always looked good in it but she rarely wore it out." she held a light grey satin low cut back dress that would've made Amanda look just as lovely as the blue outfit. "No crying back there now. I know how emotional you have been."

Too late I'm already envisioning her in the one you're carrying. "I'll keep it together, Derik has helped me focus." I assured her as the taxi pulled up.

The phone's ringing awoke Sergeant Brooks from his nap way too early. "The fool on the other end better hope this is important." as he wipes the sleep from his eyes then rolls over to answer. "Yeah, yeah, yeah, what is it? This better be worth waking me up." yawning then looking to see what time it is on his clock.

"Rufus, you old dog, you're still asleep at this time of the day? Isn't it like 1 o'clock your time?" a voice he knew but also knew he didn't care for much.

"Roger Lawrence, did my sister put you up to calling me? And why are you calling me now, at home? Is everything ok at home?" now more awake as he asks.

"Slow down dear brother, you'll blow a fuse. She's fine and so is everyone else here. I called your mess thingy and they said you were at home. They didn't tell me you were sleeping so I apologize for waking your grumpy ass up but it's worth it. I'm at work and just got some news I thought you'd like."

"It's called a mess hall and I hope you don't tell me who it was you spoke with but anyways, what news?" *and I'm not your brother but you have me listening.*

"It's about our visitor who's coming to town. Care to hear about it?"

Sarge sat straight up, totally awake now from the prearranged code signal they had agreed upon when it was first discovered and discussed. He could only mean Nibiru. "I'm all ears."

"Well remember the brains thought it'd be like a hundred years until he showed his ugly head?"

"Yeah, go on."

"Well it looks like even they are wrong with a calculator. New estimates say he'll be here within the next thirty to thirty-five years." *I got one up on him now!,* as he smiles on his end.

"Are they sure this time?" Sarge unbelievably asks.

"I'd say more so now than they were the first time. Has something to do with how it wobbles, all too scientific for you to understand." *I got another one on him, ha ha!*

"So do they have any idea yet if it'll come close or pass us by?" asking child-like.

"That's the most interesting part. The head brain that did the recalculating figures this baby will be either real close or ah...hit us." *Three for three, you're out of here brother!*

"Oh my God, what will we do?" Sarge running his hand over his head.

"No Ruf, what can we do? It's not like we can turn a wheel to avoid an accident. Even if it does come close, it'll affect us in ways we've never experienced before. It'll take more than a prayer to help any of us through this one." now he doesn't feel so wonderful about knowing more.

"I think it might be time for me to share our secret with someone I feel may have a date with destiny. At least I hope it's a possibility, for all our sakes. Give my love to my sister and tell her to write me more. See you all soon, I'm wishing."

"Will do Ruf. You be careful with who you share this with. It's more deadlier than you can imagine."

"No I can imagine and my damn name is Rufus! Not Ruf!" as he slams the phone down hard. "Hope it makes his ear ring all day, the moron!"

"I'll pay for this ride Ashley." as I hand the driver the fare. "Thank you, sir."

"Wow you are so sweet." as she gets out the door. "So I guess you'll be heading to see your friend now?"

"Yeah I hope he's conscious now. When we left the other night he wasn't. Any chance you could check on his condition for me before I try to find him?" I asked pleadingly. "It would save me some time."

"Sure thing Del. We can stop at the nurse's station and find out where he is and his progress."

"You've been a great help today. I'm grateful for your assistance." giving her a slight wink.

She giggles like a little girl would and says, "I'd assist you how ever I can." then winks back.

Sorry Ashley but I'm a one woman man and I have a promise to keep. "Perhaps sometime in the future, no one ever knows, do we?" *That should keep the peace between us.*

"Hopefully sooner." she says still giggling as we walk inside. She points towards a station just off to the right. "Over there is our station. That's Tricia with the clipboard. Watch out for her claws, they're not as sharp as she thinks they are but she will cling, if you know what I mean?"

Really, like you're not a clingy type person? "OK, I'll keep that in mind."

"Hi Tricie," Ashley being friendly and all smiles. "...can you help me find a patient?"

"Sure Ash, who's the stud? Yowza!"

"That's Del, he was Amanda's secret boyfriend only a few of us knew." *So keep away!*

"Oh man, that must suck for him. Think he needs some cheering up?" she offers.

"No, Derik and I have been taking care of that ALL day today. He came along to see his friend and assist me with Amanda's clothes for her trip home." Ashley informed her.

"Crap! I just can't seem to find a nice guy anywhere in this town. They're all losers or users. Do you know what I mean?"

"Girl you're not telling me anything I don't already know. She sure had a good one though and now she's gone. Hard to believe it." Ashley shaking her head.

"I know. Did they find any clues at your house? Got any idea who may have killed her?" Tricia asked inquisitively.

"No, no idea yet." *And I wouldn't tell your blabbering ass anyways.* "So how about his friend? Last name is Cox. GS victim."

"He's in room 204,ICU. Would that be the guy from the attack?" Tricia still looking my way.

"That would be the one. Poor guy's friend gets shot protecting him and then Amanda. Seems dangerous to be around him don't you think?" waving her hand in front of Tricia's face.

"Oh I wouldn't care. I'd die happy in his arms any day." she says with a sigh.

Girl you need some serious help or a good lay. "Well we better get going. I'll see you later tonight." and back over to me Ashley came.

"Did your friend tell you where Cox is?" I hurriedly asked.

"Yes but he's in ICU. They won't just let you in since you're not true family. I have an idea though since you like to impersonate other people but you'll have to trust me. Do you?"

"Do I have any other choices? Of course I trust your judgment, you're Amanda's friend and now mine, right?" *What a suck up I am. Geez Del.*

"Yes Del, we are now friends for life." she pats me on the shoulder.

"So, friend, why does that nurse keep looking at me so, ah, lovingly?"

"Because she thinks you're hot and can't find a guy in this town to suit her needs. Why, you're not seriously thinking about going out with her, are you?" sounding upset that I'd choose Tricia over her.

"Oh my no but I know someone who would. Let me hold the dress for a second and walk over with me. You do trust me, right?"

"Sure thing Del, I trust your judgment, you're my friend." mocking my words.

We walked over to the desk with the dress draped over the nametag of my uniform. "Hi, I'm Del and I understand you are having a hard time finding a nice guy in this big old town." extending my hand to befriend Tricia.

"That may be true but it won't be anyone as good looking as you, honey." primping her hair while accepting my hand. I placed a small peck on her soft hand.

"Well what if I said he was as good looking or better? Would you be interested?" focusing my attention deep into hers.

"Please, do tell me more." batting her eyes.

"This is Sergeant Brooks again, is Conrad still in his room?"

"He should be, I haven't seen him go anywhere. Should I check?" the desk sergeant asked.

"Ah, yeah, why not, but don't wake him if he's still sleeping." *He better be in bed.*

"Give me a few, I'll be right back."

"I can't believe you set up Tricia with a date and not me." Ashley was now pouting.

"Trust me, you wouldn't want Kelsey. He's a woman user and he'll just add her to his "stable" as he calls it." attempting to reassure her. "He'll give her what she needs."

"Ohhhh, I see. Good one!" as her light bulb went on inside her head.

"So where are we going?" I asked Ashley.

"First I, I mean we, need to drop these clothes off for Amanda. Are you alright with that? You do know where we have to go?" she quizzed back.

A chill went up my spine. *Is she referring to the morgue? God I hope not.* "I'm not totally sure but you'll tell me before we get there, right?"

"Del, if you're not ok with this, I'll understand. WE need to take these to the morgue. That's where they are holding her. That's where they hold all the deceased bodies." acting like I didn't know.

"Yes, Ash, that much I knew, I just didn't know I was going with you to drop off clothes when we left your house. I'll be ok. I'll be strong like I said I would." feeling a lump in my throat.

"Just let me do all the talking and everything will be fine. The guy who works the morgue is cool. He's a stoner from California but he's cool."

I nodded my head as the elevator dinged and the doors opened.

"Yes Sergeant Brooks, he's sound asleep in his bed. Curled up like a little baby." he chuckled.

"Thanks Sarge for checking." and then he slams the phone down. "Beat you to that one, buddy." *I should check on Cox while I'm awake and see how he's doing.* Sergeant Brooks dials the number he was given at the hospital.

"Hello, this is the main directory, if you know your extension, please dial it now, if not remain on the phone for an operator."

"I hate this new automation stuff. What's next? Home computers?" as he punches in the extension numbers for ICU.

"Hello, this is ICU, how may I help you?"

"Ah, yes, this is Master Sergeant Brooks, I'm checking on the status of one of my soldiers in your care, a Corporal Cox."

"One moment Sergeant, his new doctor is checking on him now."

"Take your time son, I've got all day."

"Hi Carl. How's it hanging dude?" Ashley strutting like a California chicken.

"Oh hey Ash, it's hanging." in his California surfer guy tone. "What brings you here? Oh hey dude, what's your name?" directing his question at me.

"Hi, ah, dude. I'm Del?" unsure what to say to the stoner.

"Funny guy, Ash. He doesn't even know his name. What have you two been doing?" laughing like a surfer dude.

"Question Carl is what have you been doing? Did you smoke some before work?"

"Ah, no."

"Then why are your eyes all bloodshot and red?" Ashley probed.

"I just got Amanda in and wasn't told she was killed until after I uncovered her. I think I almost shit myself. I looked at the calendar to see if it was Halloween or April fool's day thinking someone was playing a prank on me. Imagine my surprise when I went to tickle her and she didn't move? I'm serious, I think I crapped my pants. Will you check for me?"

She tried hard not to laugh considering the grim reality of her friend's demise but knew he was truly serious. "No Carl, I won't check them but thanks for lightening our day. We needed a good laugh."

As I peered around the room attempting to ascertain which sheet covered my lost love, Carl asked Ashley, "So who is he? Your new boyfriend? Is he cool?"

"He's cool Carl. Actually he's Amanda's secret boyfriend that only a few of us knew. You can keep it a secret we were here, right dude?"

"No problem Ash. Your secret is my secret. So, should we let him see her? I did."

"You pervert!" Ashley said softly. "What did you do?" hitting him with her hand.

"Huh, huh, ah, no Ash, I didn't do anything like that. She was too nice to me. She always shared her lunch with me if I was having a munchy attack. Why do you think my eyes are red?"

"Sniffing embalming fluid? I don't know? Why are they Carl?" glaring into his pupils.

"I was crying. That's why." he seemed offended.

While they continued to talk, the eerie thought that one other person I had known was here also, Gabby. I wasn't going looking at toe tags for fear I'd find Dr. Marshall's before I'd get to Amanda's or Gabby. I jumped at the touch of Ashley's hand contacting my shoulder.

"Sorry Del, I didn't mean to make you jittery. Carl asked if you'd like to see Amanda one last time?" her expression of doubt showing. "I didn't know what to say." now trying to comfort me while I made my decision.

"I hadn't really thought about it. I don't want to lose the image I have of her when we were together but on the other hand, it may make it stronger. Will you go with me if I do?" begging for her to go also.

"You know what? I think if I knew her as well as I think I did, she'd want us to say goodbye considering our circumstances. You're heading back to the states and I'll be here so yes, let's say our farewells here." She turned back around to Carl who was biting his nails and said "Carl, we'd like to see our friend one last time. Please."

"Right this way lady and gentleman. Please keep your hands in and run if one touches you. Heh, heh, just kidding."

Chapter 19

Saif was on hold waiting for his superior to pick up. They had known each other since their days in the IDF. He respected Moshe as much as he respected Saif, perhaps more. Saif had once dated his sister before they joined the MOSSAD so they treated each other like brothers. Moshe had proved to be a great leader and valued the hard work his men sacrificed citing they would be repaid in Heaven for their commitment to Israel. "Shalom, Saif, what news do you have?"

"Shalom, director. We have questioned an American soldier and I have Aviv checking on the A.I. officer who is handling the investigation. All indications suggest the attack was the work of Al Atta but we are still unsure of why here and now. Have you spoken with the U.S. State department you told me you'd phone?"

"Yes, I spoke with them this morning. I was quite surprised the American was up so early but he seemed worried about the actions in Berlin. Why is Aviv checking on this officer?"

"Call it my sixth sense but my experience tells me something is not complaisant. He received a call while I was in his office but he seemed nervous, fidgety." Saif explained. "You know how that always stirs my intrigue."

"Yes my friend and it has saved us more than once. God has blessed you with a unique gift and I'm glad you're on our side." They chuckle together. "Tell me about this American soldier."

"He is strong, yet weak in some ways. He is a devoted soldier and believes in himself but gets blinded by love." Saif never believed in true love or any kind of love other than for God and Israel. "We have butted heads a few times already so I know he doesn't like me but he just doesn't understand the whole situation."

"Then make him understand so he is your ally and not your enemy. You can't get honey if there are no bees Saif. I trust you'll find a way to make him see we both fight for the same cause, he just fights for the Americans." again they laugh.

"You are correct as usual Moshe, I mean director. All the Americans think about is money, sex and more money. Once they realize there is more to life than those two things, the world will be better."

"Ah, but until then we must keep fighting our fight. If we let organizations like Al Atta to continue to operate unobstructed then we face certain death. That is all they desire which is worse than the American way. I have cleared your restrictions in Europe with Interpol. You may use deadly force if required. I hope you do not but I don't want to lose one of my best agents."

"Thank you sir and Aviv and I will be careful. I must go now and get ready to meet with the American officer. We are comparing notes, I can only hope he has done more homework than me. Shalom, Moshe."

"We'll speak again soon Saif, Shalom."

Reaching into his now unlocked gun case, Saif pulls out his weapon of choice, an Israeli Army issue Browning Hi-Power 9mm Luger pistol. He liked it because of the feel when he shot it, the accuracy he had developed from years of shooting one but most of all because it's magazine held thirteen rounds compared to the average nine in others giving him a distinct advantage. "I hope the director is right and I don't need to use you." he says as he opens the breach to inspect it. Moments later Aviv walks in and grins because he knows they are cleared for force. "Yes Aviv what have you found?"

"The American officer from A.I. has lied to you. He wasn't talking to anyone from America, he got a local call from here in Berlin." he is grinning wider now.

"So the plot thickens. Do all Americans lie? Get yourself ready, we have a dinner date with this storyteller and we don't want to be late." a glimmer of dissatisfaction coming from his face.

Over to the row of tables Ashley and I walk following our guide to Amanda. This is new to both of us although Ashley had been down here before just not under these circumstances. I hold her hand and can feel her shaking. "We'll be ok." I try to encourage her. She just nods approval in believing my words.

"Well dude, she's here. Are you both sure you want to go through with this? Last chance to back out."

He was right, we had walked this far, would we turn our backs to her now? "No, I'm not stopping now." I reconfirmed my decision in my head too.

As Carl began to uncover Amanda's lifeless body, the last part of my dream replayed in my head. It wasn't Cox though this time, it was Amanda. He only went as far as her neckline so as not to disturb either of us. "If you need to puke, there's a bucket behind you."

Amazingly, a gentle calm came over me like she was behind me caressing my shoulder and telling me everything would be fine. I could almost hear her saying "Thank you." as though she was reading it from the box I had given her. She looked as lovely as the previous night, like her makeup was still on. Instead of breaking down crying like I anticipated I'd be, I stood tall and held Ashley as she cried. When it felt like she was ready to leave, I allowed her to go but I wanted to stay for just another moment. "I'll be there in a second." I told her. She looked at me like she understood what was coming next. I knelt down on one knee and bowed my head. "Lord as my witness, Amanda Kelley, I'll get whoever is behind all of this and make them pay for taking you away too early." As I stood back up I added, "I never got a chance to tell you... but I love you too." then leaned down and placed one final kiss on her cold lips. Ashley couldn't bear watching me standing alone any longer and rejoined me, her strength rekindled.

"You're a good man Adel Conrad. God _will_ grant your wish, I feel it in my heart."

As we turned back to leave, Carl was in the doorway crying. "See, this is why my eyes are bloodshot and red. She lightens up a room even in her darkest hour." We gave him a hug and thanked him for our secret meeting.

"Let's go see your friend now, Del." Ashley said as she laid her head on my arm going to the elevators.

Yeah, let's go see my friend.

"Sorry for the wait Sergeant Brooks but the doctor was busy going over your Corporal's charts, Dr. Marshall's handwriting wasn't the most legible."

"I just wanted an update, not his blood count or vitals, understand?" Sarge said firmly.

"Yes I do Sergeant and that is what I was waiting for, understand me?" firing back.

Who is this guy? I hope he isn't working when I go in, I'll have him understanding me! "So how is he?" getting straight to the point.

"He is still in a coma but shows signs of coming out of that but we won't know how soon. He lost a lot of blood and it's been hard to replenish it with just fluids but we have him stable and monitored twenty-four seven. So to fully answer your question, he is critical but stable."

"Thank you, ah...." he waited for a name.

"My name is Pat." saying smugly.

"Thank you Pat for your help." then he hangs up the phone. "Great, now I'm not sure if that was a guy or a woman with a manly voice." He shivered from the thought while making a yucky face.

Back up to the first floor to find for me a suitable outfit so Ashley could get me into the ICU to see Cox. Admittedly, her plan was good and would keep my face concealed and my identity unquestioned. She escorted me to a linen room where we found the necessary items and began my transformation. "Wait, what about you? What are you wearing?" I requested.

"I'm not going in to his room. I can help you better by being outside and distracting the doctor while you do what I have told you to do. My way will get you in to see him without raising any suspicions so long as you do what I've planned for you. Don't do anything less and definitely nothing more. It will work. Trust me." she said the last with a big smile.

Trying to do my best imitation of Carl, I replied back, "Ah, huh, huh, ok dude." to which she giggled loud then catching me off guard tip-toed upwards and sisterly-like placed a quick kiss on my cheek. "What was that for?" asking somewhat red faced.

"Luck but mostly because I wanted to all day." she was pleased with her action.

"So how do I look? Do I look like a doctor?" knowing that wasn't the desired appearance.

"No, I'd say you look exactly as I had planned." she smirked like she knew something I didn't yet. She was right, again.

After comforting his wife and making sure she was sound asleep, Maloney sat down at their kitchen table to prepare his note to her. He was on edge with his daughter's capture, the base attack and the gut feeling that there was more to these events that tied together. His cup of coffee was ready and so was he as he wrote:

My Dearest Olivia,

I promise to you that I will do whatever I can to get our daughter back, safe and sound. These are not normal men I'm dealing with, they would kill their own daughters for their glory's sake. I have a meeting later tonight and hope I can arrange her release. I also hope I make it back from that meeting alive. Know this, if I am not fortunate, I love you with all my heart. I'm happy for the life we've had together, the places we've seen together but mostly the times we've just held each other.

Love Always,
William

A tear rolled down his aged cheek as he sealed the envelope with his note in it. On the outside he simply wrote: Only open if I don't return. Love, William. He grabbed his coat from the hall rack and headed out, never looking back.

"Well now that I'm up I may as well do something. I better check in at the mess hall and I can see Conrad after that. I'm feeling a little hungry so I'll grab a bite to eat on my way over to the hospital to see Cox. What do you think there Merlin? Sound like a good plan? See Cox, go to the mess and then check on Conrad." Merlin was his pet Sun Conure. He saw him at a local pet store and loved Merlin's colors and the bird loved being held plus he didn't need to leave him outside like a dog. The companionship they shared was all he needed and the only family he cared for other than his Army family. Both were his lifelong loves but Merlin was the one he could go home to after a long day. Merlin approved by bobbing his head up and down then gave him a kiss on the side of his cheek. "Ok then buddy, back in your cage you go." He fed Merlin his favorites, papaya, peanuts, some coconut flakes and the best of all, walnuts. He was Sarge's outlet to life and he smiled whenever he looked at Merlin. "Time to go get ready." To which Merlin approved again with his head bob.

"This is Officer Maloney, someone pickup." he demanded over his car radio. He was never the most polished of officers but his dedication to his job was second to none.

"Yes sir, go ahead."

"Who is this?" Maloney didn't recognize the voice.

"It's Tony, Tony Bosch, sir. I just started two weeks ago, sir."

"Oh, ok, I remember you now. Well I'm checking back before leaving my house. Are there any messages for me?" Maloney was waiting for word on Saif's choice of a place to meet.

"Just one sir, from a Saif, he says he'll meet you at Cicciolina's at the time you agreed on."

"Great, I know the place well, been there with my wife a few times. Thank you, Tony. If anyone needs to contact me I'll be at the hospital. I'm going to check on the soldier who was wounded in the attack."

"Ok sir, have a good night."

I hope it is a good one. Maloney thought as he started his car.

A new corner stand had opened a few weeks before Sergeant Brooks found out about it. It was an old Army buddy that decided to stay in Berlin, mainly due to his new wife being from there but also because he loved the city. His main dishes were chicken and fries but he also made a mean potato salad that Sarge couldn't resist. He'd finally have a chance to visit and patronize his old friend. The thought of food made his stomach growl. "Hold on down there…" while rubbing his belly, "I'm going to get food now." His former Army bud saw the jeep pull next to the stand and immediately recognized his face, drawing him out from the food wagon.

"Sarge you old dog, you finally came to visit. Or is it to eat?" he laughed loudly while giving a big masculine hug that Brooks returned. "How have you been?"

"I came to eat and I'm doing fine, considering how things are at the base. So you stayed in Berlin."

"Yeah the wife didn't want to go to the states so we took a shot at opening our own stand. This way she can see her mom whenever and I get to make money cooking." still smiling.

"So how is business? Got them lined up I see." Sarge commended.

"Business is booming and I can't keep the chicken cooked fast enough. Actually it's my potato salad I think they come for." they chuckled at his boasting together.

"So are you going to make a hungry man wait or can I get one of those meals?"

"Coming up, with fries or potato salad, like I need to ask?" he headed back inside. "Here you are Sarge, on the house!" prompting a swat from his wife. "What? The man's starving for good food."

"Thanks my old friend." Brooks giving him a half salute.

"You're welcome, Rufus. Hey, I better get back to work before the boss tries to fire me and I'm sleeping on the streets." and gives Sarge a quick choppy salute back.

"See you later Pete."

"Ashley, I feel ridiculous. Are you sure this will work?"

"Del honey, you'll be fine. Just clean the trash in the room and I'll do the hard work of distracting the doctors. Just watch for my signal."

The elevator door opened and I pushed the heavy service cart through. Unsure which direction to go, I waited for Ashley to lead the way. She patted me on my buttocks as she passed by and giggled softly. I guess she finally got something to show for her time with me that pleased her.

"Hi guys." Ashley chimed in.

They all knew her for they had just been talking about her roommate and what happened. Almost all tried to give a cheerful "Hello." back.

Following her and her hand signals, she waved me on with her hands from behind her back, I proceeded past the nursing station and into the ICU rooms.

"Hey! Don't forget to put your mask on and empty the bed pan from bed two, he filled it pretty good and the last cleaner didn't get it and it smells." said the jubilant nurse watching me as I entered.

Yeah sure, was it Carl's pot smoking party companion? "Ok, I'll make sure it's taken care of this time." *Yuk! My damn luck!*

"He's new here isn't he Ashley?" she asked.

"I wouldn't know. I've never seen him before but his credentials were on from what I saw when we came up. He didn't speak much on the ride up." she tried to ease her curiosity.

"Maybe I should check them? We have some big wig coming in and I don't need a butt chewing." she started to stand.

"Oh just check them when he comes back out. I'm sure everything should be ok. Do you really think someone would just come in to clean bed pans?" again she tried to calm her inquisitive nature.

"Yeah, you're probably right and I'm just on edge. Come to think about it, who would want to just come in here to clean those stinky things? Poor guy, I hope they pay him well." she laughs then Ashley joins in laughing with her.

Oh if you only knew. "So who's coming in, do you know?"

"All I've been told is that an investigator was coming to talk to the GS victim from the attack. The guy is still in a coma. How's the fool going to talk to him? Mental telepathy?" she laughs some more.

"Which one is he?" Ashley inquires.

"Oh that's the one in bed two who filled his pan. I hope this guy doesn't miss it like the last one did."

I had already started on the far side of the room and was waiting for Ashley's first signal while trying not to look too suspicious. When she raised two fingers in the air while pretending to stretch, I wanted to grab a clean pan and hit Cox myself. *Oh wonderful buddy, you filled it just for me?* I gave a fast thumbs up so she knew I received her message. I saw her giggle and knew it amused her. I finished the room I was in and headed to the next to do it quickly. Cox was the next after that and I wanted to hurry so I'd have time to see him.

"I guess you've heard about Amanda by now?" Ashley quizzed.

"Yes we did you poor girl. I'm so sorry to hear about your friend's death." she offered a hand for comfort. Now some of the staff has either left or are checking on their patients.

"That's what brought me in today. I had to bring clothes for her trip home."
Again she signals, this time a subtle wave while she stretches. I'm clear for the moment.

Walking into his room I can understand why the nurse wants the pan taken out. "Geez bud you stink." I say under my breath. "How you doing in there?" knowing he is out but hoping he can hear me. "You hang in there and get better. OK?" patting his hand with mine. The touch made him stir some. *Can he feel and hear me?* "I'll get who is responsible for everything. You have my word on that." I decide to pat his hand once more. His eyes barely open enough to let light in but he seems to be looking directly at me. "Can you see me?" I ask. With a rising of his thumb, I know he has heard me and I smile under my mask. I feel a sense of relief only to have it quell when the doors to the elevator open. "It's Maloney, but why is he here?" I go back to acting my part of cleaning.

"Hello nurse, I'm Officer Maloney." showing his I.D. "I've come to see Corporal Cox. Has he come out of his coma yet?"

"No sir he hasn't. He's in bed two. Over there where the custodian is now." she points my way.

Ashley knows it's now only a matter of time before he decides to join us. "Hey can I ask you a personal question officer? I see you're a married man, do you think my boobs are big enough or should I get bigger ones?" she holds her breast in her hands.

Last signal, time to go.

"My boyfriend thinks I need larger ones." Ashley continues to try to keep Maloney occupied.

"Ah, well, miss, I'd say tell him they are yours and that's all you have to offer. If he's not happy with them he should find another pair, after he leaves." he smiles awkwardly from the question.

"I like that answer." she accepts.

"Hell me too Ashley." says the other nurse. "Your wife must love you." she smiles at him.

"Ah, bed two you said?" he's anxious to leave.

"That's right sir. Bed two." Ashley says loud enough so I can hear.

"It's time for me to go buddy. I hope we can see each other again." I give him a slightly firm hand shake. This time he responds back with his own grip of my shirt. His monitors start to sound causing the staff to scurry to his bed.

"What happened here?" the first doctor in asks me.

Remembering my name tag has "Juan" for my first name I answer in my best Spanish speaking voice. "I don't know doctor. I just clean room. Then bells go off."

"Ok you can leave us, we need the room." he orders.

Others have started to filter in along with Officer Maloney. "Is he coming out of his coma?" he hopingly asks.

"Who are you now?" the doctor replies.

"I'm A.I., Officer Maloney. I'm here to see this soldier for questioning."

"Well officer that will still be some time. As you can see he just started to come out of his coma. Didn't I tell you to leave custodian?" he peers at me.

"Yes, doctor, I leave now." I can see Ashley starting to panic from all the activity in the room.

"Hey wait sucker, I told you NOT to forget that pan, so you better grab it while you can." the stubborn nurse quickly added.

Crap! Literally, crap! Just when I thought I could avoid it. Quaveringly I grasp the pan but it's fuller than I anticipated. The fluids begin to spill and they are going all over Maloney's shoes. The nurse jumps back to avoid getting hit also. "Sorry, I clean up." laughing to myself under my mask.

"Oh! Just throw some towels down for now!" the nurse yells now madder than a hornet's nest.

"What about my shoes?" Maloney asks.

"Here you go sir, sorry." I reply throwing a towel over them then quickly exiting. *Glad that's over!* I head to the last bed for it's trash and to hear more.

"Corporal Cox, this is Dr. Roth, can you understand me and what I'm saying?" he waits for his response. Cox blinks and gives him another thumbs up. "Good, very good. Can you grip my fingers?" he holds two fingers out for him to grasp. He is able to but only lightly. "Ok soldier, you're doing fine." He uprights himself and looks at Maloney. "You might be able to ask him a few questions but not now. Come back later, ok?"

I've heard all I'll hear and determine now is the time to leave before Maloney does. *I can't be caught in the elevator with him. He'll know it's me.* Quicker now, I push the cart to escape. Ashley has already summoned the elevator to our floor and it opens as I arrive at the door. I give her a wink going in and she holds the door.

"Goodbye, Martha!" she yells to the nurse. "Thanks for the talk." and waves goodbye from within our exit pod.

"Whew! That was too close! Thank you Ashley, you performed amazingly."

She busts out laughing in hysterics. "You dropped poop on his shoes!"

Sergeant Brooks was licking his fingers as he pulled into the parking stall. "Damn good chicken." he said with a smile. "Now I need a drink. I should've got one at Pete's stand." He brought along his remaining potato salad. Once inside he'd head to the vending machines for that drink and some towels to clean his hands off. He passed by the nurse's station where Tricia was checking her make-up. "Nurse, can you tell me which way to the vending area?"

She never stopped to acknowledge him but answered him with a point in the direction to go.

"Thanks dear." he continued on the path figuring he'd find another more conforming individual to assist him. As he approached the elevators, our door dinged and opened.

Oh shit! That's Sarge! "Alert!" I managed to inform Ashley. She looked back at me confused.

"Excuse me orderly, can you tell me where the vending area is?" Brooks asked me still not knowing it was me under the disguise.

I patted Ashley on her rump and she jumped forward almost into Sergeant Brooks. She must have understood what the alert was now about.

"Oh I can help you with that Sergeant. It's down that hall, then make a right at the end and follow the signs."

"Well thank you miss?" he hoped for her name.

"Ashley and your name?" she inquired back.

"Ah, ah, it's Rufus." he replied shyly.

"That's a nice unusual name, I mean unique name." she awkwardly admitted.

I laughed just a bit too loud provoking Sarge to respond.

"You find something funny with my name?"

"Oh no sir, it's a nice name." and I began to push the cart out.

"That's good because the only thing funny is the smell coming from your cart. No wonder you're wearing a mask. I would too if I had that job." and he allowed me to pass.

Ha, ha, I'd like to drop some of this poop on your shoes too. If you only knew it was me. "Thank you." and back towards the linen closet I went. *Wow! Two close calls, that's enough for me. I'm out of here.*

"Thanks again Ashley, you were more help than that nurse over there." pointing back at Tricia and down the hall he went.

She hurried to catch up to me. "Who was that?"

"That my dear was my Mess Sergeant and if he would have caught me I'd be cleaning more than poop."

"So doctor, can you give me a time estimate of when I may speak with this man?" Maloney asked.

"Come back in an hour or two and someone will let you know if you can."

Checking his ten dollar watch, he determined he might have just enough time to make his dinner meeting with Saif if he stayed for an hour but no longer. "Okay, I'll come back in an hour."

"I'm glad to be out of these clothes and I'll never do that job ever again, that's for sure." I moaned.

"You did well up there. You'd make a great custodian someday." She giggled.

"Thanks for all your help today. I couldn't have done it without you." then leaned down and placed a kiss on her forehead.

"What was that for Del?" she timidly asked.

"My way of showing appreciation without losing the friendship we've made. Someday you too will find the love of your life just as I did with Amanda."

"How could you know in only one night? Is that possible?"

"Do you believe in love at first sight?" She shook her head yes. "Then I believe in my heart she was the one."

"There will never be another is what you're saying?"

"That is up to God. It is all a part of his master plan." I answered.

"Then I hope too that you find another love to replace the love you lost. Don't lose faith and it'll find you again."

"That I'll believe if it happens. Now don't forget to give Derik my address. Okay?"

"May I write you also? Friend." she pleaded.

"Certainly, I'd like that. Friend." giving her a kiss on her hand goodbye.

Maloney strolled into the vending area hoping to find a coffee machine. When he saw Brooks sitting at one of the tables he walked over. "Hello Sergeant Brooks. What brings you here? Potato salad?" looking over at his dish.

"Yes, it's potato salad and no I didn't come here for it, I came to see how my soldier is doing but needed a drink." holding up the can of soda and feeling displeased with his presence.

"Well I'll save you some time. I just came from seeing his doctor. He's coming out of his coma but they won't let anyone see him for at least another hour."

"I guess that gives us some more time together." Sergeant Brooks glazed at Maloney.

"I guess it does now, doesn't it." Maloney smirked back.

Chapter 20

I better hurry back to base before Sarge decides to go back. My thoughts were running wild now with almost getting caught off base. My only reprieve was that he had said I'd start out processing tomorrow not today. That in my mind gave me clearance to do what I wanted today. I didn't have enough time to hit the bank before leaving base so I only had a few more marks on me. "Guess it's the bus I'm taking back." I told myself. Buses never bothered me and you have the luxury of seeing more plus they go slower most of the time. This would more than likely be my last ride on one and with daylight soon evaporating it allowed me the opportunity to watch the transition. So much had happened so quickly over the last few days, I forgot to relax and take in the splendor of God's creation. I just hoped I wouldn't fall asleep and miss my stop.

"How much longer will he be?" Kelsey spoke out loud. "It's been four hours already and I need to pee and I'm hungry." he finished. He couldn't wait any longer to hit the bathroom but eating could. He looked both ways up and down the hall, no one was around. Quickly he ran to the bathroom, opened the door and almost passed out on the spot. The desk Sergeant was in using the facilities also. He lowered his head hoping he wouldn't identify him and grabbed the first stall closing the door behind him.

"Wow someone needs a crapper bad. Who was that that flew by so fast?" he laughed about it.

"Kelsey, Sergeant." *Shit you idiot, wrong name.*

"Hey you're Conrad's roommate right?"

"Yeah."

"Tell him Sergeant Brooks was looking for him earlier."

Oh no! He was here? Was I sleeping and missed him? "Did he say why he was looking for him?" Kelsey inquired.

"No he didn't, he just called to see if he was sleeping. I guess the guy is leaving sooner than he thought."

"Okay I'll tell him when I see him."

"Why? Isn't he in your room?" the nosey Sergeant asked.

"Ah, I don't know because I didn't stop in the room. I had to go bad." proud of his fast thinking.

Zipping up his fly now, the desk sergeant walks over to wash his hands and pounds on the stall door. "Don't forget to wash your hands." he guffaws. He hears the sound of Kelsey dropping his shot. "See I helped you."

He almost jumped out of his pants. *Yeah big help, glad I was sitting for that one.* "Thanks for the help. Someday I'll return the favor."

An hour had passed so Brooks and Maloney decided to see if they could get in to see Cox. Sarge was glad too because the chat was boring. Getting off the elevator they were almost ran over by another custodian leaving the floor.

"Hey watch where you're moving that thing." Maloney barked out at him.

"Sorry sir, I did not see you." he said in a Spanish sounding voice.

They both looked at the other and just shook their heads. Had they looked closer, they would have seen it was the same "Juan" from earlier. "Man this is a clean place. They have guys cleaning crap all day around here." Sarge bellowed.

Maloney looked down at his shoes and didn't find it funny. "Yeah I had one from earlier drop some on my shoes."

"So that's what I smelled. I thought it was coming from you but didn't want to hurt your feelings by saying something."

They lightened up some by laughing together then almost instantaneously came to the same conclusion. "Conrad!"

"If that was him, he'll clean my shoes all week until he's gone." Maloney said ticked off by the thought it might have been me.

"I'll do worse than that I'll kick his butt all the way back to the states!" Sergeant Brooks added.

"So you were telling me downstairs he was leaving. Have they decided on a date yet?"

"Yes but why do you ask? Aren't you finished questioning him?" Brooks' curiosity peaked.

"No reason, just continuing our small talk. Let's check on Cox shall we?" Maloney concluded.

No not small talk, you want something. Sergeant Brooks' senses were keen from years of service. "After you, sir."

"The meeting time is set for 6 o'clock at Cicciolina's. Saif will be there as will Maloney. We can take them both out at the same time." the caller informed the Al Atta operative.

"Good work. You will be rewarded by Allah in the next life." Then he hung up the phone. "We must prepare quickly. We have an hour before their meeting. Get me a map of the city."

"You're back, officer ah…" the doctor hesitated.

"Maloney and this is Corporal Cox's Sergeant. He'd like to see him too if possible but I must if I can."

"He is responding with hand and eye signals only for the moment. His breathing tube has been removed but his throat will still be sore from it so don't expect him to talk or push him to talk. Understood gentlemen?" the doctor ordered.

In unison they agree. Together they walked to Cox's bed where he immediately recognizes Sergeant Brooks from the Mess hall. A small smile appears on his face.

"So soldier, are you ready to go back to work?" Brooks jokes.

Cox gives him a thumb up.

"Hello, I'm Officer Maloney with A.I. can you answer a few questions for me?"

Cox signals with another thumb up.

"Good. Do you remember speaking with a Specialist Conrad on the night of the attack?"

He looks at Sergeant Brooks unsure where this is going but responds again with his thumb up.

Sarge sees the difficulty he is having and asks, "Would it be better if you answered with eye blinking? We can ask you yes and no questions for now. Blink once for yes and two for a no. Is that okay with you?"

He blinks once.

"Superb idea sergeant." Maloney reluctantly admits. "Did you give Conrad a secret message the night of the attack?"

This time he blinks twice. He thinks to himself, *that was for him not you.*

"He told us he did. You wouldn't lie to us would you?" Maloney questions.

Two blinks. Then a half smile.

"Would you like some ice water? They told us it would help sooth your sore throat." Sarge generously asks.

Cox gives him one blink with a bigger smile.

"Well it's obvious he likes you better. My questions are done for now but I'll see you tomorrow when you can talk more. Okay?"

One last time he satisfies him with a single wink.

"Good night gentlemen, I have a meeting to go to now." and Maloney left them alone.

Sarge patted Cox on his hand and he countered by snagging his which startled him. "Is everything okay?" he asked.

Two blinks. Then he tapped Sarge's hand.

"What do you need? A doctor?"

Two blinks. Then another series of taps on Sarge's hand.

"I don't understand what you want Cox." Sarge was baffled.

Cox tried to speak. "Open." he managed to get out.

"Open...open sesame?"

Idiot! No! Not sesame, it's says me. Cox blinks twice. "Hand."

"Open hand?" Sarge inquired.

One blink and a smile. *Now he's getting the idea.*

Sarge opened his hand and Cox felt for it. He drew with his finger an "n" but Sarge missed it. "Sorry buddy I didn't get that, do it again for me." This time he was looking and Cox repeated it slowly. "That was an "n" right?"

Cox replied with a single wink then spoke, "Conrad." while doing the "n" one last time.

Sergeant Brooks was even more bewildered by this but before he could ask for more the doctor interrupted.

"That's all for now Sergeant. He needs to regain his strength. You can see him tomorrow if you'd like."

Sarge respected doctors and knew he was right, Cox needed to get stronger if he was to recover from his ordeal. "I'll see you tomorrow son. You rest now."

Cox smiled and blinked once at the same time knowing Sergeant Brooks would eventually understand his message.

"Where are we?" I asked the bus driver. His response was not what I wanted to hear. "Let me off here please." I begged. "I missed my stop." He pulled the bus over and allowed me to get out. I was two stops further than I wanted to go. "Thank you." I said as he closed the door while pulling away. Wiping the sleep from my eyes, I figured I needed to hightail it back to the base if I'd make it before dark. Hearing my old Drill Sergeant's voice in my head saying "move it soldier" gave me an added inspiration. It took just under fifteen minutes to get back and I was feeling exhausted from the long day. Passing through the gates, I thought about how long I'd been gone and how Kelsey managed while I was out but knew he'd be happy once I shared my news. Luckily the desk sergeant was busy on the phone as I hurried by at about the same time Sergeant Brooks was entering the base. A few minutes more and we could've been entering at the same time.

"Where have you been Specialist Conrad? Sergeant Brooks called earlier looking to see if you were here."

"Sorry Kelsey for the long day but I got a surprise that you'll like." hoping it compensated for the time.

"What, food?" he replied. "I don't see any?"

Now I knew he was upset so I didn't delay in sharing my personal conquest for him. "Here is a number AND address to a nurse that works at the hospital. I told her all about you and she was a hot tay!" I delighted in telling him as I pulled the piece of paper from my pocket and handed it to him. His expression changed as he accepted it.

"Wow what a guy you are! I hope I can be as good as you one day. Thanks." he exclaimed with joy.

"Well you are not me and I'm not you anymore so let's switch shirts before someone catches us." I told him about Tricia and what she was like fabricating some of it of course as we exchanged gear. I knew he'd like her more if I fibbed a little and also estimated it would take one date before he realized that's what I had done. As long as he got what he wanted and she got what she needed, I figured no foul no harm. I started tucking in my shirt which looked like I had been sleeping in it for days when Sergeant Brooks walked into our room.

"Going somewhere Specialist?" he asked.

"Just down to the ATM Sergeant to get the money I owe Private Kelsey. That is here on base you know." trying to act relaxed but it came out wrong to him sort of like I was being a smart ass.

"Yes soldier, I know where the damn thing is but you're not going, not like that." he pointed at my shirt. "Get a better looking shirt on." He was obviously grouchy from being tired as was I but I didn't show it.

"Sorry Sergeant, I should've known but I just got up." I hated lying to him but had to cover my tail.

"At least one of us got some sleep today." he huffed.

"So what brings you in here tonight?" I questioned.

"I just came from seeing Cox at the hospital."

"Really? How's he doing?" I acted excited to hear.

"He's out of his coma now and should get better with time. The doctors are happy with his progress." He saw I was finished changing shirts and ready to do as I had planned. "Why don't you meet me down at the Mess and we'll get something to eat together after you're done with Kelsey. That is unless he wants to join us?"

"I sure will Sergeant Brooks. I'm starved. Haven't eaten all day." he complained.

"Why's that son? That's not like you to miss too many meals. Were you out running women again?" Sarge laughed loudly looking for us to join along.

"Oh that's a good one Sergeant Brooks." I commended winking at Kelsey to go along.

"Yeah good one Sarge, I mean Sergeant." he looked for forgiveness for his error.

"You two get your thing done and meet me. I'm parched more than you are hungry Private and don't let that happen again." grinning and shaking his pointed finger at him.

"Oh I'm in trouble now." Kelsey anticipates.

"You'll be fine, just let me handle him when we eat. Besides, I have less time than you and can afford to push his buttons a few times." We laughed heading out of the barracks.

"Team one will set up here." using a broken stick to point at the spot. "Second team will be here."

"And the signal, sir?" the marksman asked.

"After Allah has ordered the first shot, then you may join in his fight. To Allah!" the terrorist cries out.

"It looks like no one is here eating. Good more for me then." the hungry young Private delighted.

"Over there is Sarge." I acknowledge seeing him with a high hand wave. "How about some of that meatloaf, please?" I asked Jaminski.

"There you go Spec. a nice big piece. Sorry to hear you're leaving soon. I hope your new station is nicer than here. Have any idea where they're sending you?" He was just curious as most guys are when the people they like are shipping out.

"No they haven't shared that with me yet. I guess I'll find out tomorrow." and gave him a hand slap as we often had done in the past. "Keep Kelsey in line for me. He's a good soldier and a better man."

Kelsey looked up from admiring his plate of food to giving a "Thanks" type look. "I'll keep him straight for you. Later guys." and back to work he went.

"Did you really mean that Specialist Conrad?"

"What to keep you in line?"

"No, being a good soldier but a better man." he referred to.

I stopped and turned around to face him. "Yes Kelsey, you are and someday you'll believe that too. Now let's eat." and we joined Sergeant Brooks.

Maloney pulled into the parking spot that had just been vacated. *Seems the God's favor me tonight.* Or so he thought. Getting out he saw Saif sitting at one of the window tables and waved.

Saif returned his wave. *I hope this goes quickly tonight.* That was his mind set. He watches as the officer draws nearer then stands in politeness. "I thought you were not coming."

"Sorry Saif, I went to see the other soldier from the attack in the hospital. He is out of his coma." first shaking Saif's hand then taking his coat off and hanging it on the back of the chair. "Have you ordered anything yet?"

"Just a casual drink so far, so any news from the soldier?" he inquired.

"Very little I'm afraid. He is unable to talk because of that tube thing they use so we had to use hand and eye gestures."

"WE? Someone else was with you?" Saif looked intrigued to discover who was with him.

"Ah yes, Sergeant Brooks went along. He is Cox's superior or didn't you know that?" looking back at him for his response over the menu he now held.

"I'm not sure that was ever brought up in any of our meetings but now I know." pleased that he had something to start with from tonight's dull meeting. "So you were there for a while?" holding his menu up to scan for a dinner choice.

"They only gave us ten minutes to talk so no, I wasn't there long. What have you done with your day? Get any new leads to follow?" it was now becoming a sparring match rather than the typical good cops sharing information meal.

"Team one in place. I have a clear shot path to Saif." sniper one reported.

"Team number two is moving ten meters to the left for a better angle. I had blockage from a car but I'm almost in place." the second sniper shared.

"Hurry gentlemen. The sooner we finish this the better. Marduk wants to leave tonight." a third voice adds. "May Allah be with him."

"Hello gentleman, I'll be your server tonight. Here is your drink you ordered earlier sir." he sets down a bottle of water with a glass of ice.

"A casual drink eh." Maloney snuffs. "I'd like a large beer, bitte."

"Very well, are you ready to order also?" the tall college looking student asks.

"Everybody in position?" mystery voice three leads.

"One is a yes."

"Two is a yes."

"Take your shots in three, two, one, Now!"

"I'd like the..." but before Maloney can finish a bullet burns through his chest erupting his pulmonary artery. A second bullet crashes through the thick glass deflecting it's trajectory and hitting the college waiter instead of it's intended target. He falls to the floor in pain as Saif takes cover.

"Aviv, did you see where they are coming from?" he yells to his partner.

"I believe they came from that roof top over there." he shouts back as patrons yell and scream on their way out to safety. "I see movement at 2 o'clock top floor."

Saif pans the area and catches the movement Aviv has seen but he's sure there's another team somewhere out there. He looks to the left of the first presumed team. Another flash of light sending a third round narrowly misses his head. "Second team, second floor, nine o'clock do you see them?" he shouts back to Aviv.

"I see them sir. I have my side covered if you need to move."

He rolls forward to relocate behind a stone wall giving him better cover and an angle at the aggressors. "I'm in position."

"Damn it! It looks as though I need to finish what these incompetent idiots can't. I guess that's why he sent me along." the mystery man fumes. He lines up the cross-hairs of his rifle firmly on Saif's position. "Number two, draw his attention and when he clears to shoot I'll nail him."

Saif's pulse was pounding from the adrenaline. He looked back at Maloney who was lying on the floor not moving. Another round broke the fleeing silence hitting the stone wall. He looked up to return fire bringing his 9mm to the top of the wall for balance.

"Got you now Saif." as he began to pull the trigger. He never finished for Aviv had seen the glimmering of his rifle as he aimed at Saif and placed one perfect shot into his head.

Saif ducked back down behind his wall looking over at his partner who gave him a fist pump. "Ah ha, enjoy your trip to see Allah." he rejoiced with a smile.

With a hand prayer gesture he thanked his old companion for saving him yet again. Out of the corner of his eye he saw the other gunman on Aviv's side. He had switched to full auto now and was spray shooting. Saif rolled again this time towards Maloney and aimed. A direct hit found it's mark and the firing stopped. Aviv ran over to cover him from the last known sniper position but no more shots rang out. "Thank you my friend. They must have left." he said while looking down at Maloney. He was in bad shape and Saif knew it so he had little time to get any answers if he was to get any at all. "Why did you lie about the call you received today in your office?"

Maloney was spitting up blood but had to reply if he was to help his daughter. He reached with his hand inside his pocket and pulled out her picture. "She's my daughter, they have her. I'm sorry. Please save her, for me." and he expired in Saif's arms.

"We must find her and fast if we are to save her." Saif told Aviv.

"But where do we look Saif? We don't know which way they went."

"Check the warehouse where the call came from, I'll bet she's there. Hurry, Go!" he grabbed Maloney's walkie-talkie and called for assistance but never told them he had been killed. The *Polizei* began arriving with their guns pulled. He placed his on the ground and showed his ID, they immediately stepped back and he holstered his weapon. "Time to check who these people were. I'll start with that one." As he pointed towards the mystery mans location.

Chapter 21

"Move faster! We must get back to warn Marduk that Saif is still alive." the sniper terrorist yelled at his partner.

"How could you miss him twice?" he was trembling from the reality that their leader would reprimand them both. "We are dead men for sure."

"He still needs us. We are not dead to him yet so shut up and move." they were almost back to their car.

Aviv was running as fast as he could. It reminded him of his childhood days playing in Tel Aviv which is how he got his name. His mother chose it because he was born in the Spring and she had a dream he would grow tall like the crops. She was correct. He was very lengthy at over six feet and ran like a gazelle. That is why Saif choose him to follow and he was narrowing the gap. He could hear the assailants ahead yacking while they ran, a deadly combination but perfect for Aviv's keen hearing. The sound of an automobile starting slowed his gallop to a jog as he searched the streets for the source. *Lights show me lights.* He thought. About a half block up to his right they came on as the engine gunned.

"Run him down." the passenger ordered.

The driver was hard on the gas aiming directly at Aviv. He stood his ground and fired one shot into the driver's side of the windshield. It was his only planned attempt to halt the driver, it did not work and he was still coming faster. Aviv could see his face and just smiled as he pulled the trigger twice again. The first one catching the driver in the forehead, the second ripped through the passenger's upper left shoulder as the car careened into the other row of cars. He ran up to the passenger side as the remaining attacker crawled out from the mangled heap. "Get down on the ground! Drop your weapon or I'll shoot you again!" his nerves on edge.

"Help me, I'm hurt." the dumb idiot begged.

"Yes, I know, I shot you and I'll shoot you again if you don't tell me who you work for. Now tell me!"

"I'd rather die by his hands than yours!" and he spit at Aviv's shoes.

"Who or you won't get that chance. I'll send you to see Allah and he won't be happy to see you. Tell me!" and he stepped on the man's wounded shoulder.

He cried out from the pain grimacing for relief.

Harder Aviv pushed placing almost all his weight on his shoulder. "Tell me!" he screamed while gritting his teeth. It was more than the man could bear.

"Marduk! We work for Marduk." he cried as Aviv relaxed his pressure.

Unsure if anyone remained behind, Saif and the German *Polizei* scaled the floors one by one until arriving at the third floor. Here they discovered a lone gunman in the room above the second team. He was sprawled out on the bed where he landed after Aviv detected his presence and shot. "I'm glad my partner trained with the C.I.A. last year." he joked with the Germans but they didn't understand. "Does anyone here speak English or Hebrew?"

"I speaka zi English." one of the younger men says in his broken dialect.

"Tell your bosses I have jurisdiction over this crime scene area by order of INTERPOL. Have the rest of your men secure the perimeter and PLEASE don't shot my partner if he comes back. Is that understood?"

"*Yavol!* I mean yes sir!" and he gathers his men and explains their orders. "They understand and I will send our Captain up to assist you." and then scurries out the door.

"I don't want or need anyone!" Saif yells out but it's too late, he's out of ears range. "Fast little guy but you weren't as lucky, were you?" he chuckles as he turns back to the dead man. "Let's see who you are?" He began searching the stiff's pockets. Nothing in the front pockets, back to the rear ones he looked. "Imagine that, he carries a wallet, odd for most terrorist." He opens it and looks at the ID and drops it to the floor. Saif crotches down to pull the mask off the attackers face. "It's one of Maloney's men." The ID is A.I. and the name is Tony Bosch. "I remember him from the meetings." He looks back into the wallet for more evidence that might help. He pulls out a folded twenty dollar bill and inspects it. "What is this? How can this be?" he murmurs.

"I am Captain Zimmerman. You will stop all you are doing until INTERPOL confirms who you are and your jurisdiction here. Do I make myself clear?" he stood behind Saif with his weapon pulled and ready to fire.

Saif slowly stood upright while turning back to face the captain. He raised his hands when he saw the gun. "There's no need for that Captain. My ID is in my upper pocket if you'll allow me to show you it?" He moved his hands behind his head now to conceal the evidence he found. "Or you can get it if you wish."

The captain could see his holstered weapon. "No tricks, you get it." he replied.

"Very well sir." and Saif reached in with one hand dropping the twenty in the pocket as he pulled out his ID. *An old magician's trick. Sleight of hand.* He thought. "Here you are sir." as he hands it over to the captain smiling.

"Now that was some good chow." Kelsey said as he belched.

"Sounds like it from your stomach comment." Sarge and I laughed. "So do you have any plans for tonight Private Kelsey?" Sarge asks him.

"I was thinking about going to the hospital to check out the nurses." he replies.

"And why would you do something like that?" Sergeant Brooks says as he looks at me.

Kelsey is rubbing his belly due to it being full and comments, "I hear there are some good looking ones over there." in turn I lightly kick him under the table.

"Oh? Where did you hear that from?"

"One of the guys in the barracks is dating one and he told me so." as he offers a wink at me.

"What do you think Specialist Conrad? Are there any good looking ones there?" Sergeant Brooks asked with his hands now folded on his belly.

They both look at me for my conclusion. "There was only one that I knew of sergeant and now she's gone." It deadened the otherwise tranquil mood so much that Kelsey stood up to leave us.

"Well gentlemen, I thank you for sharing that meal with me. I'm off to find a woman." and he laughed as he left.

"Great guy and good soldier Sergeant Brooks. Take care of him after I leave."

"You mean like how he took care of you today?" he poked.

Stunned at his cunning attempt to make me stumble I replied, unemotionally, "How did he do that?"

"I can't prove you were there but you and I know you were." still trying to stumble me up.

"Where sergeant?" I countered. *I know he knows but how does he know?*

"To see Cox." Just a small amount of eye movement was all he needed to confirm his suspicions. "He gave me something when I went to see him today. I'm not sure what it means but maybe you can make some sense of it?"

"I have no idea what you are referring to but go ahead." I still played dumb.

"Hold your hand out and I'll give it to you."

Not being sure where this was going or what he had, I obliged and held my hand out.

"He said 'Conrad' then did this." and he drew the letter N in the palm of my hand. "Mean anything to you now?" he probed more.

"Nothing Sergeant Brooks."

"Nothing at all?"

"Sorry but I can't help you with that." I insisted.

"I get the feeling you don't trust me or many people right now and I can't blame you, son, but I AM on your side and I'll prove it. I have a story I want to share with you but I need you to be honest with me first. I guarantee you it's worth you listening to it and possibly more. I believe it is your God given destiny. Interested in hearing about it?"

Trust is a hard thing to give freely and against my beliefs, it should be earned and I always felt Sergeant Brooks had. It was now or never to see if that trust was as strong as I felt it was. "Okay, you have my attention. Yes, I was there at the hospital today with Amanda's roommate but you never said I couldn't go anywhere today. You just said I'd start my processing tomorrow."

"Yes soldier I did say that and I honor your honesty. Want to add any more?"

"I want to hear some of your story first and not here." I held firmly.

"Ok then, we'll go to my pad and share our tales."

"Stop your belly aching and drive, scumbag." Aviv urged. "You better hope it's the right place too."

"Just let me stop and you can kill me now. If you don't then Marduk will kill you too." the driver begged.

Aviv was eased back on the seat, his length filling the whole passenger side but he could see. If anyone was positioned outside the building, he'd see them before they saw him. "How much farther do we need to go?" he irked. He was getting uncomfortable from the hard seat.

"Two more blocks maybe?"

"How about being precise?" and he grabbed the man's shoulder sending a jolt of pain through his body.

"Yes, I'm sure it is another block around this next corner."

"Good, pull over here." Aviv directed.

"Why stop here? To shot me like the pig you are? Allah will..." and with one whack of the butt end of his pistol, Aviv knocked him out.

He tied the wounded annoyance and gagged him so he couldn't speak then placed him in the passenger seat. Again he had to adjust the seat but it would only be for a short trip. He knew terrorist always have look outs posted around a building and he had the address from earlier so the area matched. He shifted the car into gear and drove around the corner. "Allah is on my side tonight." and he smiled when he saw just one building with people. *Destination arrived time to find the girl.* Aviv noticed one of the gate guards was opening it up upon seeing the car. What he hadn't anticipated was another person driving it. Aviv was smart to have brought his silencer along and installed it when he bound the passenger. His first and only shot dropped the guard where he stood. He was relishing the C.I.A. training for it was now proving to be a valuable tool. Before the next one had time to draw his gun, he fired twice both hitting their marks. That eliminated the ground crew so he stopped the car just outside the rear door entrance. "Don't go nowhere." he amused himself when he tapped the unconscious man on his head. Carefully he exited the car running for the doorway. He opened it quickly and peered inside, coast was clear. He could hear voices in the distant reaches echoing off the interior walls making it difficult to determine where they were coming from. His training suggested waiting for backup to arrive but time was of essence and an innocent girl's life hung on his every move. He inched his way forward hoping for a better listening post. He found it and stopped, his sixth sense had kicked in when a vibe sent chills through him. Around the corner, now lighting up a cigarette, was the next victim for Aviv's night. He could see the exhale of the smoke from the terrorist and decided it was his time to move. Like a blur he jumped pointing his pistol in the smoker's direction. The guard's mouth opened wide enough from the frightening sight of Aviv that he could place his silencer in his mouth. In Hebrew he asked him how many more there were inside. The taste of metal made him lose his bodily function but not the will to live. He tried to answer but it was muffled so Aviv told him to be smart and he'd live. He nodded that he understood so Aviv slowly pulled the piece from his mouth. The well trained guard softly answered then started to alert the others to Aviv's presence as Aviv's reflexes fires one blast. "Idiot, you could have lived." The commotion caused the remaining fighters to act sending them towards Aviv's position. He could either fall back to take refuge outside and wait for help to arrive or he could go it alone. The only acceptable choice for him was to fight on for the girl's sake. He thought of his own daughter back home and how he'd fight for her safety, he wasn't going to stop for another man's. Their sound drew nearer as he readied himself behind some barrels. He counted five more, all very well equipped. Then he saw the man of the hour, Marduk. He had been ordering the others where to search while shielding himself with the little girl. *Coward to use a girl, what honor is there in that?* Aviv started devising a plan of attack against the closing group. He executed his first two shots. The rest ran for cover not knowing where the shots came from. Marduk yelled more commands and then left from view. Aviv had no choice now but to attack full assault against the remaining three as he heard the girl scream from her night of terror. With precision marksmanship he fired while moving towards them. The last one managed to get a round off hitting Aviv in his thigh. The sensation of burning searing lead halted his advance temporarily. He fired one last shot into the last gunman's eye blowing out his internals. His lifeless body plummeted along the wall leaving a bloodstain and grey matter splattered. "Marduk..."Aviv yelled as loud as he could. "...leave the girl she has nothing to do with this!" He waited for a response but only heard the sound of the girl still screaming. *Yes, keep screaming so I can follow your sound.* Her dad must have taught her that old trick when she was younger. He was in hot pursuit again but the pain was excruciating. It began to slow him down as he lost blood. He heard another scream but this one was a man's. The sound was closer this time and then he heard the sound of footsteps running towards him. Aviv waited for them with his pistol drawn. It was the girl, she had bitten her kidnapper and the blood was on her face. "Come here sweetheart." Aviv beckoned her.

"I bite him! I bite him as hard as I could like my daddy taught me to." she was crying hysterically. "Don't let him take me away mister. Please!" she begged.

"You are safe now my child. I will protect you." Aviv assured her. He stood back up and headed for the way she came. They had made it back outside as they watched a truck leave the building area. "Run you coward but we will find you." He collapses from the loss of blood as his vision fades.

"My god, how much longer must I wait? I have a man out there in pursuit of the attackers." Saif screamed at Captain Zimmerman. "At least let me use your radio or his." pointing at Maloney's covered body that lay on a cart.

"You can use his, he won't need it."

"May Allah visit you in your dream, you smug arrogant bastard!" Saif scorned as he located the hand radio. "Hello. This is MOSSAD agent Saif, is anyone there?"

"Go ahead agent."

"Has my partner Aviv been located at the warehouse?"

"They just arrived a few minutes ago. He's been shot sir."

Saif's blood chilled. Had he sent his friend to his death? "Is he...is he alright?" Saif asked concerned.

"He and the girl were found. They are both going to be okay."

"Thank you for that news." a sigh of relief sounds from his voice. "What about her kidnapper? Was he caught?"

"No sir, your other agent said he got away but we have the description of the truck he fled in and we're looking for it now."

Saif pounds his fist on the police car's roof. "Someday we will get you Marduk. Someday." Finally a call comes in from INTERPOL.

"Yes, this is Captain Zimmerman...he is? Okay sir...sorry we didn't know. We will assist him the best we can." He drops the mike on the seat and approaches Saif timidly, "We are to assist you with whatever you need, sir." and he comes to attention.

Saif snickers and says into his face, "Good, you can start by getting me a glass of ice water." And heads back for the building to search for more clues. "And your chubby ass can bring it to me up there." as he points to the roof top.

On the ride over to Sergeant Brooks' pad, I began assembling the pieces of clues I had been given in my head. I found ADELS, then my dear Amanda gave me TEI and now Cox finished it all with the N. The first part I though was some type of clue directed at me because of my name being in it but "Adel's what" I pondered. The second part was puzzling. Was it an element or a word that meant another word? But the last one being how it was just a letter was the most confusing.

"Trying to figure something out, Del?" Sarge asked. He was seriously trying to make me see he was on my side with his first name usage.

"None of it makes sense, the clues, the attack and the murders. Why here and why now?"

"Good questions you ask, so at least you're still thinking. Now think outside the box for a moment." slowing to park the Jeep. "How do you connect to all of it is the real question son. Let's go in and see if we can solve this riddle."

First thing I heard was Merlin squawking as we entered his pad. Sarge turned on some lights then removed his outer shirt to relax. He had some tattoos I had never seen before on his upper arm just under the t-shirt he wore. "Nice looking tats, what are they? I've never seen them before." I asked.

He walked over to Merlin's cage and opened it to feed him but Merlin had another idea and flew over to me, landing on my shoulder. "Damn bird, does that every time I have company, even to women. It freaks them out like a bat flying in their hair or something. I'll get him if he bothers you?"

"No don't, he's sort of cool. He can stay for a while."

"So you were asking about my tattoos, want something to drink? Maybe a beer for old times?" he tested my reserve.

"I really shouldn't but one with you does sound good." He smiled as he popped two caps off and handed me one. "Thanks Sergeant." as we tapped bottles.

"You're welcome Del and please call me Leroy." he gave his distinguishing grin.

The first cold swallow went down smooth but the taste was disgusting after months of being sober. I made a face that brought out laughter in Sarge then like the snap of fingers I said "I thought your name was Rufus?" realizing after it blurted out what I had done.

"Where did you hear that?" he responded semi-angry.

"Ah um ah I don't recall, Leroy?" trying to escape with the name he gave me to use.

For a moment he just looked and then he snapped his fingers. "Elevator guy! That was you, you sly shit!" now laughing at the thought. "I knew something smelled...wrong! So who was the girl?"

The time for honesty was upon us so I laid the whole story out to him. "So you told her your name is Rufus but now you are telling me it's Leroy, which one is it?"

"My real name is Leroy Rufus Brooks, there you are one of a few who know the whole thing now." looking to see how empty his bottle was. "Need another beer?"

"Sure, one more won't hurt. I won't tell anyone Rufus. You should be proud of your name."

"Are you proud of yours?" he asked as he hands me the next cold one.

"No. I never liked it and got teased a lot growing up because of it, so no, I hate it actually." putting down the new bottle of suds.

"You know every name has a meaning, yours, mine even Merlin's. Much like this tattoo you asked about." He pulled up his shirt sleeve to reveal a helmet on top of a rifle with a pair of boots at the bottom. The words "All gave some" crested the top over the helmet and "Some gave all" adorned the bottom. On the right side running alongside the rifle the words "duty, honor and country" completed it. "I was nineteen when I got this reminder inked on me. Thought it'd be fun one night on R&R to get one, now it's with me for life." I could almost see a tear shedding as he told his story. "That brings me to your story, the one I promised to share with you." as he shook off the ghosts' from his past.

Chapter 22

As he began the story of how he came to know it, I instantly knew he wasn't making any of it up. The details of the existence of this government hidden planet and why it was being withheld from the public made perfect sense in some ways but in others it did not. "If they had speculation in believing it's trajectory was on a collision course, wouldn't it stand to reason to involve as many people as possible to reach a solution?" I asked with apprehension. "Do they not believe anything can be done?"

"You're right. More people should be working to solve this but they still aren't sure it will happen so life goes on to them. It's business as usual until..."

"...until something happens and it's too late to do anything about it, I know, my father says the same thing all the time."

"Del, society has always been that way. The panic will only set in after the ugliness shows and then they need to deal with it just like here in Germany. Hitler was around a lot longer than the war but it wasn't until after the war started, that action was taken. If this planetary object is like our world's going to war, we need to do something before it has struck not after." He was dead serious and completely accurate.

"But what can we little men do against our governments to make them listen or hear or act. It takes power to get to the top, like being a president or ruler of a country and that takes money, lots of money. How do we make a splash instead of a ripple?"

He sat back looking at me, an admiration erecting. "We do it with tenacious means. We devise a way to do it against the will of the government...or it's knowledge." He sat forward now. "We keep secret what they know but use it to help our cause."

"What cause is that?"

"The one that says people have a right to know and make their own decision based on facts, not lies. You know governments don't own all the money, right?" he takes a swig of his warming beer. "Yuk! Got to get another one, you ready too?" he points over.

"One last one, then I'm done." I was feeling a little tipsy from the others. "So who does own most of the money?"

"The Church does and they love life more than any government will or has. They have the ability to help hide a cover up or reveal it, it just depends which side of the church you're sitting on." he smirked.

"I think you and I have had enough beers for one night, especially you." I started to laugh. It didn't set well with him and he slammed his beer down causing Merlin to fly to his cage.

"This is serious and you need to take it that way." He got up and closed Merlin's cage and covered him. "Good night buddy." and Merlin replied back with his kissy sound. "That's what I'm talking about, love. Love for everything. He loves me like I love him but we are two separate parts of life. Together we are happy. Now do you understand?" he was wobbling around.

Yeah you're drunk as a skunk and I'm tired. "Explain to me about the Church having sides?"

"Ever stop to notice when you walk in, there are two sets of pews? That's not so the bride's family can sit on one side while the groom's sits on the other, oh no. That's because in God's perfect world there are two of everything. Two birds to make one, two sides of an argument, two hemisphere's hell two balls." he holds his scrotum. He realizes that maybe I'm correct about the beers and sits back down before falling down. He holds his head for a moment to collect his thoughts then begins again. "There will always be right and wrong so it's safe to say there will always be a side of the church that sees everything good and a side that sees the bad. Find the one that can help your cause and God will do the rest."

"Perhaps we should get you to bed."

"Perhaps you're right again Del." He manages to stand with some tiny help from me. We are looking almost eye to eye. "Marduk is the bad, I believe you are the good. It is your destiny." He mumbles some more while heading to his room. I watch as he closes his door, then he opens it and throws out a blanket and pillow. "You are staying here tonight." and closes the door once more for the night.

Over to the couch I carry my bedding. "I should clean these bottles up." now feeling the effects of the poison I've reintroduced back into my veins. Merlin sounds off with another kissy. "Crazy old goat. My destiny? Yeah my destiny is that couch."

"I'm glad to see you are doing well my friend." Saif smiles at Aviv. "Next time you must wait for backup or God may not be so kind."

"If it hadn't had been for the girl's quick thinking, I'd be visiting him now, I'm afraid. She ran and got one of the belts and made a tourniquet. Her father would be very proud of her. Has anyone told her yet?" Aviv asked while looking her way.

"No. Her mother is outside the room being briefed."

The mother walked in moments later and held her daughter tight repeatedly saying how much she loved her and that everything would be okay. She looked over at the two MOSSAD agents and carried her precious love their way. "I want to thank you gentlemen for saving my daughter's life."

"I should be thanking her for saving mine." Aviv said. "Her father? Does she know?"

"I couldn't do it, will you help me?" she asked Aviv.

He knew someday someone would be telling his family the same thing he was about to tell poor Chelsea. "Sweetheart, listen to me, I have something important to tell you."

"Yes, Aviv?" she replied.

"You know how when we go to heaven, people come to visit us?"

She gave him a puzzled look.

"Have any of her grandparents gone to heaven?" he asked her mother.

Chelsea responded with "Grandmom went there last year." She seemed happy to know the answer. "Isn't that right mommy?" she still smiled.

"Yes, Chel, she did."

"Chelsea, your father has gone to be with her. He is safe in his mother's arms just as you are now. They are with God." he fought back the tears. The innocence in the eyes of a child was more than he thought he could face.

"Will I get to see them someday?" her young curiosity mused.

"Yes my dear, all good girls go to see their daddy's in heaven." Aviv could take no more and walked away to wipe his eyes. A little girl's tenderness had undone a rough and stern MOSSAD agent better than any terrorist interrogation ever could.

Saif walked to her and pressed his lips to her forehead. "You are very special, remember that and someday you will receive God's reward." He turned his head to her mother, "If there is anything, anything we can do, please contact us." and he gave her a card with their numbers. "We must go now."

"Will she be okay?" Aviv was afraid to look back but found the strength. Chelsea, still in her mother's arms, waved goodbye to both of them as they left.

"Something tells me she will be fine my human friend. You did well with her. Her father is smiling down from heaven. Now let's get you some more medical attention, shall we?"

During the middle of the night I had another dream. It started out rather odd. I was in a dark tunnel like object. I could feel smooth walls all around me. Suddenly a door that I hadn't felt before opened and Amanda was on the other side.

She had on the soft grey outfit that Ashley and I took to the hospital. She waved me through and said "Come with me. Come on, follow me."

I went through the opening, I felt like I was floating. I asked her "Where are we going and how did you get here?"

Her reply was "Follow me and I'll show you my love. I have something you must see."

A flash of light blinded me temporarily then the universe appeared to revolve around us. "Where are we?" I asked. "Is this heaven? Have I died in my sleep?"

She giggled her familiar way and said "Always so full of questions. No silly this is not heaven and you are still sleeping."

"How can this be then? You have died. I have touched your cold body with my own lips."

"Del, as long as my love still lives in you, I'll never die. That is why you must find a way to save our love and unite with me again. You have been shown a way. Now you must follow the path that leads you to the end where I'll be waiting."

"What way have I been shown? Who showed me? Is this all real?" I was confused.

"You must stop and think or you'll drive yourself crazy. The man you admire has entrusted you with a secret that the world must know but only when the time is right. Now is not that time. You will know when it is right. Until then I must go and wait. Keep me in your heart and never stop loving me Del." she said as she floated and diminished into a cloud.

"Wait! Amanda!?! May I have one more kiss? Just one more? Please?"

She faded back in, just her head. "Yes my love." And her warm lips touched mine. It was as heavenly as in the taxi. "Now go Del."

Suddenly the phone rang at Sergeant Brooks' apartment waking us. He finally came out from his bedroom to answer it. "Sorry Leroy I wasn't sure if I should answer that or let it ring."

"That's okay." he yawned before picking up. "Hello...yes this is Sergeant Brooks. Oh no, what happened? Oh...ok we'll be there. He's here with me. We were talking last night. About different things, I can do that you know. Well you just woke me up how should I feel? Alright, we are coming in now." he scratched his head and yawned some more. "Get dressed. We have a trip to make."

"Where are we going at this time of the morning?"

"That was our buddy Saif. Officer Maloney was killed last night and they want you in protective custody."

"Oh that's funny. Is this some kind of joke? Did Kelsey put you up to it because of the nurse. Wow what a guy. Set him up with..."

"Shut up! It's not a joke, Del." Sarge was still feeling the effects of the alcohol. "Sorry. My head hurts from last night. I didn't mean to blow up on you my friend."

"Shit this is real? Now I feel stupid for acting like that. I'll hurry, you go get dressed, friend." and offered a warm smile.

They say the third times a charm, being back at A.I. didn't feel anything like a charm and the last place I expected to see again before leaving Berlin. There were a lot more personnel on the base than I'd ever seen before and for this hour of the morning. They all looked focused like an attack was being prepared or an assault repelled. Aviv sat next to the MOSSAD car with Saif nowhere in sight. His leg properly bandaged but showing signs of combat was propped up on another chair. Sergeant Brooks parked our Jeep next to him, their non-expressive faces following the other. Aviv broke the silence "You are to go with me in my car. Saif's orders and they are not negotiable. Get in." as he opened the passenger side back door.

Sergeant Brooks halted my forward progress with his stiff arm and glared into the tall Israeli officer's gaze. "He told me to bring him here to meet him. Are we staying here on base or leaving? And my terms are not negotiable either. Specialist Conrad is still my soldier under my command so that makes me responsible for his safety."

"Not any longer Sergeant..." Aviv stood leaning on his good leg."...he has orders from the State Department to fly out tonight. They are claiming it is now a matter of National Security and want him back in D.C. for questioning. That is all I know and have been briefed."

"Leaving tonight? What about all my personal gear? All my clothes? My friends?" I asked with great grief. "How will I get to say 'goodbye' to anyone?"

"I'll make sure that's taken care of Del." as Sergeant Brooks rubbed my back for comfort.

"We must go now, Saif is waiting."

Saif sat on the end of the hood waiting for our arrival. It was a small strip adjacent to the main runways that was mainly used for diplomats, dignitaries and anyone deemed "NOYB", none of your business. Only small planes flew into this area and monitoring of the passengers was not necessary. If they were using this strip, they had more reasons to be here than you had asking, just that simple. From here they'd fly me to Frankfurt where another flight would take me the remaining way. Three days before this I was planning my smooth transition, a quiet retreat from the city I had fallen in love with, suddenly my whole life was escaping me and I was leaving it all behind. Aviv stared in his review mirror. "We are almost there. I wish you the best young soldier. May God see you home safely and may you do good work in your life. Take the path of righteousness and it will comfort your way. Shalom, my new friend." he ended as we stopped alongside Saif's car.

"Hello again Saif, will you please tell me what is going on? Why am I flying out in such a hush, hush way?" I pleaded.

"Come inside and I will show you both." He hand gestured towards the waiting plane. I felt like someone very important as I walked through the tiny door. It opened up to a spacious and comfortable seating area. "Please, take a seat anywhere."

"Wow. I get to fly in this? Did I hit the lottery?" looking amazed at the luxury.

For the first time since meeting Saif I saw him openly laugh. "No Mr. Conrad or should I now call him Sergeant Conrad?" he looked towards the rear of the plane. Sergeant Brooks and I swiveled our chairs back that way where an Army Colonel sat watching. We hadn't noticed him in the darkness of the rear when we got in.

Unsure whether to attempt to stand in the small confines, we both sat straight in the chairs hoping to present an attention stance. "At ease men, I am Colonel Nathan B. Ford, I am here to escort you, Sergeant Conrad, back to the States." He was a burly man with a clean shaven appearance. Years of service had altered his hair from it's original black to the white shade it bore now. His uniform was spotless, all the medals placed in order, his buttons shined like the sun and the crispness of his shirt sent a hint of starch. "This is an unofficial flight, Sergeants' that never happened. Is that part clear?" We acknowledged by shaking our heads. "Good. I know you both have many questions and the answers will come but our time is limited. So allow me to explain and hopefully most of them will be answered. Agent Saif and Aviv have been working with us for some time on the apprehension of a terrorist only known as Marduk that much you already know. What they and now you didn't know was Officer Maloney was here also monitoring intel but he wasn't Army Intelligence. He was with the C.I.A. unbeknownst to Aviv who trained there, last year was it?" Aviv confirmed. "He was our inside man or so we thought. Last night during the ambush of Saif and Maloney, several assailants were killed. One of the men at the restaurant was, we feel, the leader of the assault. He too was an Army Intelligence officer by the name of Bosch." Sarge and I looked at each other in disbelief, we remembered him from the meetings. "Gets better gentlemen, Saif searched him and the others. In Bosch's wallet he found this note." He held up the twenty Saif found. From a distance, it's appearance seemed different. "Please come closer and take a better look." We walked hunched over to his seat and looked at the bill.

"It's a fake." Sergeant Brooks huffed.

"And how do you know that Sergeant?" Colonel Ford asked. "Look closer." he directed.

I gazed closer to examine the finite detail. It was definitely not like any twenty I had ever possessed. The picture was odd and it had a peculiar shine to the ink. Then I saw it! My eyes widened. A gasp went out from my mouth.

"It's obviously some other countries attempt to forge our money." Brooks firmly went on.

"No Sergeant Brooks look here!" as I pointed at the questionable bill. He leaned closer seeing the same thing I had pinpointed.

"That can't be right. They messed up the year, the idiots." He laughed. That was until the Colonel turned the bill around and he saw the writing on the other side. "Oh dear God!" he let out.

Chapter 23

On the back of the bill a list of names was written in ink. At the top of that list is what was the most frightening, it said HIT LIST in bold letters. Amongst the names were Cox, Maloney, Saif, Aviv, Gabby, Kurn, Bishop, Richard and Conrad. Gabby's name had been crossed off and Cox's had a question mark. My name was at the top with under it in parenthesis 'must kill' added. Colonel Ford broke the confusion. "Forget the fact that the bill has a date of 2006 printed on it or the way it has been printed. When it was first discovered by agent Saif and we were notified, the mint was contacted also. They have just started to design the concept of these bills. They haven't even put them on paper yet! Still, here we are looking at this one with this list. No one can seem to explain how it got here or make sense of the list it contains. Sergeant Conrad, besides the people you already know, do you know any of the other three names on the list?"

Still looking at my name being first and what it said, I looked up at the Colonel with genuine fear. "No sir. None of the other names I know. I have never met anyone with those names in my life."

"Del, I know this comes as a shock but think as clearly as you can, anyone with the name Kurn, Bishop or Richard? Anyone?" Sergeant Brooks asked as a friend.

"No Leroy, I'd remember those names. They are not your usual name wouldn't you say?" looking with absolute affirmation. "Sorry sir, I can't help you with them."

"That's ok for now son." Colonel Ford gripped my shoulder to show his belief. "We need to separate the rest of you to ensure your safety and the safety of our nation until we can understand the significance of this list and how this money got here in 1983. You, Sergeant Conrad, will be going with me to Washington, D.C., the remainder will receive your assignments later. No one and I mean no one is to contact the other for anything or under any circumstance. Is that understood?" Everyone in the plane nodded. "Saif and Aviv, our nation thanks you for your involvement and help. Your Director Moshe will contact you with your orders, may God be with you. If you two wish to say your 'Goodbyes', I'll allow you five minutes and then we must leave."

"The confines of the plane are small, may we step out?" Sergeant Brooks asked nicely.

"Stay close to the plane. Five minutes men, starting now." and he looked at the time on his watch.

We exited as quickly as we could. Sarge turned around at the bottom of the steps and grabbed me tight. His hold was strong for a shorter man but reminiscent of my father's when I left for Berlin. I, after taking in a breath returned his embrace but not as hard. "Well I didn't think we'd be doing this last night but I'm glad we had the time to know one another. Remember all I have taught you and mostly the things we've talked about recently. They will help you get through this ordeal, I just know it. I'll make up some story that you had to go home suddenly for a family funeral or something but we'll get you your things, don't worry about them. I am very proud of you Sergeant Adel Conrad." He finished with a smile and a handshake.

"Master Sergeant Leroy Rufus Brooks, you have been a better father figure to me than my own. I will never forget you, what you've shown me in life but most of all, your friendship. May we meet again someday, friend. Our secret is safe with me and I'm beginning to understand what it is I must do. Now I just need to find a way to do it, for all our sakes." I gave him one last salute, uncustomary for non-commissioned officers but in this instance, I felt obliged.

He saluted back and added these words "May you sit on the correct side of the church. God speed."

"Aviv, Saif, I know we never saw eye to eye but I hope you don't hold that against me. May God guide your paths' in finding Marduk, before I do. Somehow I know he is behind all of this and responsible for Amanda's death. I'll kill him if I have to in her honor. Shalom."

"Mr. Conrad, God will guide your way in doing what you must do. We will be there to help you, if he sees the need. Shalom." Saif walked to his car.

"Sergeant Conrad sounds good for you. A leader of men you are, God has chosen so. I have but one daughter and I love her more than anything. Watch her for me if I am not able. Okay?"

"Sure Aviv." unsure of what he meant. "Shalom, friend."

"Shalom to you my American friend."

The Colonel popped his head back out and said "Time to go Sergeant."

"Yes sir." I barked out, then one final look back at the others and up the steps. At the top I waved and then disappeared into the plane.

None of the three on the ground said a word more but they were all thinking the same thing. *God Speed!*

As the plane began it's taxi run to our strip for take-off, the Colonel commented "I think you'll like your new duty station when we get back to D.C."

"And why is that, sir?"

"Everyone likes Pentagon duty soldier and we can protect you best there. No one attacks the Pentagon, not even terrorist."

The flight to Frankfurt went fast and before I had time to relieve myself, we were on our next leg to Washington. Colonel Ford had given me some literature to study on the Pentagon. The place is huge and a city of it's own, much like Berlin, but with walls. With approximately twenty-three thousand people wandering around, it was no wonder they chose it for my hiding spot. I'd be positioned in one of the dining facilities with minimal duties until they could conclude their investigation. It would take some time to master the layout but I never worried once. I knew my own chaperone would escort me anywhere I needed to go. All the reading made me tired once the excitement wore off. "Sir, I'm going to try to get some sleep since mine got interrupted, if I may?"

"That's fine, I was just thinking of doing the same thing." He picked up an intercom phone and notified the pilot to wake us half an hour before we got to our destination.

The seats were not real comfortable but they laid back and I found a blanket so I was set.

"Del, dear." a voice spoke.

"Yes?" my eyes not wanting to open.

"You are on your way. Don't forget me, will you?" the voice continued.

Alarmed by this comment, I opened my eyes. It was pitch black. "Who is that? Who's there?" I asked disconcerted. Feeling with my hands extended, I became unsettled when nothing presented itself.

"Find the men and you'll find me, my love."

"Amanda? Is that you?"

The darkness turned into light and the same universe from my previous dream with Amanda circled around me. I could see our Earth, it's moon, Mars, the rings around Saturn even tiny Pluto but no one else was present. A rumbling sound from behind me made me twirl and I saw another universe entering our solar system. It had four planets circling a burned out Sun or an illusion of what once was a Sun. The planets collided with others in it's path sending debris outwards. Destruction and waste lay in it's wake due to it's mammoth size. Nothing escaped it.

"Time to wake up Sergeant Conrad, we are almost to the airport." The Colonel informed me while wiping sleep from his vision.

It was odd hearing myself being called a Sergeant now so between the dream and his reference I hesitated for a moment. "Sorry sir, what did you call me?"

"Oh, ha ha, guess that's not what you're accustomed to being called. I felt that way when I went from a Lieutenant to a Captain. Hell I kept saluting other Captains for a couple of months until I adjusted. You'll get used to the new title as soon as we get that part straightened out with a new ID. Now let's get you ready for Washington and the Pentagon."

"Yes sir." I smiled thinking about the promotion. It was already daylight when we flew into Edwards Air Force Base. An array of vehicles stood ready to shuttle us over to the Capitol area. It resembled a Presidential motor parade drawing more motorist attention than probably hoped. A perennial "who's that" of questions and "was that the President" speculations. The drive reminded me in ways of my rides through Berlin but they were never this exciting or meaningful. I was here due to urgency and my own desire to conquer a quest. I would use them as much as they planned to use me for any information. No doubt it was the best place I could have wanted to be in this time of need.

"When we arrive at the Pentagon, you keep on my ass and don't get separated from me. There will be armed escorts so they will help but there are also a ton of people who won't know shit from shingles. I have all the necessary paperwork right here to get you through so let me do the talking and you follow. Okay Sergeant?" he was like a grandfather speaking to the favorite grandson at a ball game wishing not to get detached from each other. Always hoping for the best but prepared for the worst.

"Yes sir, on your ass, sir." I grinned. *Never got to ride a Colonel's ass before and doubt that will happen again.*

"After we get through security, we are headed for a short briefing and then they'll take you to get your ID and new clothes, at least until your stuff arrives. Don't concern yourself with how you look. They all understand you've been flying all night. Just answer their questions as honestly and accurate as you can. You'll do fine." his hand tapping my knee.

"Their questions sir? How many people will be at this meeting and who?"

"Oh just a few of the Joint Chiefs, a few Senators and Congressmen, oh and the Vice President is sitting in for the President on this one." he said in a matter-of-factly way.

"Oh just, ha ha. Sir, how do I fit into all of this?"

"That is what we are all trying to find out. Well, here we are. Time to earn that pay." He chuckled as he prepared to exit.

He moved fast for an old soldier. Time behind the desk didn't slow his pace and I had fun keeping on his tail. The first guards snapped to attention as we proceeded through evidentially from their past recognition of the Colonel. The next set also came to attention asking for ID to which he pulled from his packet of papers a single document, flashed it in their face and continued on. I saw one guard eyeball me as I stayed with my superior. *What is on that paper?* The last pair of guards he stopped at as they saluted him. Again he showed the document, his ID was scanned and then he pulled one last page from the packet. "This is the man. Here is his authorization, from the Vice President." He looked back at me, still had the stern all business look, as I stood at attention waiting for us to advance. A quick call to notify we were there and onto the meeting room. "See what these birds can get you?" I nodded. "Respect. Nothing's worth more than respect." he ended. As we entered the great room of questions as I called it, a hush transpired.

Sarge broke the news to Private Kelsey that morning after he asked him where I was. "Wow, I'll never get to thank him for setting me up with that nurse. She's great and just what I was looking for."

"Well you can always write him and tell him."

"I don't have his address. Can you get it for me?" Kelsey asked.

Sergeant Brooks knew it wasn't breaking his agreement if Kelsey contacted me so he told him he'd get it for him. "I need someone to pack his things up so we can ship them. Do that and I'll get his information for you." Shaking his head in disbelief that I was no longer there, he turned and asked Kelsey "Are you going back to the hospital today to see your new lady?"

"You bet I am."

"Will you do me a small favor then, go see Cox and tell him Conrad has gone home. I just don't want to face him now."

"Sure Sergeant Brooks and can I have tomorrow off to pack all his things?"

"From the look of it you'll need a day, so yes Private, off tomorrow." He smiled then changed back over to his usual stern look. "That means it gets gone before you go see your new floozy." he said heading out the door.

"She's not a floozy, she's my angel." He picked up one of my pictures from my night stand. "Thanks Del, now I owe you one."

Saif and Aviv were packing their clothes when the room phone rang. Saif nodded to Aviv to answer since he was closer. "Shalom? Aviv." He cleared his throat from the chips he'd been eating. "Yes sir. I will tell him. We will see you in Tel Aviv. Shalom." He hung the phone down then looked over at Saif. Saif sensed there was something wrong.

"Director with bad news?" he asked.

Aviv just shook his head for a moment.

"What is it Aviv?" worry grew in him.

"Sit down my friend." Aviv instructed. Saif did as he asked. "Your family has been...killed. A bombing hit your home and the surrounding area. I'm sorry my friend, they had no notice."

Saif cried out in horror, anger and sorrow as his friend held him to comfort him.

"We will persevere over whoever did this. I promise you that." Aviv assured his partner. "We must go back to our homeland to prepare."

As Saif's tears subsided and hate began to fill the void he uttered "May God deliver to me the hand that killed my family for I will kill theirs if they have any."

All eyes were on us as the Colonel closed the door behind us. The escort guards now stood watch outside. "Colonel, sir, have my parents been told I'm back in the US? They watch the news and if they hear anything from over there, well I know how they'll react." I asked in a soft voice.

"No Sergeant, as of this minute not many people have knowledge of where you are and we are keeping it that way, for now. Well, let me go over with you who the more important people are here. Of course you should recognize our Vice President, then from left to right you have the Navy Admiral Mcdonald of U.S. Atlantic Command, next to him is Army General Wickham, Chief of Staff, Air Force General Gabriel and Marine Corps General Kelley, Commandant of the Marine Corps."

"Kelley Sir?" I quizzed. "Any relation to..."

"Yes, my young man. That is her father. He'll drill you the most I bet but after the meeting is over. He wants to know why his daughter is gone and who's responsible. He's one pissed off Marine right now and you know how they get?

I shrugged my shoulders.

"They get revenge any way and at any cost. Gung ho son's of bitches. God love's Marines though. Or so they think. Anyhow the first suit is Senator Kennedy with fellow Democrat Joe Biden, your state's Senator Arlen Specter and another Republican Dan Quayle plus Bob Dole. Over there is Arizona congressman John

McCain, Harry Reid of Nevada, two more of your Pennsylvanian's Tom Ridge and George Gekas, Tennessee's Al Gore and then Dick Cheney of Wyoming. Now there are others here and I don't expect you to remember who all of them are, just answer them truthfully and this will go quick. Do your country proud Sergeant." and he patted my arm for good luck.

I sat down on the first available chair and waited my fate as they began the proceedings. All the background information was divulged along with who was present. I could see the questions lining up and each face begin to focus in my direction. Colonel Ford finished his presentation and announced me to the stand. I concentrated on the task at hand and my own wishes. *Respect, win their respect. I need contacts to complete my quest. This is for all humanity.* I was nervous and then a soft voice ran through my head.

"I am here my love. These men can help you." It was Amanda.

"Sergeant Conrad congratulations on your promotion, I see you still wear a Specialist uniform?" Senator Kennedy started.

"Yes Sir. It happened on our way from Berlin to here or so I've been told."

"You're not sure son?" John McCain interrupted.

"John, let him answer. He's nervous, let's give him some breathing room." Kennedy defended.

"Well if he's not completely sure of his rank, how are we to believe anything he tells us? Huh,Ted?"

"Gentlemen, we are going to get nothing if we bicker over small things. Let's get to the subject." Vice President Bush intervened. "Continue Senator Kennedy."

"What can you tell us about the counterfeit bill MOSSAD agent Saif found on a Tony Bosch?"

"I didn't know it was a fake. All I know is it has a list of names and didn't know that until it was shown to me by Colonel Ford."

"Didn't that same Tony Bosch watch you alone in your interrogation room the first time you went to A.I.?" Senator Specter inquired.

I had to reflect back to that time but then I realized he was right. "Yes sir he was the only one there with me for a short time."

"Did he find it on you or did you pass it to him then and concoct a story to cover your guilt of counterfeiting money?" Specter poked.

"No sir. None of that is true."

"Sergeant your fingerprints were found on that bill. Can you explain that to us?" Specter continued.

I searched for an answer that would suffice but could come up with nothing. "That can't be sir. How could that be? I've never touched that money!" I began to unravel.

"Settle down Sergeant!" General Wickham exclaimed. "Act like a soldier. We are only asking for information that can help us understand how that money went from 2006 or later back to 1983? From what I've been told it is real and not counterfeit even though it's only 1983. Somehow that money came back in time."

The room emitted with moans and conversations amongst the other members until finally a man from the rear of the room stood in the blackness. "Are you suggesting it has 'Time Traveled' from somewhere around 2006 back to 1983 General?"

My focus had been on Amanda's father who sat silently fixed on me the rage in his eyes made his face as red as cupid's outfit but no love showed with him. My shoulder felt Colonel Ford's hand as he leaned forward to familiarize me with who the new stranger was. "That's the President's personal advisor, Mr. Kudra M. Stein." Still staring back at the hefty Marine, the only word I heard was Stein. "I'm surprised he's even here, I was told he was out of the country which is why the Vice is present." A few heads turned in the way of the darkened figure now just coming into light.

"Mr. Stein, I didn't know you were here. Back so soon from your trip?" the General joked. The President's man never cracked a smile just looked at the military man still waiting for an answer to his hypothesis. "Sorry sir, what I am offering as an explanation is a slim possibility, yes. Many years away but still a chance this is what has happened." the general looking around at his colleagues for their understanding and approval.

"But for what reason General? What would there be to gain with one twenty dollar bill? Why not say go back in time, steal money from our time and take it forward? That might be more acceptable to all of us but travel back with just twenty dollars? You can't get a good taxi ride with that little bit." The distinguished men found some humor in his statement.

The general felt he had been mocked and fired back his next shot. "Well then Mr. Advisor, how do you explain the list on that bill with two dead people, another in the hospital and this soldier here in front of us?" The room quieted all waiting for the response.

"I can't any more than you can. Perhaps we need to watch how things progress over time." He was satisfied with his conclusion.

"Horse hockey!" all heads turned back forward. It was General Kelley, Amanda's father interrupting.

"Now General Kelley, I understand you have a personal connection to this matter but please keep your demeanor." the Vice-President intervened to calm the man.

"Sorry sir but you didn't lose a daughter through all of this. I want to know if that man had anything at all to do with her death. This is more than just National Security in my mind."

Finally his inner rage had broken. He'd never listen to what I'd have to say about his daughter or that I was not to blame. I wanted to stand and tell more of my side and what I knew. The secret I held had to be known but I just didn't feel now was the correct time or place. I may have earned some respect but not to the degree I had hoped for. UNLESS...

Chapter 24

I knew it was time to see who here would be truthful with me. I already knew about the threat from the outer reaches of our solar system. I knew they also were aware of it's existence. Would they deny it? I had the perfect way of testing my theory, my dreams. I stood slowly coming to a full attention and waited for someone to address me. Much to my surprise it was General Kelley.

"Do you have something more to add Sergeant?" he asked still enraged.

"Yes sir. Please, I ask that all of you listen to what I'm about to say with your fullest scrutiny. I have been having repeated dreams during these past few days and have no idea what they may mean. My most recent was on the flight over here." All focus and attention was now in my control. "In my dream a planetary system came into our solar system and caused much havoc destroying other planets along it's way. It is headed straight for Earth. Nothing can be done at this time to avoid it." I paused to see what reactions there were and to ready myself for my next part.

"Please continue." Mr. Stein motioned. "This sounds interesting."

"What if someone has sent a warning to us? Say someone like myself to awaken us to the existence of this fulmination? That could explain my finger prints on the bill and the general's suggestion of time travel."

"That's preposterous young man!" Stein laughed about it. "The ability to time travel is nonsense and if there were another system on a direct path to Earth, our best scientist would know about it before you having a 'dream'." More laughter ensued. "This is reality not fantasy Sergeant. Nice theory though wouldn't you say Mr. Vice President?"

The Vice tried to laugh along but his facial tone suggested more behind the illusionary mask. There shown genuine worry as he pulled Mr. Stein down to say something in secret. They talked back and forth for a short time then Mr. Stein broke through the clatter.

"Gentlemen, please, let's conclude this so we can all get back to more important things. Sergeant Conrad, your idea is unique but it is just a dream. We suggest you keep it to just that, a dream. As for the rest of us here please remain seated as the sergeant is removed from the room. Thank you for your dedicated service to your country."

The colonel whispered into my ear that he'd be out when they concluded. He wanted to ask me a few things. Ten minutes later they began filtering out and the colonel attached to my arm. "We'll go get that new ID now. You made quite a splash back there with that dream analogy. You got some heads rolling that's for sure. Well it seemed like a realistic possibility to me, for the future that is."

Yes, I know I did and no one in there confirmed my story. They are hiding the truth. "Sir, am I staying here at the Pentagon for duty?"

"Yes you are. They want to keep you close until they figure all this technical mumbo jumbo out. And there's still the terrorist concern. Like I told you, you'll love it here."

Before we could leave the area, an individual cleared his throat then asked "May I have a word with you Sergeant?"

The colonel and I both turned to see the statuesque figure of one General Kelley. Now face to face, I snapped to attention faster than the colonel. His spotless uniform made my unkempt appearance seem enervated but that was the only difference in my mind. He was a man just as much as I was and I'd stand toe to toe with any man, even my own father. I showed him my respect now I hoped he would not repudiate mine.

"Colonel I'd like it to be alone if we may?"

"Yes sir. I'll be there waiting for you when you've finished sergeant." he gestured towards the bathrooms.

Watching as he left the area, the general faced back and grinned, giving me some relief. "You got our full consideration with that theory of yours. And I'd like to say I thought you were more honest than those stuck noses. I'm impressed with the man my baby was with the night she died. Would you please join her mother and me for a dinner sometime after you've settled in to D.C.? I'm certain she has questions of her own, as do I."

"Thank you sir, I'd appreciate that very much. Your daughter from what I had time to experience was a wonderful person. You know I'm not sure if you know this but I only knew her for about a day."

"She went out with you in just one day? That I did not know. You must have made one hell of an impression on her."

Yes, I believe I did. "I wish she would've had a chance to tell you in person or a letter maybe."

"Yes that would help make the difficulty I feel right now into believing some things." his examination of me still progressing. "Well here is our number and address. When you're ready to meet, contact us. Good luck here at the Pentagon."

"Thank you sir, I'll be in contact." I watched as his old soldier gait made him vanish in the crowd. "Time to find the colonel."

About a week went by and I was still waiting for my things. I had settled into Pentagon life at the new dining facility and made a few friends but I still missed my old ones. The investigation continued into the mysterious money and attacks. All known leads had produced nothing. It was as though Marduk and his group had fallen from the face of the Earth. I kept looking for new recruits to help with my plans being cautious as to what I said and to whom. One morning I was exiting the kitchen through the swinging doors going to fill a drink dispenser when I almost ran the President over, literally. He had stopped in to grab a quick thirst quencher and about got knocked on his tail. With him were his aides, security men and the Vice-President plus his son, George W. Bush. The scene was awkward for me but funny to the president so much that he pretended to wrestle with me. As he began shaking my hand the Vice cupped his ear and whispered. He gave an even firmer grip and told me how proud he was of my service. "You are what being an American is all about." then proceeded on his way. The vice president's son stopped to speak with me after a brief conversation with his father.

"So you're the infamous man from Berlin. I'm the vice-president's son, George also, with a W., he he." he laughed at his own joke while waiting to shake my hand.

"It's nice to meet you, sir. What do you do?" figuring it couldn't hurt asking.

"I'm in the oil business. Do you know anything about that?"

Only what my dad gripes about, blood suckers, he he. "We should not be fighting over oil? Really, aren't there other alternatives?" I was truly serious.

He paused and stroked his chin with his hand then offered, "I see what my father saw with your open mindedness. Well I'd like to stay and talk more but I better be catching up to the others. If you ever come up with something on that alternative idea, call me. Better yet contact me. See ya." and did a terrible salute trotting out.

"Wow, hope he never gets into the White House. Lord help us." Then I finished my task I had set out to do.

"Sergeant Conrad, you have a call." my new mess "Daddy", as he liked to be called, Sergeant Ortiz hollered from the door.

The title still struck me as odd but I liked it and the new stripped look on my clean uniforms. "Be right in."

"No, now!" then he cupped the phone. "This guy you don't want to make wait." He urged me to hurry fast.

"Who is it?" and he shoved the phone into my hands. "Hello, this is Sergeant Conrad."

"Did you forget about my invite Sergeant?" went a grumbled voice.

Oh shit! It's General Kelley! "No sir, I did not. Sorry they've kept me busy." I attempted to reconcile.

"Horse hockey! I'll deal with them. The misses and I have made plans for a nice get together. She really wants to meet you now. This Saturday evening, at 6 p.m. so be ready by 5 o'clock. I'll have someone pick you up so you don't get lost. Got it Sergeant?" he was all business.

"Yes sir, 5 p.m. I'll be ready. What should I wear, sir?"

"Why? Don't you have your gear from Berlin yet?"

"No sir.

"I guess I need to get on some more asses then. You'll have your things before Saturday son. See you then." click went the phone.

Sergeant Ortiz rushed back over to me for the gossip. "So tell Daddy what he said?"

"He said you're not my 'Daddy' and to stop asking everyone to call you that. Oh yeah, I'm to have off Saturday, all day Saturday. If you don't believe me, call him back, Daddy. I'm sure it would make his day better." and proceeded to make salad for the lunch.

At first he wasn't sure, so I gave him a little wink and that nudged him on. He grabbed the phone and asked for the general's connection. As others started observing the conversation, they soon realized he was on the ropes and the general was delivering the knock out blows. "Yes sir. Ah, yes sir. Certainly, sir. I'm sorry sir. I will let them know sir. Thank you, sir." he was beet red and we were pissing our pants. "Good bye sir and I hope you have a nice evening with Sergeant Conrad. He is a nice person and good soldier." As soon as he hung the phone up he turned to me, embarrassed, and apologized for making us call him "Daddy" and we were not to do it anymore. "Enjoy your Saturday off." was the last we heard from him that day.

Sure enough, the general was correct my belongings were in my possession by Friday. *Impressive, is it the stars or the man?* "Guess I'll have a chance to find out this weekend. I know just what to wear." I smiled as I unpacked. I could tell by the writing it must have been packed or readied for shipping by Kelsey. His penmanship needed help but not his ability to pack. I remembered when he arrived at Berlin he had like three boxes where the average person would have used five. I almost dreaded opening my boxes for fear of an explosion of clothes or worse. "Open first? Oh this should be memorable." I began to chuckle. He knew I wouldn't pass on opening that one first, so I carefully cut the tape from around the edges. As it sprang to life, my heart raced from excitement. What was in this one? Folding back the box flaps, I noticed an envelope with just one word written on it, Del. Anxious to see what was inside I ripped it open and pulled out a letter. I began to unfold it when something fell out of it and hit my lap. The pictures concealed inside had landed upside down so I turned them over. The top picture was one of Kelsey and me standing outside our barracks. The onset of memories and tears ensued. As I went through them, each new picture brought back more and I realized how much I missed being there. The last two brought a welcomed change of happiness. They were of him and Tricia, one at her place and the other at one of our old hangouts. Next I went for the letter. It was the first one I'd received from anyone since my hasty move to D.C. It read:

Hey Sergeant Conrad,

Yeah I heard from our old 'boss' that you got a promotion before leaving us. I'm glad someone like you earned those stripes. Bet they look good on you too. Well if you haven't looked at the pictures I sent along do so now. I'll wait.

Thank you. For introducing me to the last woman I'll ever want, need or plan to be with. It was love at first sight, for me, not her right away. But that all changed when, well you know, (WINK). Now she won't leave me alone.

So how did you like those other pics? I have doubles so don't worry, keep them. I'll be writing you more so stay in touch because others here (WINK AGAIN) want to hear how things are going for you in D.C. Old Ruf is hoping to stay up to date on things. He says he'll help me get my next promotion if I keep up the good work. I hope so because I hate being just a private. I want to be like you, a Sergeant someday. So tell us how things are in the Pentagon when you write back. It would sure be great to know everything is working out for the best. Our friend says to give you his brother's number, just in case you need an ally there. Well I got late shift and then a later shift with Tricia, what a gal.

Talk again soon,
Kelsey

Ps (202)870-5859

I guess it was a good thing for me that I had my own room now since being a sergeant had some privileges. For the rest of the night as I unpacked and wiped more tears away, the sorrow subsided and it was replaced by loneliness. Again I was all alone.

Saturday night could not have come quicker. Sergeant Ortiz's mishap with the general left a bad taste in his mouth and my body aching from all the extras he made me do. My ride for the evening was prompt but not what I expected. It was a brand new Rolls Royce Silver Spur limousine complete with an English chauffeur. It pulled up and the driver got out, opened the back door and in his English accent said "Mr. Conrad I presume? I will be taking you to the Kelley's this evening."

Wow, did I make that much of an impression on the general to send a limo?
"Thank you. Where are we headed this evening?" I boldly asked as I entered.
He answered as he got back in. "Bethesda, Maryland sir."

I was always taught never to mock someone but this English gent made that rule hard to follow. What helped ease those thoughts were the Rolls, it's luxurious feel of the soft leather and the smell was memorable. It made the ride along the Potomac that much more special. Here was a small town guy riding in a once in a lifetime automobile to a general's home in Bethesda, that a month ago I never knew. What was next out of this incredible week? I sat back and enjoyed.

"Did you tell him there would be company?" the general's wife asked.
"No, I thought it would be better to wait, just in case the other doesn't show. No sense in getting the young man all restive if I don't need too. Right?" he laughed.
"Just don't use those big words when he's around. Hell, I hardly know half of them and what they mean. Do you think he will?" she laughed along with him. "Besides, I don't think Amanda would approve if we did and you know she's watching us, especially tonight."
"Yes dear, our little girl is watching." as he gulped the last swallow of his drink down. Just then the doorbell rang. "I'll get it, it's probably him."
"OK but please watch how many of those you have, for me?" she almost instinctively begged. She watched him wink before he gave her a kiss, then he went to answer the door.
"Hello, thanks for coming tonight." He welcomed his guest.
"Are you kidding me? I wouldn't miss this night for anything." as the general closed the door behind them.

"Are we soon there sir?" I asked the driver.

"Just a little ways yet sir, do you need something?"

A bathroom break would be great. I should've gone before I left. "Nothing that I can't wait for...ah, I don't know your name?"

"It's James sir."

The name is Bond, James Bond. Oh stop it! Your mother would kick your... "Strong name, doesn't it mean..."

"...it means something over used." he interrupted.

"Actually I was going to say inferior but you don't seem like that to me. You, I feel, are defined, educated, cultured." I detected a slight grin in the review mirror.

"Thank you, sir." *At least someone knows dignity.* "Were you educated in Europe sir?"

"The Hotel Excelsior in Berlin, James, I studied with Chef Heising."

"Bernhard Heising? He was a teacher? Great Scot, what did you learn to make? Bratwurst and beer?" he joked I assumed.

"No we learned to make French dishes from him like Boeuf Bourguignon and Coq au Vin. They were two of my favorites to prepare but I really liked Cassoulet."

"The English variety sir?"

"There's an English version of Cassoulet? I did not know that James. Do you have a recipe for it that I might be able to try?"

He was delighted to see someone with cooking interest such as his own. "I'll get you one that's better than Bernhard's, you'll see the difference." He smiled back again. "We are here sir."

The house he drove up to was opulent. It made the house I grew up in pale in comparison. The driveway arched in the front for easy turn around or parking. The outside resembled an Italian villa with stucco facing that hid the inner beauty I had yet to see. I peered upwards from inside the limo where I saw two shadowy figures standing at one of the upper windows. The one I thought was the colonel possibly standing guard while watching for my arrival. The other's face seemed like I may have known them but they walked away too fast for me to focus. James was quickly at my door and opened it as the lady of the house greeted me at the front door. *Odd, I guess that wasn't her up there if she's down here so fast?*

"Hello Sergeant Conrad or can I call you Adel?" Amanda's mother's greeting was warmly magnanimous. I could see just where Amanda got her charm from.

"You may call me Del, please. Your home is phenomenal." still awestruck from the size.

"What, this old place? I got it for after I retire next year. Come inside Del, we have another guest who'd like to talk with you some more." the general smiled.

Chapter 25

It felt like walking into the Wizard of Oz's castle with the great arches and huge windows. The décor was modern and gave the appearance it was for show only. All around the room sat flowers that had aged in their vases. *These must have been given to them for Amanda's funeral.* No, this was a greeting room, not for sitting and talking. Where we went next was for socializing and where I was reintroduced to the second figure from the window.

"Hello again sir, you are the President's personal advisor, correct?" I asked unafraid now. *I had been invited here for a reason, perhaps this was why?* I pondered. I was glad I had worn my "preppy" look, as I fit right in.

"Good memory for a non-commissioned officer." He jokingly looked at the general for his applause. "Maybe we should see if a commission is in his future? The Army could use some bright young men as officers." as he still awaited the general's approval.

"That Mr. Stein would be his choice and not mine nor what we invited him out here for tonight. So gentlemen let's have a quick toast and then join my wife for dinner. Shall we? Do you drink Del?"

"I only drink socially sir and tonight's about being social so yes, I'd like to share one with you men."

"I hear you on that Del. What an unusual name? How did you get it, do you know?" Mr. Stein inquired.

"My mother chose it for me in memory of a grandfather. I never knew him and no one seems to have any pictures. She said they were burned in a house fire."

"And where are you from?" he prodded.

"He's from here in D.C. now, Mr. Stein." as the general poured us a nice glass of red wine. "Cheers gentlemen."

"Salud." went Stein.

"Prost." I proclaimed as we clang our glasses together.

"So you were in Germany? How did you like it?" Mr. Stein asked.

"Yes, I was in Berlin. Beautiful city, ever been there Mr. Stein?"

"Oh please call me Kudra while we are here, anywhere else Mr. Stein. I insist."

"Ok, Kudra. Have you ever been in Germany?"

"Some parts of Germany, yes, Berlin I have not experienced yet." his eyes twitched.

My mother always did that same thing when she was out being a harlot, as dad would put it and he'd ask where she was. So what is he being deceptive about and why? Our eyes matched looks waiting for the other to speak.

"My, my, if I didn't know any better, I'd say you two could pass for brothers. Wouldn't you agree Paul?" said Mrs. Kelley as she changed the subject quickly.

I hadn't noticed but she was onto something. He looked like an older me.

"Woman, have you been drinking the wine too? They look nothing alike." the good general analyzed. "How soon until dinner? I'm hungry."

"I'll check dear. No fighting while I'm gone." and back to the kitchen she went.

"So what nationality is Kudra from? I've never heard that name before." I dug for more information. *And I didn't like the stare-down you gave me.*

"It's Indian, my father was from Bihar and my mother was German." he offered to fulfill my curiosity.

He doesn't look Indian at all, still hiding behind lies. Let's rattle his box. "So have you thought anymore about my theory on the money and my dreams?"

He about choked on his wine when I asked in regards to those topics. "Ah, well, actually I did do some research especially on the planet part. Our best telescopes in our country have detected nothing like what you described, so I'd say they are just dreams. Nice dreams but just dreams."

"So how's that Sergeant Ortiz been treating you since our last conversation, Del?" admiring his choice of pre-dinner wine. "Having any more trouble with 'daddy'?"

"He's been tolerable sir. And I corrected his use of that title using your influence. I hope you don't mind."

He laughed joined by Mr. Stein and after feeling the opening I blended along. The lady of the house came back to inform us "Dinner is ready gentlemen. I'm glad to see you enjoying yourselves. Del, I have a special place reserved for you." She gestured with a come-hither way.

"You better follow her or she'll drag you there." the general said as he finished his glass of wine and laugh.

Heading towards her direction, lead me into the massive dining area. She was standing next to an end side chair that placed me next to her and across from the other guest for the evening. "This is your placing for tonight and any time you are here in the future." her warming generous tone welcomed.

"May I help you with yours ma'am?" I offered. She graciously accepted and I guided her into her spot.

"Ah, a true gentlemen among warriors, how fortunate I am this evening to have at least one." she smiled back as the other two took their places.

I hadn't noticed earlier possibly due to how I was sitting but Kudra had a nasty looking mark on his hand. "Ouch! That must have hurt? Dog bite?" I quizzed.

"Yes, ha ha…" looking down at his hand "…I have three Rottweiler's and they like to fight. I happened to get the bad end. Let's eat shall we?"

Quick change of subject? "Sorry I didn't mean to pry. Yes, let's enjoy their hospitality." The general just looked on.

"Saif, where are you going?" Aviv wondered.

"I have been afforded the same training as you had Aviv with the Americans. I am going to hopefully shot as straight as you when I'm done." His intentions were more but he couldn't let it show. "Will you write to me while I'm there since I have no family?" sorrow could be seen in his eyes.

"As long as I'm still around, you will always have a family Saif." and they hugged a brotherly hug. "Good luck. We shall miss you while you're gone."

Saif picked up his bags and walked to the door. "Aviv, will you send this to our contact in Berlin for me? It's just a letter." and dropped it on the desk next to the door. *God be with me on this journey.*

"Now that was a great meal." boasted Kudra. "I haven't had Beef Wellington that good ever I do believe. How did you like it Del?"

Still chewing my last bite, I nodded in appreciation of his compliment until I could render my own. A subtle swallow of wine and I was clear to speak. "Yes, that was as good as the chef's I trained with in Berlin." I felt my honesty was a better compliment than his and more meaningful. "Who prepared this, James maybe?"

The general corrected my gaffe with a bit of a smile "Almost correct on that Del. My wife prepared all of this but I'm sure James has taught her a trick or two. Her cooking has gotten better since he arrived." He held his glass up as a show of thanks but maybe more of a truce until later.

"Sorry Mrs. Kelley, I meant nothing negative by my comment."

"None took, Del. It was actually nice to hear a comparison to the great chefs of Europe." her smile extra radiant.

James entered the room with an urgent look as he went to Mr. Stein. "Sir, I'm afraid there is a call for you and they say it's urgent."

"Well then, we better not keep them waiting. Please excuse me." His manners were the better part of what I saw of him, so far.

As James showed him to the phone, I continued our dinner conversation. "This wine is very good. Is it French or from California?" I was not the wine expert at this table.

"Ah, yes, Amanda said you liked wine. It is actually from a nearby vineyard." Mrs. Kelley prematurely spoke.

"Amanda told you I liked wine? When?" She had made my curiosity peak.

"I'm sorry good people but I have an urgent situation back in D.C. and must go. Doreen the dinner was fabulous and I hate to leave so soon but you know how these things work by now." he gave an English style kiss to her.

"Yes, I'm afraid I do know how they work." looking over at her husband.

"I'll walk you out Kudra." as the general stood. Now he was looking at the misses for her previous comment.

"Good night Del. It was nice meeting you again. Maybe we will do this again." His hand extended.

I stood to accept and scope his hand more. "Yes, let's do it again, maybe your place the next time? I'd love to see your Rotties." *That doesn't look like a dog bite.*

After hesitating a brief moment he stuttered "Ah, sure, next time."

When they were out of hearing range, I asked Amanda's mother "So you were saying Amanda told you I liked wine. Did she call you the night we went out?"

"Ah, perhaps we should wait until her father comes back. Then we can talk more. I'll start to clear the dishes." her face filled with uncertainty.

"May I help? I insist please."

With her back again warm smile she replied "Certainly Del, I'd like that. She was right you know. You are a really nice guy."

Again her reference confused me but I allowed her the moment until the man of the house rejoined us. James assisted us in clearing the settings. "Are you going to share your recipe for the wellington also?" I jested.

"Oh I doubt he'll give that one up since the Misses fought so long to get it from him." my host shared.

"Great dear you're back. Del has a question for us, James will you finish while we talk with our guest?"

"Yes Mrs. Kelley."

"Follow me then Del." and back to our original room she led.

The general had started a nice fire in the fireplace while he was out which illuminated the room with flickering shadows of light. The touch was reminiscent of my dinner with his daughter. Doreen went over to a curio cabinet and removed an item from inside. From behind me I could hear her say "We have something we would like you to have." as she placed the box from my past in front of me. The writing untouched, she beckoned for me to open it. "Please open it. I think you'll like what's inside."

"Mrs. Kelley..." I tried to begin.

"Please, call me Doreen."

"Ok, Doreen, I appreciate you wanting me to have the figurine back but it would mean more to me if you kept it, please."

"Do you mean that figurine Del?" as she pointed back over to the curio she had come from.

There on the shelf was the little child nurse with a picture of Amanda behind it.

I turned back both were smiling a "we're here for you" expression. "I don't understand? What's in the box then?"

"Why don't you open it like she said and find out?"

A flood of feelings still penned inside awaited my release and as I opened the box they gushed outwards. They joined me on the couch where I was sitting and embraced me as though they were my own parents.

"Derik wrote us a letter, detailing his time with you and what he found inside the box. Ashley also wrote one to us describing her time with you and her sorrow for our loss. When they went to clean out Amanda's room they found a letter she had written to us but never had a chance to send. Why don't you read her letter to you first, then you'll understand hers to us better." Doreen still being the motherly person rubbed my back.

My dearest Del,

Although we've just met, I feel a calming joy when we are together. They say you must first be friends before you can be lovers. I hope we can become more than friends. While we are apart, I want you to have something that's a part of me to help you remember me until we can be together again. Just as you gave me the beautiful figurine, I am giving you my cross necklace. Wear it to protect you and keep you safe until I'm back in your loving arms. Your kiss lives on in my dreams.

Love always,
Amanda Dori Kelley

Ps Yes I believe in love at first sight.

Doreen removed the cross necklace and hung it around my neck. "A little small for the chain but you can get a longer one that you like." she held back her tears well. I guess when you've cried long enough the healing starts. I could almost understand why the general had been drinking. It doesn't take away the pain though. "If you'd rather not read her other letter to us we'll understand."

I was still shaking like when you lose your first love, only she was a first true love and now I undeniably knew it in my heart. I fought back the emotions by embracing the commitment I had made to her at the hospital. It was time to heal. "No, I'll be fine and besides I have you two to lean on if I need, right?"

"Yes Del, you have me for life son. For anything I can do for you in the world. You ask me and I'll die doing it if I have too." my newest ally assured me.

"Thank you, sir." I said sitting up straight in my seated position. "Now I'd like to read yours."

Back over to the curio Mrs. Kelley went. From under the figurine and picture she pulled the envelope that held the mystery message. Her loving gaze offered compassion as she handed me the letter. "We'll let you read it alone but we are in the next room if you need us." She reached for her husband's hand and he patted my back as they walked away.

Reaching deep down inside to gather strength, I calmed my nerves with the thought of a cookie. "Ok, I'm ready."

Chapter 26

Dear Mom and Dad,

The most terrific thing has happened to me, I feel. I've met a man that reminds me of daddy but nicer, just kidding dad. He's as passionate about life as you are, maybe more. We met in an unusual way but not like you two did at a dance. He came in to the hospital to give blood to help a wounded soldier. Not by donation though, he gave directly with a transfusion. Daddy you always said if a man is willing to give of himself, to help a fellow being, he's a keeper. Well I wish that were a true possibility. See, he's leaving for the D.C. area in the next few weeks and I don't know how long we'll have together. I just know you'd like him and I can't stop thinking about him. I feel like a little girl again. We are going out for dinner tonight to the one place I wanted to see when I was with what's his name, the Heising. You know how much you spoiled me with French cuisine. I hope he likes what I plan to wear. I've been fretting all day.

Dad, do you remember the story you would always tell me about falling in love with mom at first sight? Do you really think that could happen for me? I'm planning to put in for a transfer to the hospital in Bethesda so I can be closer to you and mom but also Adel, if he'd like to see me more. He has the bluest eyes I've ever looked into and a smile that makes my heart race. Hopefully someday I'll get to introduce you to him.

Mom, he's very handsome and gentlemanly. He's better than those marines or navy flyboys daddy always tried to get me to go out with. I can't quite describe it but there's something special about him. I feel sort of like he has a date with destiny to do something great for everyone. I'd like to be part of that moment.

Well I must get finished so I can ready myself for this date. I'll let you know how things went when I get back so I'll finish this letter later. Until then I love you guys and miss you. Hope he sweeps me off my feet because I'm floating already.

"She never had a chance to finish writing the letter." I heard her father say behind me holding a fresh glass of wine. "Would you like another one son?" holding his up. He had been watching from the doorway.

"Yes please, dad. Now I understand why you were so pissed at Sergeant Ortiz for his use of 'daddy'. She called you that all the time, didn't she?" the tears no longer showing.

"She was "Daddy's little girl" and my whole world until she joined the service. I couldn't make her pick the Marine's or the Navy. She wanted to fly, so into the Air Force she went and fly away she did. If she hadn't done that though, she would have never met you and from the sound of that letter, you made her happier than I ever did or could have."

"No sir, I don't believe that to be true. She admired you from the way she talked about you and how she related to you in this letter. You were still her "dad" and no one can replace that feeling a father has for his child, especially a daughter."

"Well then, I'd say her interpretation of who you are was a bulls-eye. Doreen did you want to ask him about tomorrow?" she had filtered in behind us.

"Del, we are going to the cemetery to visit her tomorrow. Would you like to go along with us?" her sincerity was genuine.

"I must work tomorrow or I'd say yes, I'd love to go."

"Then you'll stay here tonight and go with us after church. You do go to church don't you?"

"Well yeah, I mean, yes ma'am I do go to church but what about…"

"What about work?" Mr. Kelley butted in "I've already taken the liberty of notifying that imposter 'daddy' that you'll be off tomorrow. He had no problem with that, besides it's a Sunday and that place is dead on the weekends. Now let's hear all about your family. We have time." as he looked at his watch.

The next four hours we spent talking and looking at old pictures, talking some more, even shedding a few tears but it was the most pleasant four hours I had spent in a long time. The bottle of wine was empty and our minds full of comforting thoughts as we readied for bedtime. They showed me which room had been Amanda's then where I'd be sleeping. "I thank you for all you have done this evening and I wish you both jovial dreams." my hand touching the cross.

"Good night Del." and the misses of the house gave me a tender loving peck on the cheek.

"See he is a convivial type of a Guy." the general said anxious to test his vocabulary.

"Yes sir, I love fun as much as you probably." which sparked a 'huh' kind of expression.

"He's as gifted with the tongue as you are my dear." that got her a pat on her bottom as I closed my door.

"So how do you like my dad, Del?"

"He's nicer as a person than a general. Good taste for wine too may I add."

"Do you like my gift? My grandmother gave it to me for my sixteenth birthday."

"It's a beautiful cross but not as angelic as you my love."

"I'm happy that you are coming to see me tomorrow. I miss you and your kiss."

"Well pucker up honey and I'll plant one on you." pretending to simulate kissing.

"Just remember your promise. Daddy will help, I know he can." She leans forward to accept my affection. "I love you."

"I love you too."

The room lights flashed on as Doreen entered to notify me it was time to arise. "Who were you talking to Del? And I hope that kiss wasn't for me?"

Quickly trying to cover up my emotional state, I apologized for the misconception and assured her it was in no way directed at her. "I must have been having a dream again."

"That must have been some dream." she grinned looking back as she closed the door. Waiting just outside the door was the general. "I knew you should have gone in when he didn't answer. He's having dreams like you've been having, poor guy."

"What about me dear? Don't I get a poor guy?"

"You got one last night or did you forget already?" she kissed him on his lips softly then headed for the kitchen to prepare breakfast.

The drive over to the church was odder than the ride to the general's. This time I sat up front with James and the happy couple rode in the back. The church was a catholic church which I never knew Amanda was catholic. I had never gone to that type of ceremony before. "Sir, not to feel out of place but I'm not a catholic, I'm a Protestant Christian."

"Do you not want to go in? There's another church around the block that James can take you to."

"No, it's not that I don't want to go in, it's just that I've never attended this kind of service before and don't want to mess something up."

"You can't mess anything up more than me son. We'll do this together and manage to get through." He was obviously joking with me to ease my tension.

Inside was similar to my own church back home. The people greeted you as you came in the usher's would assist those in need and instead of my Pastor welcoming us, it was a Priest. Today was different though as there was another individual present who rejoiced in seeing the Kelley's.

"Welcome Doreen and Paul, so glad to see you here today. You brought another soul with you and he is?"

"He is the one Amanda met in Berlin. This is Del, Del this is our Excellency Bishop Michael Gallagher."

"Hello sir, it's nice to meet you." I did what I thought a person should do and semi-bowed my head.

"Oh, ha ha. I'm not the Pope son, at least not yet." he chuckled at my unknowing ignorance. "Is he ah...?" asking the general.

"No he is not catholic. I'm afraid Del is not accustomed to our way of worship so forgive me for not enlightening him a little more."

"God loves all of us no matter what religion we chose to follow. Perhaps someday he will join the church and follow it's path."

The dream, is he the Bishop I'm searching for and is he on the side of the church I seek? Follow the path. "And which path would that be sir?" I had to ask.

"Why the path to righteousness of course, do you believe?" his mannerism was inviting, as much as the feeling of family I had felt at the Kelley's home. His soft spoken voice would have made an excellent choice for the Pope.

"That I do. I believe in a great many things. Most importantly I agree with your belief that God loves us all. He wouldn't have created us if he didn't, right?"

He appeared to be taken back by my open understanding of what God meant to the world. "I see you wear a cross. Is that to show your belief or your faith?"

Puzzled I asked "Are they not the same?"

"To some maybe, to others they are as different as the sun and the moon. Would you like to discuss this some time? For now we must be starting service." He nodded that the pews were filling.

"Yes. I'd be very interested in sharing views."

"Let's talk after church then." and to his position he went.

"Seems like you make friends easy Del. That is a sign of a great leader you know." the general toyed with me on the idea. "Let's go sit while there are still seats."

The sermon reflected on making good decisions and often the Bishop looked our way. Was it a signal or just me thinking he was sending one? Could he offer help in my personal quest or guide my path to forgiving the person who stole the love I'd never know? I watched how he commanded the attention of his faithful followers. Not a soul slept during his sermon. When he concluded, his face glowed from self-appeasement. He had delivered the word of God and his believers were happy with what they heard. As he had promised, he met us after to finish our short chat.

"So, where were we young man, ah yes, your cross. May I see it?" I satisfied his eagerness by removing it. "Have you decided yet?"

"Decided what sir?"

"What it's significance means to you? Why do you wear it? Show it?" his questions were honest but something I hadn't thought about until now.

"I wear it in respect and remembrance of the person it came from." *Does he recognize it being Amanda's?*

"What about the faith in what it stood for to that person?"

Again another question I had not anticipated. "You know who this came from don't you?" I started to gather. He nodded he did with humbleness. "Then you would know I now wear it to symbolize my commitment to a promise I made to her."

"And that promise is a good one or one filled with hate?" he saw the path I had been heading down even before I did. "You must decide if that promise is worth keeping even if it means the sacrifice of your soul."

"What if I believe that man has been deceived by other men for their own glory or to protect that which they desire? What if God has entrusted someone to warn the world of a danger so significant that it could end man's existence? If that person did not follow his heart and what he believes, is he as guilty as the person who commits suicide by not acting on those beliefs?"

"Your thoughts are troubling. Is there more to her death that you haven't shared that you are so bothered?" now he was beginning to understand where my position in this mess was at. His eyes searched my soul like that of a caring parent.

"If you are asking me did I have a hand in her death, then no, I did not kill her. I may wonder if there were more I could have done to prevent it like staying with her but only God knows that answer. What I am bothered by is a known existence that men are not sharing. Not sharing with the world or being truthful to the danger it poses. You are a man of God if I told you my secret would it stay a secret between you and I?"

"Only our father in heaven would know. Whatever it is you wish to confide in me please hesitate not."

My belief was now being tested and I trusted that my instincts were correct. *I hear you Amanda, I trust in your sign.* "A threat to our planet has been revealed to me. When I questioned the actuality of it, I was laughed at by people of great importance. They have repeatedly denied that it is a reality."

"And what is this threat?"

"Another world colliding with ours, it would end life here on Earth." As I spoke those words, he dropped the cross from his hands.

"I'm sorry. I didn't mean to drop it." he apologized as he retrieved it from the floor. "Are you certain of this entity?"

"I have no reason to doubt it doesn't exist."

"Then you haven't seen it to verify that it does exist?" his probe was brash.

My answer was better. "I don't need to see God or the Devil to know they exist."

"You are very correct there. You're intelligence is unusual for someone of your age. Generally from my experience with the younger generation, they are naïve to the world's needs; you seem to embrace those needs. Well I see your ride is waiting and I have used enough of your time this morning. It was a pleasure meeting you, a pleasure I hope to have again. You are welcome here anytime you wish to find peace. Oh my, the cross, may I bless it for you?"

"I'd like that Bishop. It would mean something special to me when I hold it and wear it."

"Then bow your head." He placed his hand on my head and spoke these words "May God be forever in your heart, may he direct you as he so lovingly has done, may you find peace in your journey ahead and may you find the answer to your faith, bless this pendant, may it protect and watch over young Del, in God's name we pray, Amen."

Two more amens could be heard behind me as he finished, the Kelley's had listened in to his blessing. With smiles on their faces, Paul thanked the Bishop and we returned outside to an awaiting James. "Onto the next stop James."

"Yes sir." he winked at me and passed a piece of neatly folded paper. I nonchalantly placed it in my pocket for later.

The cemetery was vacant for the most part a few scattered visitors here and there. The spot they had chosen for their daughter's resting place was near a large old oak tree. During the Bishop's prayer I had secretly made a wish. *If I have picked the correct person to speak with, may a Cardinal appear and sing his song.* I chose the cardinal as my sign because of the Catholic Church, I knew it was part of it but didn't know it's placement. Much like my own life, I was still searching for my own direction. Doreen walked between us holding our arms with hers as we ventured to her daughter's mound. The soil still fresh from the recent burial, she knelt down and kissed with her hand the ground. "Hi baby, mommy's here with Del. You were right, he is a good man and we like him. Watch over him and maybe you can be a part of that special something you thought he possessed." she blew another kiss before we helped her stand back up. "Paul, let's give him some time alone with her so he can say what he wants to say. We can sit over there under the tree."

"That's really not necessary Mrs. Kelley. You might like to hear what I have to say." I advised.

They reunited alongside me, he held her closer as the winds began to swirl.

"Well hello again my dear love, thank you for your gift." I kissed the blessed cross. "Your parents have been absolutely wonderful in sharing their homes warmth which comes from their hearts. I can see where you received your humanity skills and how easy they transfer to another. I have begun to answer a calling that I know you have helped inspire. Your light will lead the way to the end. If my first choice was correct, then show me with your love by doing what I have requested. Then I will know the second choice is the one you have chosen in my dreams. I will visit you as often as I can but know this, if I'm unable to, I still love you deeply in my heart. When my task is complete I hope we both find peace for I will not stop working to achieve that goal that I have promised you. Comfort your mother in her days of sorrow and strengthen your father when he needs it to comfort her. I know you are with God now waiting for all of us to rejoin you one day. We will, someday. I will never say 'goodbye' but instead I offer 'until the next time we meet' and leave you with these words. I will find who is responsible and then do what must be done." I laid my hand upon her dirt mound and held the cross in my other hand and closed my eyes to silently pray. The pair of hands which touched both sides of my broadening shoulders felt like angel wings with the wind. Then in the howling breeze we heard a branch snap and turned in time to see a limb from the great oak fall to the ground. Their shock intensified when they realized that was the spot they would have been possibly sitting under, it became numbing when I uttered "Show me the cardinal baby. Where is the cardinal?" A mother cardinal had been pinned under the branches. She pulled herself out even with her broken wing and checked on her babies in their nest. The scene was incredible and we acted upon impulse rushing over to see if help could be administered. The mother's instincts were to protect, until his hands opened.

"Come to me good mother and I will care for you and your family. I will not harm you." spoke the once spiritless warrior general turned gentle giant. Her song of grace was only overshadowed by the light of the sunrays that pierced the remaining tree limbs and beamed like the face of Christ. Inside the nest were two crying babies barely old enough to see the world. He lifted the mother in his hands cradling her frail body against his. "Del, take the nest back to the car and have James place it in the blanket that's in the trunk. Instruct him to put it in the rear seat with us so the mother can see they are alright." his voice as urbane as the Bishop's was earlier.

"Yes sir." I still opted to show my respect for his position over me. He never amended my homage.

With mother and children safely inside the car he disclosed his love for birds and how he once cared for a robin that had fallen victim to a similar event. His eyes filled with tears as he faced his own personal strife and his wife knew why. Her demeanor urging him to let out the demon he was holding inside. "Go ahead dear, tell him everything."

He knew she was precise in her conviction. Now was the time to share all. "Del, we would like for you to have complete understanding of what we are about to share with you and agree to keep silent what we tell you." I looked over at James with a nod. "Don't worry, he already knows."

Another secret to remain hidden? Why? "Is it about Amanda?"

"No, but it is something you have asked about though." he held for my answer.

"Then yes, I'll keep your secret silent, until I feel it is no longer a secret. Then I have my own to share."

He was totally caught blindsided and searched for reasoning to my answer. What secret could I have that he would want, must have been running through his brain. He finally accepted my terms and started his confession. "When you first came to the Pentagon, you asked about the planet theory and again you asked at our home. I too have been having dreams since Amanda's death, just as you told Doreen you had one this morning. They lied to you about there not being any threat or that they couldn't see it. They didn't lie that it can't be seen from our country, at least not yet. It can only be seen from the southern hemisphere in Antarctica. An outpost on the southern tip of Ross Island just below New Zealand detected what is now known as Planet X. In my dream last night, you saved us from being crushed by a tree. You and Amanda were also holding baby cardinals. So when you said 'show me the cardinal baby', I think it hit both of us. I knew Doreen was aware of my dream and yours but you didn't know about mine. The most unexplainable part of mine was when the Bishop dropped your cross. You somehow save his life because at the end he is thanking you for your sacrifice." He paused for a moment to give me time to absorb everything. "Now you had something you wanted to share?"

Chapter 27

"Ah, are you Saif Kabak?" the tall young and tanned man asked.

"Yes, I am Saif Kabak. And who might you be?"

"My name is Brandon Richard. I'll be your liaison during your training. Welcome to the United States of America. Is this your first time here?"

"Thank you Brandon and yes my first time here. Did you know my partner Aviv Maciar when he trained here also?"

"Hmmm no. No I don't recall that name. How long ago did he train here?"

"It was two years ago."

"Well that would explain why I don't know him. I have only been with the agency a little more than a year." He seemed rushed for time constantly looking at his watch. "We need to go so we can get you settled in. I'll help you with your bags."

Saif felt uneasy with Brandon's actions and hastiness. He himself had always been a thinker and never hurried unless in pursuit or action and even then he thought clear headed. This man was in too much of a rush for a Sunday. "Are you late for something important?"

"The Redskins are playing a preseason game today and I was hoping to watch."

"So you are a Redskins fan."

"No I'm a San Francisco 49er's fan."

"Are you from San Francisco I would assume?"

"Actually a suburb north of it called Fairfax." he said proudly.

"I thought Fairfax was in Virginia?" Saif questioned.

"It is, I know ironic huh, but I believe in those types of things."

"What types would that be?"

"Destiny, you know, being where you need to be, when you need to be there."

"Like you in front of a TV soon?" Saif eased his previous misconceptions.

"Oh we are going to get along real good. Do you play football?" Brandon asked as they continued walking and talking to the car.

"Del, please tell us what it is you wanted to say." Mr. Kelley urged.

"There is a list of names on the bill that was found in Berlin, that much you should know already general."

"Yes, go on."

"Have you seen that list?"

"No I haven't but I chose not to look at it because of my rage at that time."

I took a deep breath before proceeding "On that list was the name Bishop. Amanda told me in my dreams that I should follow the path. Your Bishop this morning told me the same thing, to follow the path of righteousness. When I said out loud for the cardinal to show, my use of baby was to Amanda, not about a baby cardinal as you thought. She also told me in my dream that you could help me in my quest. Would you if I told you what it is?" my strong gaze locked on his.

"If I thought your quest was worthy, then yes."

"Would finding the man responsible for her death be worthy?"

He looked at his wife briefly then back to me. "I don't understand what you mean Del? They know who killed her. It was her ex-boyfriend."

"Yes, it was him but what if another man say ordered the attack on her, would he not be guiltier of her death?"

Still he looked puzzled. "Please explain."

"Was the German soldier who killed the Jews as guilty as Hitler who ordered it to be done?"

He paused for a moment. "Now I'm beginning to understand your concept." he agreed. "They are both guilty of the act but the one who initiated the order would be accountable twice fold. Yes but I still don't see the connection between my daughter and the threat."

"I have made a promise to her that I intend to keep by exposing the threat and her killer. You're going to help me along with the Bishop."

"And how do you propose I do that?" he said with a slight chuckle.

"You're a General. They are skilled in strategizing war plans. This in a sense is a war, a war against time and another skilled killer. That is what I think she was trying to convey to me about your part in this. If I stand any chance at succeeding in my mission then you need to show me the path!" my frustration beginning to build.

"Paul, I believe in what he's saying. Can't you help him plan a way to reveal the lie without getting yourself into trouble?"

"Yes Doreen, I could but his way is about revenge, not justice!"

"No sir you're wrong! It's not for revenge it's for the justice your daughter deserves!"

He finally saw the truth in our eyes and knew he had to do what was asked of him. "Yes, I will help you plan and guide you. I wouldn't want your death on my conscience also if something were to happen to you." He was looking down at the mother bird that had rested in his hands. "This is just like in my dream but her figurine says 'Your babies are in good hands.' Here I hold the mother and her two children are counting on me to see her through. Doreen, you must be the strength for all of us." tears rolling down his cheeks, he missed his daughter.

"So how long have you been with MOSSAD?" Brandon asked.

"Almost seven years."

"Do you like it?"

"Some days are better than others but there's no place I'd rather be. Do you like the agency?" Saif asked back.

"Oh yeah!" the openly enthusiastic young yet mature man exclaimed. "I like the toys we get to play with." beaming with a smile.

"What other things do you like besides toys and games?" Saif was beginning his own investigation of his intermediary.

"Anything Hi-tech especially computers, I believe they will change the world."

"I hope for the better." Saif voiced out while watching the scenery pass by. He didn't like the sound of a world run by computers. "Do you own one?"

"Wow! I wish I did but I can't afford one on my salary! Maybe someday when they're less expensive."

"Do you use them at C.I.A. Headquarters?" Saif continued to probe.

"Yup! That's what got me into the agency. I went to Berkeley for computer science."

Saif's attention was drawn back to the intelligent gent. "Perhaps one day you'll design a computer?" he was being suggestive more than questioning.

"I doubt that."

"Why do you doubt it?"

"It takes money to do something like that Saif. Unless you know someone with a lot of money to burn, it will always be a doubt." the prudent agent finished. "We'll soon be there. Do you have any questions on the facilities or what you can and can't do?"

"No, I'll find them out later. Let's just get me settled in so you can watch your game." Saif smiled because he knew he had a friend here now.

James had already dropped us in front of the house and parked the Rolls in the garage when he entered the kitchen where Paul and I worked on the mother's damaged wing. She would still need to feed her babies so the next step was finding food, worms to be exact. "Here you go sir." James updated the General. "I dug some up from out of the flower garden." still as mellow with his accent as when he picked me up the day before. "Shall I find more?"

"No James that should be a good start. Now, if you'd be so kind as to fetch us a pen and pad to write on?"

"Yes sir." and into the other room he went.

After he disappeared I asked Paul "So what do you think would be the first step in our plan?"

"Well traditionally you'd know who your enemy or enemies are but in our situation we know one but not the other. Or do you know the other?"

"Only that he goes by the name Marduk. The pair of Israeli MOSSAD agents from Berlin were also in pursuit of him."

"Then they would know more about his structure. We need to contact them."

"We can't. Maybe you can but I've been restricted from communications with them until after the investigation has concluded." I informed the general.

"Ah ha, there you go momma. You should heal in time. Now feed your babies." his compassion was incredible for being an instrument of war. "I will contact them then to gather what intel they can share. Thank you James." he had returned with the items. "Please take her to the sunroom with her infants so they can eat. That will be all then for today."

"Yes sir. Good day sir Del. It was nice to meet you." He then motioned like he was writing something on his hand.

The note he gave me earlier. I almost forgot. I gave a quick wink back. He grinned.

"What other names are on the list? Do you remember?" the general asked after we were alone.

"The only other two you wouldn't know are Cox, Cox I wonder how he is?" I transfixed for a moment.

"The other?" he patiently waited.

"Sorry sir, the other was an Eljer Kurn."

"Who did you say?" he said in disbelief.

"Eljer Kurn. Why? You act as though you know him."

"Not personally but I know who does, if it's the same person." He stood to stretch. "I'll be right back. Find us a good bottle of red wine over there."

I scanned the selection of imports and domestics. I didn't know grapes from apples so I looked for one that appeared newer hoping it was. Combing through, I pulled one and noticed a familiar symbol. On the bottle label was hand writing. As soon as I could distinguish what it said, I stopped and slide it back. I reached inside my pocket and removed the slip of paper James had given me. It simply said 'Any recipe you'd like is in the kitchen. Just look for the recipe box. The ones marked "special" are from my brother, Eljer. Enjoy, James'

"How are you feeling today Corporal Cox?"

"Better nurse. Will I be able to have visitors soon?"

"Why? Aren't I good company?" she replied back in her southern laughter.

"Certainly you are I just wanted to see my friends. Sarge only says so much when he comes in and, don't tell him this, he's sort of boring."

"Well you'll find out later today when the doctor comes in I'm sure. Just ask him. Now, do you need a back wash?" she smiled.

"Welcome to Langley agent Saif. Here is your ID for while you're here. Agent Richard will show you around and assist you in settling in. Everything is in your packet. You have a meeting in the morning." The guard also seemed rushed. "Oh yeah win another one guys!"

"Excuse me?" Saif muttered.

"Sorry sir. I'm watching the game on this little black and white."

"Oh, another Red potato fan?" he mused.

"Red potato?"

"Skin of a potato? Redskins?" *And these guys are training me? Not much intelligence here.*

"Oh! I get it now! Good one, I'll have to remember that one. Good luck to you sir." and back to the game he went.

"General Kelley? Are you out here?"

"Over here Del. I was just speaking with James."

"You knew in there?"

"No, I suspected."

"Is his brother the one on the list?"

"How do you know?" James asked.

Holding the note, I replied "I didn't until I saw his name on a bottle of wine. The last name on the list is your brother, a chef? How does a chef end up on a hit list?"

"He's my half-brother actually and he hasn't always been a chef. He does like to mix things though." to which the general and he lowly laughed.

"And you two find it funny?" I must have seemed furious.

"No it's not funny. The inside joke is my brother is also a chemist. He's worked on a theory for many years but even chemist must eat. So he gave up on his dream and decided to try cooking other things."

"What was he working on, may I ask?"

He looked at the general for his approval. With his nod he answered. "A process to make a new fuel source, one that would eliminate the need for oil and it's dependency."

"So he never succeeded and stopped? Well his idea sounds like a reason to put someone on a kill list. What do you think sir?" locking eyes with the general.

His arms crossed, "Absolutely. Any threat to Big Oil and who knows what they would do."

"Then he must be warned." I stated firmly.

"That's just what I was about to do young man. Maybe you can ask him for his recipe for Cassoulet." James joked.

"So now that I have you established in your room, how about we go have a beer and watch the game?" Brandon asked Saif.

"Sorry my friend, I'm tired and don't drink. Some other time maybe?" he offered a hand shake.

"Sure Saif any time. I'll see you in the morning then." and they shook hands.

Saif looked through his "Welcome" packet and found a pad with the C.I.A. letter head. *This will be a great way to relax and get a letter ready to send back home to Aviv.* He'd tell Aviv about his newest friend and what he thought about the huge facility, of what he had seen so far. His training would last six months and a hard six months Aviv promised him they'd be. He was mentally focused after the death of his family. He planned to use his time here to solidify his abilities and escape the pain back home.

"Hello dear brother, how was your day?"

"James, are you okay?" he asked because his brother rarely called.

"I'm fine, you're the one I'm worried about." He got straight to the point. "I need to see you, here in the states, as soon as possible? Like yesterday maybe?"

His brother knew it was of utmost importance if he was directing it that way. "I'll grab a flight for tomorrow if I can."

"No need my good man, a mutual friend of ours will arrange a confidential pickup. Just bring your recipes, all of them."

"All of them? Something tells me this is not going to be for a cooking contest. I'll see you soon then. I'll bring a good bottle of wine this time. I couldn't stand that last stuff you tried to have me swallow down." He put the phone down. "What on Earth does he need my recipes for?" he mused.

"You can make your calls sir. I'll take Del and explain some things I'm sure he has questions to." and back to the kitchen we went. "Would you like a good cup of tea maybe?" the house servant offered.

"That does sound better than wine at this time of day. So, are you and your brother close?"

"We've had a difference or two but we have always remained friends. You have never mentioned any siblings of your own. Do you have any?" as he measured the tea.

"No." I said sadly hanging my head down. "I was an only child. My mother could never have any more."

"Too bad sir, you would make a dandy brother." He smiled trying to cheer me. "Did they spoil you as their only one?"

"No, my father didn't want me growing up like that and becoming tarnished. He wanted me to appreciate the things I worked for and earned."

"I'd say he did a fantastic job then. You value more than others would, had they been in your spot. Don't change for anyone or anything Del. It is your greatest asset." He slid the fresh hot cup of tea to me. "Now enjoy while it's hot." We talked awhile more until the General joined us.

"Ok James, your brother is set. Tea, Del, what about our wine?" he frowned. "Where was I? Oh, he will be flying into BWI aboard British Airways flight 4705, it was the best I could do on short notice. I'm sure he'll like the first class seating."

"Oh I'm sure he will too, I just hope he isn't soused by the time he arrives." We all chuckled. "Sir, I've been wondering about something. If my brother's idea say could work or someone gets it to work in the future, would that create a way to time travel?"

"I can't see how, it was just an idea for another fuel source wasn't it?"

"What makes you ask about time travel? What kind of fuel source is it James?" I had to question.

"All I know is it was something the Nazi's were trying to develop in hopes of keeping their war efforts alive. Speculation was, had they succeeded, we would all be under Nazi control."

"And it wasn't nuclear or anything similar to that?" I was becoming intrigued.

"No young man nothing like nuclear, this was a clean energy source that would outlast even oil. He would brag to me that it would enable man the ability to travel the stars. I always knew he drank too much but this idea of his was obsessive. It killed his marriage and almost himself. Then he had an awakening and turned his life around one day. No one knows why or what happened but I can still see the strife in his face when we see each other. His look is like he is entombed just waiting for the end to come. He has no, how do you say it sir? 'Gusto' left in him." he said with a little jolly ho arm swing.

"Well then James, let's put some back in his step." I announced. "Sir, I think I need to pass on your wine invitation. It's about time for me to head to my home. Care to give me a ride?"

"What's the hurry Del? Do you have something better to do?"

"Not better sir but something that needs to be done."

"Ok, I'll grab my coat. James please let Doreen know we are leaving. I'm sure she'd like to say her goodbyes."

"It's never 'Goodbye' sir, only 'Until next time.' I've always said."

"I like that Mr. Del Conrad. I shall use it for now on." James said on his way to inform the misses.

"I'll work on our 'Plan' when I get back tonight Del. It's been great having you here. You're like the son I never had."

"And you are like my father, a man of few words but words that count when said. Amanda told me you were special. I'd have to agree."

"She was a good judge of character just like her mother, how that other guy got through, I'll never know."

"But that doesn't matter now does it dear?" Doreen said coming down the stairs. "She still had good sense when she met this handsome young man." She placed a kiss on my cheek. "I look forward to seeing more of you. We have much to talk about still."

"Thank you Mrs. I mean Doreen. I look forward to more of those great dishes I saw in the recipe box."

"You do what I tell you to do! I know where our problem is, he's here in D.C.! Now get here and kill him as you were instructed to do in Berlin!" the irate voice screamed over the phone.

"It was not my fault sir. The team you sent didn't do their job. Now I have to clean up your mess? Very well, I will, but it will cost you more. We need more guns and weapons that I'm sure you can arrange with your contacts there." the ruthless negotiator waged.

"I'll get what you want after you get what I want! Him out of the way! If he discovers my secret, I'm ruined!" he couldn't have been more forceful with his plea. "You will be ruined as well." The words stung as he said them to the hired assassin.

"I will accomplish my end. You better hope you do too." he said as he slammed the phone down. "It seems as though our connection is coming undone. We may need to sever our relationship when we finish the Berlin job. Prepare to go to America. You've been there before so you are perfect for this task."

"I won't let you down."

"Thank you sir for the ride home, will I see you tomorrow?"

"Possibly Del, I mean Sergeant. Remember to keep the professionalism when we are in uniform." he said probably to remind his own self.

"Will do sir, have a safe trip home. I wouldn't want something happening to you now." An exchange of hand signals and the Rolls was off. My thoughts were on writing back to Kelsey so he could relay a message to 'Ruf' about the update. "How can I tell Sarge without Kelsey getting involved? I can't just come out and say it in the letter. I can't risk sending a second letter within the other and say it's for Sarge only. I got it!" as I reached the housing doors and showed my ID.

"Thank you Sergeant. Your picture is better than mine. Have a good day."

Yes my pictures are good thank you. "Thank you Sergeant and you the same."

Chapter 28

August 6, 1983

Hello my buddy Kelsey. How is old Sarge treating you? I hope you're still with Tricia and I'm glad you two hit it off. Don't forget me if you have any kids, alright? Well duty here at the Pentagon sure is different than Berlin. I get to lounge around all day and watch TV. Your favorite team is on now I think? Don't you like the Redskins? Just kidding about lying around, I have a jerk for a mess sergeant but things will get better, I think. Thanks for the pictures, they brought back old memories. I've sent some along from here and doubles for my other buddy "Ruf" so just keep yours and make sure he gets his pack. Good luck with your promotion, I'm certain you're in good hands and should get there in time. Oh oh, your team just lost in overtime to Atlanta, sorry. I'll keep in touch and send more pictures when I write. Maybe someday we'll be stationed at the same place again.

Later everyone,
SGT. Del Conrad

"Well that takes care of that part. I'll just mail this out tomorrow. Now, I wonder if someone is at home." I dialed the number from Kelsey's letter to see. It rang what felt like an eternity and just as I was about to hang up, the voice on the other end said 'Hello.' "Ah hello, is this Roger?"

"Yes my name is Roger. Who's this?"

"Is this Roger Lawrence, brother to Leroy Brooks?" I wanted to confirm.

"Yes. Is this one of those damn sales calls because if it is I'm not interested." Click went his end. "Damn fools."

"He hung up on me." I was agitated by his action and not listening to me further as I redialed.

"Hello."

"Rufus says don't hang up on me again or he'll thump you a new one." *That should get his full attention.*

"Who the hell is this?"

"He said you were stubborn, boy he wasn't lying. My name is Del and I served with him in Berlin. Do you know who I am now?"

"The one sent back to the states because of Nibiru?" using the code word to confirm.

"Only because they lost Marduk." was my confirmation phrase.

"Are you okay? Do I need to get you?" he sounded anxiously nervous.

"I'm fine, thank you. I contacted you so you could relay a message to Sarge."

"Sure thing young man, what?"

"I'm sending a letter over tomorrow with pictures for him. I taped them together back to back."

"Why would you do something like that?" he interrupted.

"If you let me finish, I'll tell you. I hid some notes inside their centers, he'll understand. Can you remember that?"

"Of course I can. I'm not some dumb old Sergeant now am I?" his humor lacked skill.

"No I guess not. Thanks and I hope you're not a Redskins either." and quickly hung up.

"Hell no I'm not a Redskins fan. I'm a Cowboys fan." he yelled back into the dead phone.

"Did you have any trouble getting Del home?" Doreen asked her husband.

"None dear, we talked most of the way back. He likes us very much. He would have made a superb son-in-law."

"Sorry to tell you but your team lost today in extra innings."

He laughed and corrected her once more "It's called overtime dear and it's only preseason. It doesn't mean a thing to me and they lost all of them last year and won the..." he waited to test her knowledge.

"The World Series?" she timidly replied.

"Close my love, it was the Superbowl." he loved that she tried and that was all that mattered. "I have some work to do so I'll be in the study if you need me."

"Ok my dear. I'll check from time to time to see if you need anything." They kissed as loving couples would, embracing the time they still shared together, their love never stronger than now. The way they looked at each other now held more meaning than when they first met. She never felt safer in his arms and found it hard to let go. "And you know where I'll be, if you want me." she said with a daring look.

Although they went their own paths, they were still in each other's heart. He needed to think about the plan now; there would be time to cuddle after. "Okay Del, now that I'm in the dog house, let's go to work."

Roger hadn't spoken with Leroy in about two weeks. The last conversation was urgent but he expected this new news would pale in comparison. He heard the phone click. "Leroy? Are you there?"

"Roger? Why are you calling so soon? Has something happened to my friend?"

"No, he says he's fine. He contacted me tonight about a letter he's sending out tomorrow. There will be pictures for you to look at and look closely inside them."

"Are you sure it was him? And he said that?"

"Yes I'm sure he knew our phrases."

"Ok, I'll check them out when they get here. Anything else?"

"Yeah, your Redskins lost in OT to Atlanta! Ha, Ha! Brother!" and off he went.

"We'll see who's there at the end of the season again, brother!" looking over at his poster of their past Superbowl victory. "Right Merlin!" he nodded up and down and let out a squawk.

"Why must you go to America again daddy?" the little girl visibly upset. "You promised to take me to see the Western Wall and Grandmama."

Seeing the hurt in her face and knowing he had made those promises, he offered as his wife watched "How about we all go tomorrow? We will spend the day together before I go. Does that sound good to you, Avivah?"

"Oh yes daddy! Can we mommy? Can we?" her innocence of age showing.

"If your father says he will, then we will." she smiled her appreciation to him for keeping his vow to his only daughter. "I'll prepare a basket of fruit for us."

"Thank you daddy, you're the best in the world!" and she hugged his neck tight.

"I'd do anything for you, anything. Now go help your mother while I get packed for my trip." and he kissed her forehead before sending her on her way. After she left, he reached behind a section of their home's wall and remove a wrapped packet of documents. He hurried through them and found the one he wanted. "This passport should do just fine." as he snickered and returned the others to their hiding spot.

His wife reentered the room "Sorry I was going to ask which fruit you would like but I see you are busy." she turned back in disgust.

"Geva wait! You know this is what I do. I do this to protect us."

"And when will it end? When!?" she rushes out.

"When the war between our people and theirs is over, that's when." He spoke softly.

"Who are you talking to daddy?"

"I'm talking to God, my little one. He hears all our prayers." and she nods a yes.

"Daddy, are we going to see Grandma today?" Aviv's daughter asked.

"Yes Shira, we are and we are going to the Jordan River to see an old friend." His mother now lived in Jericho and a fellow MOSSAD agent lived nearby and had invited them. Caleb was as trustful as his own partner Saif and he was there for Saif's family's funeral as support to Aviv. "Do you remember him from the funeral?" he pointed at his picture on the wall.

"Yes, I think I do? Was he the big man that mommy said ate all the food?"

"No." he said laughing. "Mommy over exaggerates sometimes. He only ate half of it." His beautiful wife, Shoshana, whose name meant rose, was as celestial as his daughter, joined them. She apparently heard the last part by her look as he became apologetic. "Sorry but you really should be careful of what you say to her. She repeats everything these days."

"You're right Aviv, she repeats everything she hears you say." she laughed with them. "I'll be more attentive in the future as will you." She loved them both with all her heart but deep inside she feared the same could happen to them as had happened to his partner. She never told him though for she didn't want him to stop doing what he loved. "Come Shira, help me finish getting things loaded in the car."

"Okay mommy, she is so bossy sometimes." another saying she heard her father say many times.

"Now Shira, your mother is not 'bossy', she loves us very much and that is how she shows it, at times. Come here so I can give you a big hug." and she did so he could. "I love you my princess." and he pressed his lips to her head.

"I love you too daddy and I hope I can marry a man as wonderful as you. That I heard mommy say." and she ran to help her mother.

He went into their bedroom and pulled a locked box from the closet. He opened it hoping he wouldn't need the pistol he removed from it but was always armed when heading into a sometime hostile land. "I hope this is not needed."

"I hope it isn't too." his wife said with uncertainty behind him. They just looked into each other's eyes and said not another word.

Cox was sitting up in his bed eating when Sergeant Brooks appeared. "Attention, soldier." the old master joked. "Is that junk any good?"

"Horrible, but better than that liquid diet I was on." referencing the near empty IV bags still hanging.

"Did they give you any idea when you might be out of here?"

"Doc said maybe another week. Why, do you need me that bad?" he joked back.

"Well they didn't wound your pride I see. No, I don't need you but maybe a friend of ours might?" he tested Cox's memory.

"Fill me in while I try to fill up. Start from the beginning so I know I haven't missed anything."

After Sarge had finished telling the tale with the newest update, he asked Cox "Do you think you can help him?

"And you are certain he understood what the 'N' was for?"

"Yes, I watched as he wrote each letter down to combine them. It all spelled 'Adelstein', was there more?" Sergeant Brooks inquired.

"Just this, Gabby and I had compared stories we got from home, the soldier from the little girl's story was Conrad Adelstein."

"And what does that have to do with Sergeant Conrad?"

"I'm not positive yet but...I think there's a connection." He paused for a drink. "There's a part of the story not many know that is too coincidental." He stopped again, this time to look Sarge straight into his soul. "The redeemer would enter into a self-conquest because of a lost love." He could see the wheels turning in Sarge's head.

"Then we must help him." the old chieftain suggested.

"That we will Sergeant Brooks."

"Grandma!" Shira screamed. It had been well over a year since they last saw each other.

"Oh my how you have grown in one year. She will be taller than both of you." she told Aviv as he gently embraced her. "Any longer and you'd be coming to my funeral."

"Don't talk like that Idra." Shoshana scolded her. "She'll believe you and one funeral in a month is enough."

"I'm sorry my son. I know it hurt you when your friend lost his family. How is he doing?"

"He went to train where I did mother. It will help him to get his mind off of things."

"Or make them worse and want to kill someone." Aviv's mother opinionated.

"Now who got killed?" little Shira asked innocently.

"No one." her mother and father said together.

"But grandma said..."

"She said something she should not have said." her mother quickly interrupted.

"Let's go inside and talk. The neighbors are so snoopy." the elder of the group recommended.

"So they're not like you Idra?" Aviv's wife poked.

"Ladies please, no fighting while we are visiting." his look of clemency directed at both said all it needed. They unloaded their bags and began heading in.

One of the nosier neighbors saw them outside and hollered "Hello." and waved at Aviv.

"See what I mean? Now everyone from the Dead Sea to the Mediterranean will know I had visitors."

Aviv not wanting to be ignorant returned the gesture. "Momma, who is that?" he asked her going into the home.

"Another Palestinian I think. They come in groves. Soon they'll own this land if we are not careful."

"Your mother's now the philosopher, just great." His wife murmured.

"You know, someday you two will need to see eye to eye."

"I hope not too soon my dear."

"I want to leave early so bedtime will be sooner, Avivah. Go give your mother a kiss good night and then to bed."

"So soon but the sun is just setting."

"And we will be up before it is, young lady."

She knew not to argue so she kissed him and went to find her mother.

He continued his prayer now that he was alone. He focused on his visit to see his mother and his trip to the states. "May Allah be with me during both times and help me rid the world of the infidels. They know not what evil they prepare to unleash upon the Earth."

His wife stood back in the shadows unseen and said her own prayer to God to forgive his obsessions.

"Well now, that looks like a plan worthy of God's blessing." the general said assuaged. For the first time in days, today made him feel at peace with his accomplishments.

"I have dinner done early so we can relax afterwards. I gave James time to get ready with his brother coming tomorrow." She had changed into something a lot more relaxing too.

His eyes gleamed with delight from her glowing freshly washed hair to her fragrant European perfume. "Let's eat later I'm hungry for you, now."

Chapter 29

"Mother your Shwarma is the best!"

"Thank you Aviv. How did you like it Shoshana?" she asked gloating from her son's approval.

"I must admit, it is better than my mother's." then under her breath she directed to her husband "But not as good as mine is it dear?" They chuckled.

"Grandma, what did you make for me?" Shira anticipated a treat.

"Why, your favorite of course Shira, sufganyot. This time with raspberries." she told her smiling from seeing her pleasure of the news. "I'll be right back with them."

"Well, your mother went all out this time."

"She hasn't seen us in so long she just misses...mother you made enough for the whole neighborhood. Are you selling them too?"

"No but now you can take some along when you leave tomorrow." her sorrow because of their planned short visit showing. "Maybe next time you'll stay longer."

"I can't get him to stay home for a day or two and you want him to stay longer? I'll believe that when I see it." Shoshana groaned.

"Maybe you can't get him to stay but I could if I had to." they began bickering again. "Are they good Shira?"

With the filling from the inside of them smeared all over her face she tries to say 'Yes' but with her mouth full it is impossible. She just nods hard and smiles.

"No more after those you have, okay young lady?" her mother scolds.

Her smile now turned upside down was righted again by grandma's approval that she could have more tomorrow.

"Would you like something to eat now Paul or are you still hungry for me?" Doreen flirted.

"Yes dear, let's go eat before it gets cold if it isn't already."

"I'll warm it up for you if it is...and maybe later too?"

"Insatiable you are woman. Go ahead and start it, I'll be down after I make a quick call. He waited until she was going down the stairs then dialed. *Ring. Ring.*

"Hello?"

"Hello Kudra, this is General Kelley. Can we talk?"

"Why certainly my good friend, what do you want to discuss?"

"Nibiru."

Kudra hesitated then looked to choose his words wisely. "That subject is better conversed in private, not over a phone Paul."

"I know which is why I want to meet with you tomorrow morning. Is your schedule open?"

"If it isn't, I'll make sure it gets open. Is everything alright? Has that young man influenced your silence?"

"No he has nothing to do with this. Just meet me and you'll understand."

"Okay Paul, I'll see you in the morning. Give my regards to the wife please."

"That I'll do sir. Good bye." and down to join his wife he went.

"It is time to leave Avivah, help your mother. I'll grab the bags."

"You always leave so early Rafe." his wife griped.

"That is so we don't hit much traffic and the guards are eager to pass you through so they can change shifts."

"If you worked an honest job we wouldn't need to hide like we do."

Her comment angered him and he grabbed her arm so tight that welts were imprinted. "Don't tell me I'm not doing honest work when I'm doing as God has asked of me. Someday you'll give credence to my work and see why my mother named me Rafe." He fully believed in the name he'd been given and it's meaning. God has healed. "Now get in the car and don't say another word until we get there."

"What are you doing up so early Shira? Do you need a drink?" Aviv asked his daughter while lying in bed.

"I had a dream and it woke me. I'm scared for you."

"Now why would you be frightened? What was it about?"

"You shot yourself and we had to bury you like Saif's family." A definite chill in her voice startled Aviv.

"I would never shoot myself Shira. I only shoot bad people and only when they make me shoot them. Your mother was right, you ate too many of grandma's dessert." He kissed her forehead and assured her "It was just a bad nightmare. Now go back to sleep."

After she left, her mother whispered "She's just like you, eat too much and have bad dreams."

"Yes but how many of my dreams have come true." he lay awake with his eyes opened. Next to him, she opened hers too now and prayed it was just a dream.

"Sergeant Conrad, did you see that game yesterday?"

"The Redskins game? No Sergeant Ortiz, I'm not a fan."

"Who do you like? Don't tell me those Cowgirls." he laughed.

"No I'm from Pennsylvania, home of the greatest football team ever, The Steelers!"

"Oh they cheat to win. Lucky for them they had blind referees or 'the catch' would have been an 'incomplete catch' or don't you agree."

"That's why the referees aren't like you. They don't wear glasses and can see."

It provoked him so much he sent me clear across the huge building with a container of hot coffee for a staff meeting. He wouldn't allow me to use a cart either so I had to stop ever so often to rest my extending arms. After delivering the coffee, I decided to check out the PX. Finding the usual items and nothing of interest, I determined I had better head back. That's when I saw General Kelley coming out of his office with the President's advisor. They shook hands, the general gave him a manila folder and then he went back inside his office. I watched as Kudra washed away in the crowd then went to the general's door. I knocked and his secretary, I heard, gave me the go ahead to enter. "Hello, I'm Sergeant Del Conrad, may I see the general?"

She noticed right away we were from different branches and asked what my business was with him. She seemed snotty to me but he liked her from what he told me. "He doesn't like being disturbed, you know."

"I promise if you tell him who I am, he'll be okay with it."

She dropped her pencil and knocked on his inner door then disappeared behind it. A few moments later the door opened with her smile and she motioned for me to go inside.

"Come in young man! Good to see you! I have great news!" he was overly excited after a visit from Kudra I thought but I wanted to hear his news.

"Well it's nice to see you too. You're in good spirits this morning."

"You will be too after I tell you."

"Ah, tell me what? Sir."

"The investigation has been concluded and...you have a new duty assignment."

The first part I was glad to hear, the second I wasn't so sure. "Where am I going, do you know?"

"I'm not certain where but I pulled a few strings and it's possible, a small base nearby called Ft. Belvoir, Virginia. It's an Engineer mostly base and we need someone who's capable of constructing our plan. No what I mean?" giving me the eyes.

"Yes sir, I think I do know. How soon do you think this will happen?"

"Best guess with these things…a week maybe two tops. Why? Got a hot date?" he joked. "You know Del, with the kind of man you are, from what I've seen; it would be a shame if you didn't try finding another woman. I know you loved my daughter but she's not the last woman on Earth."

"Not now sir. My focus is on her and my task. So you worked on a plan?"

"Yeah, I've got some ideas. We'll go over them in a few days when I've fine-tuned them."

"Very well sir. I better get going before my other boss flips out for being gone this long."

"How long has it been?"

"About an hour? Maybe?" I shied when I said it.

"Did he have you delivering breakfast to the president, at the white house? Why so long?"

"I stopped at the PX because he wouldn't let me use a cart. I wanted to find a gift for you and Mrs. Kelley."

"I'll handle this with a call. I'll make him shake in his shoes again, watch." He laughed as he dialed. "Hello, Sergeant Ortiz, please. Tell him…tell him it's his daddy calling. He'll know who it is." He cupped the phone while waiting and suggested "You better get going. I'll contact you later." then he gave a firm shake. "Hello you little bugger, what's with that other Sergeant carrying coffee all the way over here? Don't you have a cart to use?" He saluted a fair well then an okay sign as I closed the door.

"Got to love those stars, wish I had a couple."

"Shira come eat. Grandma made eggs." Aviv yelled. "So what will you do today?" he asked his mother.

"My usual, go shopping for food, see my one friend and then home to wait."

"Wait for what? Or should I say who?" Shoshana's curiosity wondered.

"Wait for my son to return is what I meant. Must you always be so nosy." still they fought between themselves.

"Momma please and you too dear. Enough, I can't stand you two fighting. We'll be gone again soon mother. May I use your phone?"

"Of course you can."

Aviv called his old MOSSAD buddy to make sure they were home. "Hello Jocheved, this is Aviv. Can we come over soon?"

"Yes my friend. We are waiting for you."

"Thank you. We will see you in a little while." Then hung up the phone.

"He is home and waiting." he told his family. The phone rang back and he offered to answer it.

"No no Aviv, I can get it." his mother quibbled.

"Shalom."

"Momma!" Rafe yelled so loud she nearly jumped out of her sandals.

Aviv saw her reaction and asked "Are you okay?"

Covering the phone she said "Yes, now go get your things packed. You don't want to make your friend wait all day."

He leaned down and gave her a kiss. "Ok momma."

"Momma? Is everything okay there? Do you have company?"

"Oh no everything is fine. Where are you?" she asked as the pair left the room.

"I think she has a friend Aviv." Shoshana grinned.

"Oh nonsense, at her age?"

"Why not? She's been lonely since your father died. She has needs too."

The thought repulsed him and he smacked her buttocks. "Don't make me think about that again." he laughed.

"We are visiting the Wall momma. I wanted to surprise you but you didn't like that when I did it the last time. We are coming to visit and should be there soon, if that's alright with you?"

"Ah, sure Rafe, in about an hour?" her voice unsteady.

"Ok momma. It's nice to hear your voice again."

Shoshana came back into the room smiling. "So someone has a man friend?"

"Mind your own business. Take some of those sufganyot for Shira so she has something good to eat. And not a word to Aviv." she shook her finger.

"Momma said another hour and we can come. Take my picture with Avivah."

His wife thought to herself, *yes this might be your last one with her.*

For the rest of the morning I thought about the possible new duty station. I asked jokingly if "Daddy" had ever heard anything about it. Even though he got ripped earlier he was generous in his sharing. "Oh that's a nice place and the town around it has many things to do. There are a lot of pretty women and the base is beautiful too. You'll like it there. Wow, must be nice knowing a general with some pull."

"That's not why I'm going there and I still don't know if I am."

"Oh,ok. Well enjoy the rest of your day."

"I will." and off to my room I went to grab my package to ship.

"Goodbye grandma, it was nice to see you again." Shira gave her a kiss and hug.

"Idra it was a pleasure to visit you. *And short.* We will try to make it longer the next time. I promise. *Don't bet on it.*" Her not so affable daughter-in-law tried to show some tolerance.

"That would be considerate. *Even for you.* Maybe you could help me cook too next time. *You're no Julia Child honey.*" It was as though they could read the others mind with how they eyeballed each other.

"Mother as soon as Saif comes back we will come to stay for more than a night. That promise you can hold me to keep." He held her with his long arms tenderly wrapped around her. "I love you, momma."

"And I love you too my son."

"One last kiss for grandma!" she hollered to Shira then handed her another bag of goodies. "Shhh, don't tell your mommy." she said quietly and winked.

"Goodbye." the intrusive neighbor waved to Aviv.

"How can my mother not like such a friendly man?" he said to his wife.

"Maybe…" she stopped herself mid-sentence.

"Maybe what?"

"Nothing dear, just a dumb thought. Let's go see your friend." *Maybe he's her friend from the phone?* She chuckled to herself.

"Hi, I'd like to send this the fastest way possible. Can you tell me how soon it would arrive?" I asked the mail clerk.

"It would take about two days for fifteen dollars."

"Fifteen dollars?!? That's more than I spent to ship things home from Berlin. What's the next fastest for how much?" I bellyached.

"Five to ten days for six." The gum smacking clerk waited.

"Ok do the six and make it five days."

"Do you want me to deliver it also?" she mused as she stamped the envelope. "Is there anything fragile inside?"

"Not anymore." I joked back wishing she'd swallow her gum.

James was glad to see his brother's plane land. He never favored flying but as he put it, "It sure as hell beats swimming across the Atlantic." Their plane had finished docking as he waited near the baggage area. It had been more than six years since they last seen the other and it was at their mother's funeral. Over the announcement speaker he heard "Flight 4705 now offloading at terminal B1." He was happy the general splurged on the first class ticket, he wouldn't have to wait as long. Fifteen minutes had gone by when the first passengers came in to view. He heard the unmistakable sound of a boiling Brit before he saw his sibling.

"James Thornton Renfield, I'm looking for James Thornton Renfield. Has anyone seen him." He was as soused as James had hoped he wasn't.

Embarrassed to admit it, he held his English derby hat high in the air hoping the familiar article would catch his brother's attention. It worked.

"Dear brother come help me with my baggage."

How much could he pack in a few hours? He positioned his hat back on and headed for the inebriated fool. "Hello brother, I see not much has changed."

His brother could see the discontent in James and adjusted to become more civilized like him. "Is this better? I wouldn't want to discown discount oh discountenance you now would I." still wobbling.

"No brother that you have already succeeded in. Maybe you can make better use of your talents and help others in need?" His confused look along with his lush habit showed James he hit a nerve. Now if he could get him to stay sober. "Come along or must I hire a taxi to help you out of here?" Now he was toying with his condition. He set down his bags and asked "Are you capable of walking to the car or do I need to bring it to the doors?"

"You think I have talents?"

"Eljer, you are capable of doing great things, when you put your mind to them. Question is, do you believe in yourself?"

"Yes James I can walk. And I'll carry my bags. And you didn't answer my question."

James knew when his brother was bitter and not to stir the hornet's nest, so he led the way. It saved his arms and helped to sober the man of the hour. By the time they reached the Rolls he looked like he was ready to puke. "If you need to regurgitate, please do so before getting in this time. The smell lasted a month the last time." He looked back and his brother had beaten him to the proposition. "Oh poor chap." was all he could think to say without laughing out loud.

"Aviv welcome. We watched from the balcony for your arrival." Jocheved and his wife lived in a large building close to the top floor. He enjoyed the view and it often reminded him of his visit to New York and the World Trade Center buildings. It was relaxing to him but Aviv favored lower floors so he never ventured out on the balcony to capture the full extent his friend appreciated. "I see I'm not the only person driving the same heap for too many years." He hugged his friend tightly. "Maybe someday we'll hit the lottery, you think?"

"Jocheved if that happens I'll buy you a new car, after we get ours." they laughed.

"Shoshana, still as lovely as the day you married him I see. And look how big Shira is getting. She is as beautiful as her mother. You will have boy trouble soon Aviv."

"Thank you Joch for the compliments to both of us. What about you and Juci, no children yet?"

"No but it's not like we haven't been trying."

"Jocheved are you embarrassing me again?" his wife blushed.

"No he's too bashful to do that Juci." Aviv recalled how timid he was when they first met.

"Oh my, my friend, we have been separated too long. Let's go inside and catch up on life. Shira looks like she could use a drink anyway."

"Momma! So glad to see you."

"Me too Rafe. Hello Geva, how is my favorite daughter-in-law? Avivah! You are prettier than all of us! Give grandmama a kiss and hug."

"Your favorite daughter-in-law?" Geva questions. "I am your only one Idra ."

"I know, that's why I said that." She tries to catch her stumble.

"Are you feeling ok momma? You acted funny on the phone when I called earlier."

Before she could answer the neighbor hollers over "Hello. Back again so soon?"

"Don't pay any attention to him, he's crazy in the head." as she imitates with her finger circling.

Rafe looks puzzled at him still waving. "Momma maybe we should get you out of here? That stuff is contagious you know."

She slaps his arm in play and says "No it's not. Now come inside so we can make lunch before I go to shop for tonight. Geva, do you know any good new dishes?"

"Yes Idra, I have one you will love. Avivah, help your father with our bags. We are staying the night."

"Oh? I did not know that when you called Rafe."

"Sorry momma but you seemed rushed when we talked so I figured we'd ask when we got here. We can stay in a hotel if it's a burden."

"No my son. You can stay here with me. It's the least I can do after missing you all these years."

"I'm glad you found me mother and I don't blame you for not being able to care for me when I was a baby. All that matters is I'm with you now and that we all love you." They joined in a circle in the middle of the lawn.

"I had to leave you with the Palestinian family. They could care for you and give you things I could only dream about." Her years of hidden sorrow diminished as he held her to his bosom. "Do you really forgive me my son?"

"Yes mother I do but why all this doubt? You, you seem to have changed?"

"I'm getting old and my wise years are behind me. Maybe I'm getting what the neighbor has, the crazy's?"

He laughed off his previous thought and put his arm over her shoulders "Let's eat some lunch. Then Geva and I will go to the market for you and you can play with Avivah. She is your only grandchild you know?"

Idra could only manage a pretend smile behind it was guilt from not telling him the whole truth, at least not yet.

"Aviv after lunch we will go to the market to gather things for dinner and let the ladies stay here to talk." His buddy laid out the days plans. "Then after dinner we will go over to see the sunset at the Jordan River it is beautiful this time of year. You missed it the last time you were here and I bet Shira would like to see it too." He bent over and squeezed her cheek litely.

She giggled from his touch. "Can I go to the market too?" she asked the big man.

"That is your father's decision, ask him?"

She turned back and before she had time to ask he said "Yes you may. She knows good fruit and could be useful." He saw his wife glaring. "You've taught her well, besides what do men know about picking good food?" he offered as a truce.

"Okay Aviv but you better not lose her, again." The horror still terrified them.

"Shoshana she'll be fine, I'll hide her behind me." Jocheved soothed her worries. Everyone found it humorous.

"We really should stop to clean you up some brother so the misses doesn't see you like this. Did you eat anything on the plane other than olives?"

His brother was beginning to feel the effects from the alcohol wearing off and was comforted by the thought his sibling had made. "Not much James and yes I'm hungry. Let's stop at one of those places. I've never been to a Howard Johnson. Is he English?" he was pointing towards the unmistakable orange roof.

James just shook his head in disbelief. "If you'd stop to read the news occasionally you might know a few more things in life. I must agree though, we can accomplish both things with one stop." and he headed for the exit.

"Saif how has your day been?" his liaison asked.

"They have everything done so I can start my training as soon as tomorrow. I'm impressed with the proficiency after being told Americans do things backwards."

Brandon found no humor in his comment and actually found it offensive because he took pride in his role as a computer operator. He strived to be perfect or as humanly possible perfect. "So what do you have planned for the rest of your day?"

"I'm going to catch up on my sleep. I'm still feeling the lag from my trip over here. What will you do? Play with your computers?"

Now Saif hit a personal button. "One day some computer person will save your life with the information they can get you. You wait and see. I'll see you tomorrow when hopefully you'll be better rested." and off he stormed.

"Gee, some guys are too sensitive with their work." and Saif headed for his room.

"Ah yes sir, good day. Would you have a room where I can clean him up?" James asked the hotel clerk.

He looked the pair over and replied through the window "We only rent rooms by the day not by the hour."

Confused, James says back "But I just want to wash him so he's clean for the misses. I can't take him home looking like this."

Now the clerk is even more daring with his next comment. "Look buddy, I wouldn't suggest you taking him home, to the, ah misses, in any shape. Does she know?"

"Yes she knows. We talked about it last night and she's excited to see him again. But as you can clearly see he couldn't hold his load and spewed on himself."

The clerk busted out laughing at the top of his lungs as James' brother leaned forward to share what he thought the clerk was thinking. James' eyes bulged about the time the clerk came up for air. "There's a shack down the road about a mile that can help you 'Guys' out with your problem."

Furious from his brother's enlightenment James tapped the window and swiftly wiped the shit grin from the ignorant imbeciles mug "He's my bloody brother you pompous ass! Now get me your manager!"

The man immediately sank into his easy chair and pressed an intercom button. "Yeah sir, I have a problem and need you to help. Please?"

Within moments the hotel manager arrived and spoke with the red-faced clerk. His expressions as he heard the story made James aware they'd soon be getting a room for free and maybe even a meal if he chose to tell them his boss was a top ranking general. "I'm very sorry sir for my employee's misconception. Please take this room key as a, ah compensation for his naiveté. When you return it, I'll have a voucher ready for a free meal." He waited for their approval.

"Thank you good man, I appreciate it more than he does as you may possibly understand why." Eljer motioned over his appearance. James was still hawk eyeing the unfortunate bubblehead behind the glass. "Let's go brother." his younger brother whiffed.

"This market is huge Jocheved. My mother often bragged about it but I honestly thought she was just over exaggerating as usual."

"No Aviv, she is right. It is one of the larger in the area. Some say it is because of the tourist coming for Spa treatments at the Dead Sea."

"Well money will draw them in. Shira you hold on to me and stay close. Your mother would ring my neck if I lost you here. Lead the way my good friend."

"Rafe, this market is wonderful! Look at all the people and the things they sell!" Geva was in her own heaven for a change. Her outlet to his hard ways was cooking. She immersed herself when she had the chance.

"Should we split up and look for different items or would you rather stay together?"

Her opportunity to relax away from him presented itself. "Good idea Rafe. Here's half for you and I'll get these items." she tip toed upwards to give him a kiss.

"Okay, meet me back here in about thirty minutes." and he left her standing with a puckered face.

"What can I see in that short of time?" she pouted then started her search.

Chapter 30

"Daddy, daddy, daddy…"

"Yes Shira, what is it?"

"I saw a pink scooter over there. Can we please go look at it? Please?" He found it hard at times to say no but all she was asking was to go look at it.

"Go ahead and look at it but stay there until I come for you. I'll be finished here soon." He gently stroked her face and watched as she headed for the object of her desire.

"Kind sir, may I see your pink scooter hanging up over there?" Shira politely asked the old man. He reached up and struggling, began to get it down.

A man close to the scooter said "Here let me help you before you hit someone with it you old geezer."

As the scooter descended and the man's face emerged, Shira saw the figure. "I'm over here daddy. How did you get there so fast?"

The elderly man thanked his helper then turned to show the sweet girl.

"Daddy come look at it with me." she motioned with her hand. Excitement from seeing the shiny scooter up close showed on her face. The man began walking away. "Daddy, where are you going? Don't leave without me." The smile changed into a bewildered frown. She pursued her father figure.

"Thank you, sir." Aviv accepted his bagged items. Glancing back he no longer saw his daughter. "Shira?" he bellowed over the crowd's noise. Still looking towards the scooter stand, he watched as the elder struggled to raise the toy back up. He hurried over still shouting "Shira!" His friend, who was only a few stands away, heard his cries out for the lost girl. Aviv, whose height helped him tower over the patrons, saw his friend and informed him "I can't see her. She's not at this stand."

Jocheved pushed through the mass to where Aviv stood. "She is not with you?"

"No, I allowed her to look at that scooter. It was just a short moment." the fear showing in his expression. "Sir! A little girl was just here to look at that scooter, did you see which way she went?"

The old man looked befuddled. "She was with you when she left. You helped me get it down."

The two MOSSAD agents tried to register his comment. "Which way did you see them going the last time you saw them?" Jocheved quickly thought to ask.

"He went that way." The man must have thought it was a joke or ploy to get the item away from him. "Now go away!" he yelled at them.

Almost instantly in unison, they pulled their ID's out. "Where is she?" Aviv's mood went from worried to inflamed.

The man now knew they weren't trying anything. "I swear I saw her with you and if it wasn't you, then it was your twin."

"Aviv, we must hurry to find her. You go that way and I'll take this path. They join back together. One of us should find her." Aviv said nothing, patted his partner on his shoulder and then began to search.

"Daddy, wait for me. I'm getting tired." Shira struggled to push her way through. She reached out when she got a little closer to tug on his shirt. When she did, the man's shirt pulled back far enough to expose to her a gun tucked in his pants. "Why do you have your gun?" she naively said.

The man turned around quickly from feeling the draft, stopped dead in his tracks and grabbed the girls arm. "You saw nothing. Now go play somewhere else, anywhere, but quit following me." his utterance frightened Shira.

"I'm sorry daddy. I didn't mean to make you mad at me."

"I'm not your damn Dad!" Rafe stared straight into her face. A moment she'd never forget. He left her standing alone in the middle of the isle, crying.

"Excuse me miss, have you seen my daughter?" Aviv had pulled a picture from his wallet and was showing it around.

"Oh you're funny. Your daughter is with your mother." the lady commented without even looking.

"You've seen my mother here? How do you know her?"

"Is this heat getting to you? We can leave anytime and what's with the new shirt?" Geva was not pleased he bought one and didn't think of her. "Did you even get me anything?"

Aviv was puzzled by this stranger's accusation. "I'm sorry?"

"You should be, now take it back and get me something instead. And you better finish your list." Geva moaned as she left.

Aviv shook it off and restarted his hunt. "Shira!"

Jocheved heard mumbling about a girl being left behind. "Where did you see the girl? She might be my friends. She got separated from us." he asked a passerby.

"Over that way, just listen for her cries."

"Thank you, kind lady." He walked and shoved through until he heard more chattering then a child sobbing. "Shira!" he yelled louder. "Shira!!"

"Jocheved!" she saw who was yelling and went shoving through.

"Oh my sweet child, where did you run off to? Your father is worried sick about you as was I."

"He said he wasn't my father and made me cry." She held tight to his arm.

"He's here? Where, I don't see him?" he peered through the crowd.

"I don't care where he is. I want to go back, now."

He wiped her tears with his shirt. "Don't say that Shira, he loves you. Now stop crying. Everything will be okay. I have you and won't leave you."

In the distance he could hear another voice yelling her name. "Shira!"

"Over here Aviv!" and he signaled with his free arm.

He finally made it to them now relieved the search was over. Trying to remain calm he bent down on a knee to comfort his child. "Why did you leave the stand when I told you to stay there?"

"You're mean and I'm telling mommy you hurt my arm." Shira attached herself to the big man again.

"I never touched her Jocheved. I was getting fruit at the stand and she went to look at that scooter. I swear." his face was sincere.

His friend looked at Shira's arm and there it was the mark from the hold. "She has bruising Aviv."

Confused he reached to see it better. She drew back. "Please let me see." he begged. She extended her arm. He saw the same as his friend did then did the unimaginable. He slowly lowered his fingers over the impressions. They didn't match. His hand was much larger. "You see my friend, I never touched her."

"Yes he did and he has his gun in his back." she argued.

Aviv knew he was innocent but couldn't explain he just offered "See for yourself, I have no gun on me."

Jocheved walked behind him and lifted the tail end and saw nothing. "Your father is telling the truth."

Shira gazed at her father's bare back. "I want to go home." was all she could say.

"Yes. We have had enough excitement for one day." Aviv agreed. When they got back to the car he offered to drive home. "You know it always eases my mind when I'm behind the wheel."

His friend allowed him to drive but with a stipulation "Don't wreck my car. Juci will kill you after your wife does, especially when she hears about Shira." He gut laughed.

That's exactly what Aviv feared the most, her reaction.

"I'm glad you got rid of that hideous shirt. Where's my gift?" Geva questioned Rafe.

"What on earth are you talking about woman?"

"I saw you just a little while ago. Where's the bag of fruit and that picture you were flashing around like an idiot?"

"Has this market gone crazy today? First that girl, now you." Rafe's facial veins were showing.

"Hey, calm down dear. I was just joking with you back there. I knew she wasn't your daughter."

"My daughter? Geva we both know who our daughter is and she's with my mother!"

Something just wasn't right to Geva but she couldn't unscramble it yet. "Ok baby, let's just get what we need and get out of here." she tried to ease his tension.

They finished their list and headed back for the car. Upon passing by the stand with the scooter, the man again apologized to him and asked "Did you find your daughter? Does she still want the pink one? I still have it and I'll give you a good price."

This time instead of blowing up, Rafe looked at his wife and things started to click. "Sir, do you remember what I was wearing?"

"Yes but it wasn't that shirt, it was an ugly green one."

Geva pulled a picture of their daughter from her clutch and asked him to describe the girl he saw.

"She was very pretty with the greenest eyes I've ever seen." he marveled.

"Then it wasn't this girl?" she held the picture close to him.

"Oh no, she is pretty to but not the same one who looked at the scooter. You remember her?" he pointed at Rafe. "You and your MOSSAD friend were looking for her."

Now things were beginning to make sense but with an awful feeling.

"I need to find a replacement to fill Bosch's role but whom?" the man asked himself as he scanned the list of names. His favorite venue was the C.I.A. and although the last had failed, he knew with their training and dedication to country, they possessed what he sought. With the right amount of finesse they could be manipulated into doing most anything and the price was perfect, they were government paid. "No, no, not him, maybe a girl? No, I need another man. They are easier to con. Wait...what's this? I can't be this lucky. Can I?" He buzzed his secretary. "Mildred, place me through to the director over at the C.I.A. and let him know it's me."

"Yes sir."

He continued checking the other names but was fixed on just one. The speaker buzzed back. "He's on line two, sir."

"Thank you Mildred, I'll take a tea too please." He disconnected from the com and picked up his phone. "Hello, old chap."

"Hello sir, how can we help you over here?"

"Are you training another Israeli?"

"That is classified as you know but off the record a strong possibility."

"I'd like to meet him and his liaison if you could arrange that?"

"Another covert op, sir?"

"Off the record, a strong yes." he smiled on his end.

"I'll set it up for later this week if that works?"

"That will suit just fine. Give my secretary the information. Going to see the Redskins soon?"

"Why yes I am, the Monday night game against Dallas."

"I'll see you there then maybe. Thanks again."

"Glad to be of service. Goodbye."

A service you are, more than you know.

"Rafe, are you thinking what I am? Is your mother capable of hiding the truth from you for so long?"

"I don't know but we are going to find out. It might explain her behavior and her neighbors earlier."

"But why keep something like that secret if it is true? Wouldn't she want you to know you have a brother?"

Just the sound of the concept made him chill. Did he have a brother... one that looked like him too?

As soon as the car stopped, Shira jumped out and ran for her mother. She began sobbing while telling her side of the story. The men brought the items in from the market and before Shoshana had a chance to scold Aviv, Jocheved intervened.

"There is something not right with her side of the story Shoshie." as he often called her. "Come with me for a moment to listen to what I have to say."

Her impulse to hit Aviv for letting their daughter roam alone was suspended until his friend was done talking. "I'll give you five minutes before I come back to give him a wallop."

They went into the next room where Jocheved began explaining what he knew but more of what he had a gut feeling about. "You said his mother got a call when you were there earlier today right?"

"Yes, I thought maybe she had a man on the side and didn't want Aviv objecting. So?"

"What if it wasn't a man like a friend but someone else?"

"What do you mean Joch?"

"Could he have an unknown brother?"

Her loud gasp of possible realization made sense but also drew Aviv in a hurry to see what had happened.

"Is everything ok?" he hesitantly asked prepared to block her blow.

Her expression had changed so drastically that he wasn't prepared for her loving hug and passionate kisses. "I'm so sorry my love. Please forgive me." she begged.

Aviv just stood looking at his friend with his arms and shoulders shrugged. He lipped the words "What did you say?"

Jocheved lip synced back "I'll tell you later." and gave him a thumb up. "Let's make some dinner!" the big man yelled sparking the pair of love birds to jump.

"Rafe, what are you going to say? You can't just come out and ask her, she has obviously kept it a secret for a reason." Geva tried to reason with him.

"Geva you heard him say MOSSAD, did you not? It's not like I could walk up to someone I just discovered is my brother and then have him ask me what I do for a living. Oh, I'm an International Assassin for hire but don't tell your friend. So I must find out if it's true. I have no choice but to put her on the spot and tell her what happened today. If she lies, it will show on her face."

"If she breaks down and tells you the truth what then, are you going to tell her the truth about you?"

"Joch come here." Shoshana beckoned. "I need you to keep Aviv occupied so I can call his mother."

"Why would you do that without his knowledge? He has the right to know too."

"Yes but she won't lie to me as she has with him."

"But we don't know that for certain."

"That's why I need to find out before he does. You have three brothers. Imagine how you would feel if your mother had hid them for years from you. Now, wouldn't you rather hear it from your wife first?"

"Why, so he can yell at you?" Jocheved offered his opinion.

"He wouldn't dare yell at me. Listen to how he's playing with his daughter after the trauma they experienced. She still looks up to him and now would be the perfect time to be able to tell him this wonderful news we both suspect."

About this time into their conversation they heard Aviv say to Shira "Maybe someday you'll have a sister or brother to play these games with. I never had a brother..." He jumped from his seat and ran to the kitchen. "Joch do you think that other stranger could have been my brother?" both excitement and reasoning on his expression.

"Momma, we are back. We found all kinds of good things at that market." He paused to hug his daughter. "Go help your mother with the bags."

"I told you there were good items there."

"Why didn't you tell me I have a brother?" he instantly sprung on her.

"Why, what ah what do you mean Rafe? You have no brother." she tried to hid her guilt. It didn't work and she could tell he saw right through it.

"Tell me the truth mother." He forcefully grabbed his own mother and stared her down. The phone rang giving her a break from his hold. "You better answer it."

Shaking from his outrage she trembled "Hel, hello?"

"Idra, this is Shoshana. You sound terrible. Are you okay?"

"Oh yes Shoshana, I'm fine."

"Who is it mother?" Rafe said out loud.

"She has company. Should we call back?" the daughter-in-law asked Aviv while cupping the receiver.

"Mother! I asked who is it!?!" this time Shoshana heard what was said.

Her eyes bulged. Everyone could see her reaction. "Someone just said 'mother' and it was a man's voice."

"Give me the phone." Aviv urged. "Mother, who's there?" he spoke to a silent end.

Rafe was getting tired of waiting. "Give me the phone."

She slowly handed it to him and said "It's your brother...your twin brother."

"Mother, are you there?" Aviv again asked.

"No but your brother is here. Hello brother."

Chapter 31

The English pair gorged themselves on the free feast. Eljer began to feel better and James was once again delighted that his brother looked presentable. Their server had just freshened up their teas when James asked "Brother, this formula you so invested your past life into, what exactly is it?"

The younger looked around for listening ears and began. "It was a Nazi plan to create diamonds but after their initial trials resulted in something more they worked profusely to perfect it."

"But diamonds come from natures processing of coal. That takes years and a lot of factors." James pointed out.

"Yes, I know." Eljer grinned.

"Did you ever get close to their results?"

"Unfortunately no but I'm sure I'm missing just one or two key elements."

"How could you know that?" James dismissed his presumption.

"Because what I've been able to make burns for a short while. The stuff they accidentally made...well let's just say, it's still burning." He smiled as his elder brother dropped his spoon.

"Hello dear. Has James returned with his brother yet?"

"No Paul. I hope nothing has happened to them." She was always a worry wert.

"Oh I'm sure they are alright or James would have called. Well, let me know when they do. I think I'll be coming home early. I have more work to do."

"Not there?" she questioned knowing how important his work was at the Pentagon.

"No, my other project with Del, I need to prepare."

"Is he coming with you?"

"Not yet, not until I'm finished, then we'll invite him back."

"Okay my love. I'll inform James as soon as I see him. Goodbye, I love you."

"Until later and I love you too."

"I think we should be going now Eljer. I'm sure the general would love to hear your story."

"James, do you like working for them? Really like it?"

"Yes, they are very good people and I feel like family to them. Much like we were many years ago." he reminisced.

"We still can be. There's still enough time to make amends." he offered a shake.

"Hello my brother. My name is Aviv. What is yours?"

"Our mother named me Rafe. I guess you're the older of us."

"Why do you say that?"

"She chose to keep you and the older is wiser." his bitterness beginning to show.

"Well we have much to catch up on. Can I meet with you now?" Aviv's eagerness could be heard in his tone.

"How about we meet later tonight after dinner? But if we do, we meet alone, just you and me?"

Curiously struck by the stipulation Aviv asked "Why, why not with our mother there to introduce us?"

"She found it more important to her to keep us apart, let us do this one thing as a memory of our own?" he was laying out the start of his own plan.

"You know what, you're right, I like that idea. How about the bridge that spans the river at sundown? That should make a memorable first meeting between brothers."

"Yes, yes it will." Rafe agreed as he prepared to finalize the idea he had laid out in his mind.

"Mrs. Kelley, we are home." Eljer announced.

"Really Eljer, must you." James didn't approve of his tone.

"Hello gentlemen. Did we stop off for some drinks?" she joked.

"No just some food, he was starved. They only fed him olives and peanuts on the plane."

"For first class, that's terrible!" the misses exclaimed. "Well he looks good for that long of a flight. They must have been comfy seats."

"Oh they were comfy I'm sure." James spoke before Eljer could.

"Well you need to call the general. He wants to come home early. To work." she said still surprised.

"Then I had better call while I still have a job." and he took his brother with him.

"So mother, tell me everything about your other son before I go to meet him." Rafe pressured. "Is he like his friend, a MOSSAD agent too?"

"I am so nervous and eager to meet with him I'd go now if I could."

"Well my friend, we have made all this good food and plan to eat it. You need to settle down and gather your wits. You don't want to act like a school girl on her first date now do you?" Jocheved laughed.

"No Joch, you're right. Let's eat even though I know I'll have a hard time."

After Rafe's mother completed her knowledge of his sibling, he knew he had no other choice but to make another call. He couldn't jeopardize his hidden identity with the trip coming up. "I need to use your phone again, in private." he forcefully bullied. The ladies left the room. "Hello this is 'The Healer'. I need some assistance tonight and soon."

The person he called knew him well from previous bombing assaults on markets. "Just tell me when and where...and who?"

"At sundown on the bridge over the Jordan river...the person will look like me."

"Excuse me? Can you repeat that last part again?"

"The man I want to kill is my twin brother."

"How do you expect me to know which one is you then?"

"I'll be the only one holding a gun, that's how." his terroristic personality surfacing. His upper lip began to quiver. "If he hasn't changed his shirt, it should be an ugly green one. If there's any outside involvement, shot them. He is MOSSAD and so is his friend that he's staying with."

After dinner, while the women cleaned up, Jocheved spoke with Aviv. "You know my friend I don't like the idea of you going alone. You heard what your daughter told us about seeing a gun on the man she presumed was you."

"You don't think just because I'm excited I'd throw my senses to the ground do you? That is why I'm taking my sidearm along...and you as my backup." he smiles.

"So you too are worried?" the big friend inquires.

"No I'm concerned. Here is a man I've never known about and he suddenly comes out of nowhere? And he's armed? Our training would have us treat this as I'm going to, suspicious."

"Don't let our everyday lives, Aviv, make distrust in a brother."

"It is not I, with the trust barrier. He wanted a meeting alone, I'd rather it be with everyone meeting as a...family."

On the other side of the thin wall was Aviv's wife listening. *Yes my dear, I agree, we should meet as a family and maybe I can help soothe the rough edges?* "Juci, would you watch Shira for me tonight?"

"Are you planning to go with Aviv? He will resist."

"I know that, so I'm going to see his mother while he's gone."

"Good afternoon madam, I'm calling to speak with the general please, tell him it's James." He knew she recognized the voice but he was still always the professional.

"Hello James, I'll page him. So when are you going to take me out like you promised?"

"Sorry Millie, no time now, my brother just came to visit. The general, please?" he rushed to change the topic. The familiar tone sounded then the general picked up.

"Your driver slash man servant slash butler is on line one." she sounded annoyed by James' objectionable behavior and brush off. She purposely allowed the conversation to be heard.

"Thank you, Mildred." He switched the connection. "Hello James, how was your brother's trip?"

"His usual sir, shall I come for you? The misses said you wanted to come home early."

"Yes I do. I have one stop to make then I'll be ready. Be here in about an hour."

"Should I bring my brother?"

"If he wants to go for a ride, sure, but I don't want anything like the last time." he laughed.

"I'll see you in an hour sir. Until later."

After he hung up, the general decided it was time to go for that short walk. "Mildred take all messages, I'm heading out for the day." He headed for my room with a second copy of his plan.

"Good luck dear, just be yourself and I'm sure he'll like you." Aviv's wife encouraged.

"I will. You ladies have an enjoyable evening too. I'll see you when I get back." He kissed her passionately, the first in a long time. She knew he was nervous then. "Are we ready Jocheved?"

"After you Aviv, remember I have your back." He gave his wife a hug and quick peck. "Shira, I will guard your father." he whispered into her ear to which she smiled.

The group waved as the men drove away. "Are you sure you want to do this?" Juci asked Shoshana.

She wasn't but pushed on. "Yes, I feel I must be there for him." She leaned down and brushed her daughter's hair then kissed her cheek. "I love you and I'll see you again soon." She hurriedly followed in their car hoping to arrive just behind them.

"Good thing Joch offered to drive him over or I'd be running." she openly said as she looked her appearance over in the mirror.

The drive was not far from the apartment house so it left little time for Aviv to think about his brother. "I'll hang back at the river side and watch you from there. That will give me a good angle and you'll be able to signal if you want me to join you." Aviv gazed but said nothing. "My friend is there something bothering you?"

"His voice Joch, I've heard that voice before but can't place where or how?"

"Well we are here. Time to tell if you're just paranoid." he tried to chuckle. He'd never seen such deep thought in Aviv's face before.

They began their walk to the bridge and parted fifty meters before it just as they had planned. The view was as spectacular as Jocheved had described. It calmed Aviv's emotions as his wife, unbeknownst to him, was parking. *I wish I had changed shirts, this one is awful like Shosh said when I bought it but I liked it.* As he crested the walkway he felt like he was looking in the mirror, watching his twin heading his way. Joch still didn't see the brother but could see from Aviv's expression he must be near.

Shoshana double stepped in hopes of seeing the two meet. Her feet ached from the shoes so she stumble stepped to get them off then ran barefoot.

"Hello brother." Aviv held his hand out. It was met by the showing of a silencer equipped pistol. "What is this all about?" he asked as he held his hands up high.

"One more day, just one more day and we would still be strangers. I can't afford to have you around to mess my life up again."

"But I haven't Rafe. How could I have?" Aviv begged to understand. Now Jocheved could see his extended arms and instincts kicked in. He headed for the bridge. Someone else could see him in this stance, his wife.

The gunman on the hill laid on his belly for stability "Come on, get out of the way Rafe. Move to the right. I can't get a clean shot." he spoke but it fell upon deaf ears.

"Don't worry brother, I'll heal what hurts you most." his eyes as cold and black as hell itself.

"That is how I know your voice. Now I know who you are!"

"No! Don't shot!" Shoshana yelled distracting the evil twin.

Aviv made a lunge for the gun. They struggled to gain control over the other. Jocheved running as fast as he could was also nearly out of breathe from the sprint up hill. A blast came from high hitting Aviv in the upper shoulder. He cried out in agony as he let go of the gun. Rafe wobbled back and began to draw on his defenseless brother. Another shot rang out. Shoshana running with all her love crossed between the sniper and her husband, the shot penetrating her back as she fell to the ground in front of Aviv. A third shot, this time a huge blast from closer came from Joch's gun hitting the armed brother's gun hand sending his armament flying upwards. The sniper had reloaded and took dead aim on Aviv as he stood numb from seeing his love not moving. The hit knocked Aviv over the side of the bridge and into the river below. Rafe saw Joch coming in closer and ran for the side he came from for cover. The marksman laid down another shot hitting Joch in his calf and stopping his advance. The big man fell out of sight from the, would be assassin, so he policed his spent brass and proceeded to rendezvous with his accomplice. Fellow bridge walkers, whom had taken cover, came to assist the wounded MOSSAD agent and his friend's wife. As Jocheved reached Shoshana and turned her gently over he wept like a baby. Her almost lifeless body asked him for one final request.

"Anything Shoshie, anything for you." Joch tried to comfort her.

"Take care of my baby." and she expired in his arms. He wailed even louder. Aviv could hear him in the distance as he struggled to stay afloat but he knew what the shrill meant. He cried along.

A knock on my door made my heart jump. It wasn't something I had experienced often while at the Pentagon. "Who is it?" I decided to ask rather than opening the door. Under the door slide a manila envelope. This prompted me to now open my barrier.

"Hello son." smiled the general. "I thought you might like that." he pointed to what I was holding. "Go ahead and open it."

He took a seat as I unstrung the tie. Inside was a small yet concise detailed plan he proposed. "This is it?" I said not wanting to offend him.

"We need no more than that. Any other variables that come along are as we know it, we adapt and overcome. That has always been the military way, sergeant."

"I guess I just expected more."

"The best plans are the simplest. We don't need to concentrate on the other enemy when we know he will eventually surface to stop our plan. What we need to focus on is getting the word out to more than just a hand full of us. Strength in numbers will flush out those we scare. Throw a match on a horde of rats and one will move, throw gasoline on that same pack and then throw a match, the mischief bastards will run for high ground." He sat back to admire his work.

"I'm sure glad you're on my side sir. This should prove to be fun."

"Del, there's no fun in trying to survive. That's why we call it life or death."

"Sorry sir, I stand corrected. So what can I do for now?"

"You are cleared to get in contact with your old friend in Berlin. I'd start with him and notably his D.C. contact for part one. That is our starting point and a crucial part it is right now." the general stood to leave.

"Sir, does anyone besides us know about this list?" I had to ask considering the meeting I had seen earlier. I wasn't going to assume anything and didn't want to offend him with speculation.

"Just us for now but I will tell you this, if you get proof, others will know within a week."

"I'm on it sir. I'll get that proof."

As Israeli police forces began arriving, Jocheved who had already provided his credentials instructed them to search the river for his fallen friend. He knew from the blood stain on the wall, Aviv was wounded but had no idea how badly. He also faced the task of explaining to Shira when he got home, what transpired. He failed to keep his promise to her. He would not fail in his vow to her mother. After an hour's long reconnaissance of the river, nothing was found. They searched further down to the Dead Sea but still no sign. "He must have been dragged under somewhere along the banks. We will keep looking sir but...well this has been a longtime as you know and I can make no promises to find him...alive." the head of the search team relayed to Jocheved. "We should get you to a hospital to have your wound dressed or you'll..."

"I'll be what!" he screamed. "Dead too? It's a flesh wound." his stubbornness controlling his senses.

"Please sir, for your own benefit."

He was right and Jocheved would be no good to either his wife or his new responsibility if he bled to death. He watched as they loaded Shoshana's covered body onto the gurney. "He's a dead man when I catch him."

I was relieved that the inquiry into the incidents and the money were closed and it opened the chance to contact my former Army buds. The first to hear my voice was the most important "Rufus, you old dog!" I blasted when he answered. "How's Merlin?"

"What are you doing calling me? I thought we were banned from that?"

"WE were but everything is over. I was just informed. There's a lot to catch up on but right now I need something from your brother. Proof of what he knows."

Chapter 32

This was not a call Rafe wanted to make nor would his employer be pleased with his news. "Hello Mildred. Is my son busy?" He hated using the term "son" but it had long been established as a code word when contact was needed.

"He just returned, I'll put him on." She put down her end and updated her boss. "Your father is on line four."

"Thank you Mildred. I'll take it in my office." He hurried in swiftly closing his door behind. "Make it quick, this line is not secure."

"I ran into a problem over here. Why didn't you tell me I had a twin brother? Both you and my mother kept it a secret from both of us?" His anger was heightened by the pain in his hand. "Now he's dead! And I'm shot in the hand!"

"Are you getting any attention for your wound?" Kudra asked concerned.

"Yes a handler is taking care of it now but I won't be able to leave today as planned. My family needs to be moved also."

"Okay here's what you do. Head to your secure area and wait a day before coming over. I'll get your family out of there before anyone has a chance to question them. I'll explain everything when you get here, just get here."

Rafe gave him the specifics then added "At least that's one more off the list."

Jocheved's pain inside his heavy heart dulled the feeling in his leg as he bent to speak with Shira. "My beautiful little girl, something very bad has happened but Juci and I will take good care of you."

"What's wrong Jocheved?" her innocence breaking through.

"The man your father went to meet has shot him and your mother was shot too." he broke down. His wife knelt alongside him.

"Your mother has gone to Heaven Shira. We don't know where your father is, yet."

"It's just like my dream then. He did shoot himself." she said amazingly calm.

Joch regained his composure "No my child he did not shoot himself, his brother tried to kill him."

Her next comment stunned everyone "Then he still lives. I've seen it."

"Hello again Eljer, I'm glad you could come on short notice. How was your flight?" he asked as they began the trip homeward.

"Very nice general and I thank you for the upgrade to first class. More leg room."

"And bags and booze and…" James started.

"And that's enough, brother." Eljer took offense to his brother's repeated bringing up of the liquor.

"You had been doing so well and then you started drinking again after our father's death. No excuses this time."

"He's right Eljer, we need you sober, always, not just part of the time." General Kelley instructed from the back seat.

"If someone would tell me what is so important, maybe I'd understand better?" he quipped.

James looked back at the general in the mirror and blatantly told him "Tell him the same way you told me sir."

With one swift sentence he looked Eljer straight-eyed and said "Our world is on a collision course with a bigger planet and we will all die."

The no longer drunk Englishman swiveled in his seat, rolled the window down fast and hurled what remained of his lunch onto the guard as they passed through the gate.

"Oh dear lord, that poor soldier." James pressed the accelerator.

"At least your brother made it out the window this time." the backseat commentator added with a chuckle.

"So you need him to get you photos of the anomaly?" Rufus asked.

"Yes and I need them as soon as humanly possible. This will get our process rolling."

"Del, do you trust this general completely?"

"As much as you trusted in me and I have in you. There's too much at stake and he wants exactly what I want. This is too real not to trust him." I stopped to ponder Sergeant Brooks' question more. "Do you have doubts of your own?"

"No. Not as long as you believe. I'll call and go over with him what you've told me. Get back to me tomorrow."

"Thanks Leroy, I will."

The guys' ride from the Pentagon to home was quiet after the general's revelation to Eljer. He strolled in behind his brother still delirious. They headed for the great study where the general had composed his plan. He gave each one a copy with instructions for each to follow. "There is no deviation from those plans unless I or…Del makes them. They are as secret now as anything you've ever kept a secret about. Only a handful of us will know what is happening completely, the others will know just their roles, just in case something was to go wrong."

"Pardon my ignorance sir..." Eljer interrupted "...but my formula has never been perfected."

"Yes it was. You even told your brother the story about the Germans and their intent. If they could do it, so will we, we must or all life could be extinguished. You have told him the truth haven't you?"

"Yes I have and I have seen proof of its existence. There is an eternal flame in a caldron that sits atop a tripod figured structure that looks much like the Olympic flame. There are no pipes to feed it a natural gas to explain how it stays lit, they do not replenish whatever is inside it because it is a monument to their fallen soldiers and guarded continuously. You Americans have your own version known as the "Tomb of the Unknown Soldier", theirs is in East Berlin."

"You mean the Russians?" James was stunned to say.

"That would be who occupies that side of Berlin brother. They got to Hitler first so the legend is known. A top level scientist was reportedly with him and they offered to reveal the formula to the Russians in exchange for their safety. Rumors were never proved but throughout the years reports of people that looked like Hitler and his scientist surfaced from South America. At his age then, he could still be alive."

"I've never heard any of this before and I'm a top ranking officer. How do you know of it?"

"Oh, no doubt our father and his crazy stories." James said with a whim.

"He was not crazy! And I'll prove it!"

James laughed at him. "How do you plan to do that?"

"I'll make it work this time!" his younger brother defiantly rendered.

"Looks like we have our scientist James." the general stood to inspire Eljer in his new found commitment with a congratulatory hand shake.

The following morning as I prepared for my shift, another knock sounded on my door. "Wow, two visitors in less than twenty four hours? I must be getting popular. Who is it please? I'm getting dressed."

"It's Sergeant Ortiz."

I threw my shirt on quick and opened the door. "Yes sergeant?"

"Your transfer orders came in this morning. You're out of here."

I accepted the papers from my former menace and grinned "Guess I don't need to go to work then, huh?" I laughed inside as he walked away rattling in Spanish.

"Ft. Belvoir, Virginia, here I come. I guess the general does have some pull."

An all-night search proved useless and the daylight hours only solidified the outcome of the MOSSAD agent's inquest. Director Moshe had been in the vicinity and got the news late evening and decided to stay. "It could be days, maybe longer, until his body surfaces Jocheved. You should start to make plans for his burial along with his wife's. I know he was your friend, he'd do the same for you."
Although it was hard to accept he nodded his agreement. "Unfortunately you are right sir. Juci and I will take care of notifying his mother."

Excited to tell the general my news, I headed for his office with orders in hand. Before I managed to get there, a familiar face came around the corner.
"Hello Del. Or should I say Sergeant Conrad? You seem in a hurry, late for work?"
"Mr. Stein or should I address you as..."
"No, no, no Mr. Stein is sufficient."
"Then please refer to me as Sergeant Conrad."
"Very well, oh I see you have papers?"
"Yes, I just got transfer orders."
"I hope you like where the General, who requested my assistance, is sending you."
"You helped?"
"Certainly, I have some pull in this town too you know."
"I guess thanks should be given." and offered a shake. A ways up the hall, unseen by either of us, was the general himself, watching.

"Well while we are out, what items do you need to start with Eljer?"
"These are a small beginning." He handed him a list.
"We can't get that can we? Isn't it like, illegal to possess?"
His brother smirked "That's why the general has you doing that part. Now let's see if you can pull your weight and produce what I need to make what we all need."
"I still don't understand how this will enable space travel as you have so gallantly boasted."
"It's actually quite simple. The trouble with space exploration is both weight and longevity. The fuel sources we use now are heavy because of their liquid and they only last for a short burst in distance. If you could concentrate and lighten that

same source, you'd solve half the problem." He was showing some pride in his knowledge.

"Only half, what's the other half?"

"Renewability. You can't find oil just anywhere but coal is a form of carbon and carbon is an element of life. Where there's another planet, there's some sort of carbon."

"Impressive young man, you have earned my services."

"Good morning Mildred. May I see the General?"

"Certainly Sergeant, go on in." with her usual pleasant smile.

"I got my orders sir, I'm headed to Virginia."

"That's great news Del. Our English partner is working on his project. How are things on your end?"

"I am to call my Berlin contact back today."

"I have a secure connection here, why not do it now?" he offered looking at his watch.

"Let's shall we." I gave him the number to the mess hall and waited for an answer.

"Hello, this is Sergeant Brooks." he sounded his familiar unhappy self.

"This is Sergeant Conrad and I have someone with me whose been waiting to speak with you. Say hello to General Kelley."

"Hello sir. I've heard nothing but good things about you."

"And I've heard equally better about you and your brother sergeant."

"They are not actually brother's sir they are in-laws." I corrected the ranking officer. "So Leroy, how did you make out with your pictures? Get any good ones we can use?"

"Boy I'll say from what he told me. There's five distinct features all traveling together or as he put it "A family out on a picnic coming to see what we have to share." You could hear him shake off the heebee geebees.

"Sergeant, when can we get them, the pictures?"

"How does two p.m. sound to you sir? I knew you wanted them fast Del so I set up a meeting with him today at the Air and Space Museum in front of Kitty Hawk herself. Don't be late or he'll walk, he gets nervous about these things."

"I'll be..." a tap on my arm from the general halted my speaking. He signaled that both of us would go.

"You'll be what Del?"

"I'll be joined by the general too and we'll see him at two sharp. Thanks Ruf."

Jocheved and his wife went to tell Aviv's mother of the sad news. Her character was stunningly unusual to him, she grieved not for a son he knew she loved much. She wouldn't even bother with Shira while they were there. Word had come in that some of Aviv's torn clothing was found with blood on them a mile downstream just before the entrance to the Dead Sea. Still she responded with no emotion. Joch offered to arrange the funerals but she disallowed it saying "They are my family I will take care of those things."

"As you wish, Idra. May we raise Shira, as I promised her mother I would?"

"Go with her and never come back. I am old and soon too I'll be gone."

Shira walked over to her grandmother and childishly kissed her cheeks. "I know you don't mean that. We'll see each other again, soon." She spoke so insightful that she made her grandmama breakdown with tears as they left.

"Joch, is she in shock from the trauma?" Juci asked.

"I don't know my dear something just wasn't right but we have this child to fend for now. You always wanted to be a mother, now here's your chance." as they left the house.

"Good job mother, I'm proud of you. Now you just need to keep our secret, a secret." spoke the voice from behind her as she watched her beloved Shira wave from inside the car.

"I hope these items will be safe at the house until we find you a better lab."

"Always complaining James? We can get a room at the Johnson's if you'd prefer?"

"No, no I'll never step foot in one of those establishments again." to which Eljer mused. "I just don't want to blow up the neighborhood."

"We won't you apprehensive old fool. Besides, this is just a small amount. Wait until we know the "Recipe" and get larger loads. Then you can complain and believe me, it won't fit in the back yard." he huffed.

"How much do you plan to make when you get it figured out?"

"As much as they say we'll need, my guess a couple of tons."

"Tons Eljer? Great Scot, I'll need to find a bigger warehouse then."

"How will we know who the person is we're looking for once we get there? Have you seen a picture of him?" the general quizzed.

I had seen some pictures at Sergeant Brooks' pad but never really studied them. A passing glance to his bathroom or occasional look towards Merlin's cage but never a long look, still, I was confident I'd know him. "By our code word sir. I'll know him."

"Must be some word, I hope not Rufus or Leroy or Sarge." He looked down at his watch as we entered the building. "Ten minutes to get there. Plenty of time."

"Sir you seem edgy, petulant? Is everything alright?"

He stopped. "I saw you with Kudra Stein earlier today, shaking hands? How should I feel?"

"He only informed me of your part in my local transfer. So I thanked him for his. You really don't care for him much do you?" I sensed the tension.

"He's a politician's mascot and is only out for what he can get. The only reason I invited him over for dinner was his insistence that you had something more to do with my daughter's death, which I now know isn't true. So I'm thinking he's up to some dirty work. They all play dirty sooner or later. We better get going."

Up the elevator we proceeded. As the doors opened, there was the plane that started the history of flight in all her glory. I scanned the layers of people that had gathered around to view the piece of history. I looked at my watch which read two o'clock on the nose. Then I saw him. "What a smart man I should have known."

"You see him already? Without the password too?" the general sounded like a little boy again. "Where?"

"Where he had said he'd be sir, over there." I nonchalantly directed my hand upwards towards the plane, at two o'clock hand sign.

"Brilliant man!" the general boasted.

I lead the way walking and talking about how I had longed to fly someday too. As I approached closer I winked and nodded to the man I spotted from the other side of the room. "This looks like a good place to see Nibiru, wouldn't you agree?"

"Only if you don't mind if Marduk gets in your way."

"Hello Roger, nice to finally meet you. This is..."

"General Kelley, Marine Corps. I served under your command when I was in 'Nam' sir." He exposed a tattoo from his days there.

"First Marine Regiment, I'd know that insignia anywhere. Glad to see you made it out in one piece."

"So Rufus tells me you have something good for us?"

"Here..." he handed me a pamphlet of the Air and Space Museum "...you might find the information in this useful." then walked a short distance down the railing.

I looked inside and saw an envelope. Inside the envelope was a microfiche. I looked at the general who was also gawking and smiled. "Here's our proof."

"If you need further information sir, I can be reached at the number provided." Roger said as he walked by us and left.

"We need to have a look at that film and I know just where to go. Come on."

"Hello again Mildred is the skipper in?" the C.I.A. man asked.

"Yes he is, hold please. Sir line two you have a call from the director at C.I.A."

"Thank you, I've got it. Hello my friend, what news do you have?"

"Your meeting is set for tomorrow afternoon. His schedule is full after that so I arranged it ASAP as I knew you'd want."

"Splendid, you keep up this good work and I'll let you stay in my box seats for a game." he knew the seats were a luxury most could only dream of affording.

"I'll keep you to your word sir. Be gentle on my man, he's a newbie."

Even better yet fresh unmolded clay. "Goodbye."

"Doreen! I'm home with a guest!" our leader yelled out.

"What is all the hollering about? Oh? Hello Del." she said delighted.

In from the kitchen joined James and Eljer. "How did you get home sir?" the elder of the two asked.

"You have heard of taxi's here right?" he joked. "Doreen dear would you help me set up your old microfiche machine, we need to use it."

"Certainly and later you can give me a backrub for lugging it."

"Ma'am let me assist you." Eljer offered. She accepted and they went to retrieve it.

"Would you gentlemen care for some tea?"

"That would be a grand idea James. Bring it to the study. We'll set everything up there." the general instructed.

After everyone reassembled and the viewer was ready, we inserted the film. "Are we ready for this, dad?" I moved the film into position for the first look of what was on it.

"I think I need a drink."

"No you don't Eljer." said Doreen.

"That wasn't me, that was James." he replied.

"Paul? Is that a cross?" his wife asked.

"Yes dear, one of monolithic size. It's time to call the Bishop."

"I agree sir." as I continued to roll through the pictures.

Chapter 33

"We will need you to call Michael, my love. He'll come over quickly if you tell him you need his prayer time because of Amanda." He could see the look she was giving him. "Don't worry, in a way, you're not lying to him."

"I better not be, you know how I hate those who do." she peered at him as she dialed. "Hi Bishop Michael, it's Doreen. Could I have a few minutes of your time at our house, now?"

"This sounds urgent. Are you okay?" he asked.

"I just need to talk with you about something. Please?"

"Okay Doreen, I'll be right over."

"Saif! Glad I found you. We have a meeting tomorrow with someone from D.C. but they won't say who."

"A meeting for what?"

"All they will tell me is it could be a once in a lifetime opportunity. We'll find out tomorrow."

"Ok Brandon, I'll see you tomorrow then." Saif shook his head as he left. "These American's are stranger than Aviv said."

Thirty minutes had transpired by the time the Bishop arrived. "I got here as fast as I could. Shall we begin with a prayer?" he genuinely asked.

"I'm afraid we will need more than a prayer father." the man of the house broke in.

"Paul, I didn't know you were home. What more could we need than our lord's love?"

"Come, see and listen, then you can decide." Behind the general the rest of us appeared.

"Something tells me this is more than just a family get together."

He followed the general into the study where he began the story to catch the Bishop up to date. "So here is the picture we received today."

"Paul, you told me that was a cross." Mrs. Kelley griped.

"He told you the truth Doreen, it's a planetary cross." the Bishop confirmed as he held his own cross.

"You mean it's that big?" and she passed out.

"I think she just realized the magnitude of this monster." Eljer commented.

"A monster in deed sir, Paul what plan have you devised?"

"We need the church to be notified, if they haven't been already." He gazed waiting for his response.

"I know nothing of this so it's possible the papacy doesn't either. As soon as I return to the church I will send word. What else do you need?"

"We will need funding or a way to funnel funding to pay for the expenses. America has become a good model for hiding monies for projects the rich want. I'd say it's time for the needy to have theirs." Again he waited for a response. "You have told me, they plan to position you within the fiduciary system. Are they going through with it?"

"Yes, Paul, I have been entrusted with those duties. Doing what you are asking me would be against my beliefs, surely you must know that."

"Are we not taught in Proverbs 14:22 *"Do not those who plot evil go astray? But those who plan what is good find love and faithfulness."* We need your faithfulness."

"But Paul, my faithfulness is to the church and my responsibility is to God."

"Your first responsibility is to life, the life of people in general, not just the life of the church. Surely you must have known I'd expect that much from you. You were hand-picked by my daughter in my dream."

"And that was just a dream Paul." he sneered.

"I had the same revelation." I added.

Then another admitted the same had happened in their dream. Someone we'd not known before that moment. "She came to me in my dream, last night. Michael, you must believe us and help us." Amanda's mother begged.

Scanning the requisition files, Kudra discovered an unfilled order that would suit his needs. "This should suffice the rebel's needs for a short while." he spoke out loud. He grabbed his phone with excitement. "Yes, this is PA Kudra, there is an order from March that hasn't been delivered yet, it will need to be shipped immediately to a new destination."

"Under whose authority sir?" the munitions commander asked.

"By executive order, the order number is…"

"Yes, Doreen, I will help to do what now appears to be God's work. How much do you feel is needed gentlemen?" everyone looked around. "Any guess?"

"How about one billion dollars?" I offered. "That sounds like a nice round figure."

"And what are we going to do with that much money, plus how am I to explain it if, no when, I get caught?"

"That's where I come in. I have acquisitions means to cover up the trail, I've already begun this morning with, some shall I say, bogus unfilled orders." the general was pleased with his ingenuity. "What we are building men is a future."

"You already planned on me saying yes?"

"No my friend, I planned on God restoring my faith. He has."

The burial for both Shoshana and Aviv were customary although his body was not retrieved, it had been ruled a death. Idra served as the Shomer for them, her daughter-in-law had requested she be hers years ago after her parents died in a bombing. She only accepted the role because her son begged her. Now she wished the woman who made her son the happiest were still there and that she had admitted the truth years before. "Jocheved, when I pass on, I want you to assist Shira with my burial. She is my last remaining family."

"But that is not true Idra, you still have your other son, somewhere."

"No Jocheved, he is no longer someone I consider family. I have disowned him after what he has done. I only pray the lord has mercy on his soul."

Jocheved's thoughts were more in depth. *Yes, may he, for I will not.*

The ground work was in motion, now the funds were lined up. The hardest was yet to come. An area needed to be chosen where the size of the ship we proposed could be built without being detected or a chance encounter would expose it's existence. "Sir, may I suggest a possible spot?"

"Certainly Del. Where do you have in mind?"

"Why not hide it under their noses? Where it was first discovered? Antarctica."

"Who is going to want to work there building anything?" Eljer blasted. "I'm not going there to work on the formula."

"No, he's right. It's cold so that would help harden the steel alloy faster. It's out of sight from most shipping lanes and we already have a post setup on it. All we need to do is fabricate the pieces and somehow get them to the assembly site where a team would piece them together."

"Legos anyone?" James blurted out.

"Well sir, it's getting late and I must get back to pack for tomorrow."

"Oh my, it is late. I must be going too if I'm to get anything done." the Bishop said as he stood to leave with me. "Del, you have a bright young mind, may the lord continue to enlighten your destiny. Lady and gentlemen let's end this night with a prayer." He blessed our plan and more importantly, our success.

"Del, James will take you back. I'll see you again soon."

"Paul, one second." the bishop interrupted. He whispered into his ear "How many people will be on the ship and who chooses the lucky ones?"

"That I leave up to the lord, and you."

The following morning I stood outside my doorway with gear ready to roll for my next assignment. The brisk air coming in from the Potomac felt exhilarating. Football season weather was here and the local fans were praying for a repeat season. I was praying for another piece of the puzzle. An all too familiar Jeep drove up and a Private exited. "I'm here to get you I believe, Sergeant Conrad?" I nodded I was the one he was looking for and began tossing my bags in the rear. "My name is Private Rudy Rue, nice to meet you." He was a very young baby boyish faced teenager complete with some acne still but it was cloaked by his thirst for life and the thrill he'd gotten since joining the military. He spoke of how much he liked being an Engineer and dreamed of building huge skyscrapers someday. His desire to become an architect was as fabled by the recruiter as my ambition to become a great chef. So we shared at least one commonality.

"So where are you from Rudy?"

"Shouldn't we address each other by our rank?" he said astonished that I called him by his first name.

"Why, we are the only ones here right? I know you'll respect me with formalities when the time comes, until then you can call me Del."

"I'm from a small town you probably never heard of before."

"Try me, I've heard of so many since joining the military." I encouraged.

"Ok then, Akron?" he said seriously.

I laughed. "Everyone has heard of Akron, Ohio."

"Yeah but not many know about Akron, Pennsylvania."

My eyes exploded with excitement "I'm from Lebanon just north of you so yes I know exactly where you are from. My parents and I would stop before going home from the 'Green Dragon' to get ice cream from the Dairy Queen in town." I made my connection and he knew beyond a doubt I was a homeboy.

"So which school did you attend?" he asked and that began our short trip to the base. By the time we arrived he must have felt like my brother. "Here is our barracks and over there is your new mess facility. I'll take you there next. First we need to check you in with the Company First Sergeant Richard. Don't let his bark scare you it's not as bad as he'd like you to think."

"Excuse me, what did you say his name was?"

"First Sergeant Richard. Do you know him from another place you served together?"

"Is he any relation to Little Richard?" I joked but he didn't get it from the way his face distorted. "Forget it, let's go."

"Saif, you have a call from your director. A Mister Moshe?" another CIA operative notified him. "You can get it up in the briefing room."

"Ok, thanks." Lucky for him he had just finished dressing and was waiting for Brandon to show for the meeting. He strolled down to the room and found the phone, still blinking on hold. "Hello, this is Saif director, what has you calling today? Checking up on me?"

"I'm afraid not Saif, I have bad news...your partner Aviv...he was shot and is missing. He has officially been deemed, murdered."

His expression was searching for something anything to say but the words held until he pulled back his senses. "Do you know who or why?"

"The who part we know...it was his twin brother. We are still piecing together the why."

"I never knew he had a brother." Saif said in disbelief.

"Neither did Aviv until recently."

"How are his wife and child taking this? Tell them my prayers go out to them."

"I'll tell Jocheved to tell his daughter, his wife was killed in the attack."

Saif slumped to the floor as memories of his own family recaptured his mind. His friend and partner had been there for him in his time of need, now his family was shattered. "Is there anything I can do? Am I being ordered home? I will surely come if that's why you called."

"No, I feel you are better placed where you are for now. I called to forewarn you that his brother has not been captured and we have reason to believe he is headed for the states. Remember, he is identical to Aviv, you may have the best chance at recognizing him if you do get the opportunity."

"But I'm in Virginia, how will I see him?"

"A call was intercepted last night but before we could get to the location, they were gone. He's headed for D.C."

"Just remember, you'll have only thirty minutes of air once we close the lid. Stay quiet and the customs people will never check a thing. Now let's get you comfortable inside, is your watch set?"

"It's ready. I'm not but let's do this anyway. I hate the thought of lying in one of these God forsaken things."

"Start your timer now." and the young Palestinian closed the casket lid. Minutes later they were offloading them onto a truck as customs watched the proceedings.

Inside the third coffin lie Rafe with his eyes shut. The darkness surrounded him like when he was young and alone. Then the kind Easterner's came to give him a new life and it did change. His wife gave him love and the man gave him the father figure he desired, until her untimely passing. The man cried out in pain from her death and Rafe vowed to avenge his new father's loss. *Soon father, I'll be back in your caring arms and together we will correct the passages of time. Soon I will deliver to you, your vengeance.*

Chapter 34

As I sat in the outer office looking at the First Sergeant's door, the lettering in gold registered as prophetic as a sign from the heavens. This was more than coincidental to me so I was overly anxious to meet the person to the name. Had I been standing at the door when it opened, I too would've fallen victim to everyone's preconceived ambition to make small jokes. He barely stood four and a half feet tall I guessed but I was soon to find out it was no barrier to him. He invited me in and as I stood, I felt as small as he was. His years of military service had created a unique kind hearted individual with a voice as big as the moon on a full night. "Welcome to Fort Belvoir Sergeant, I've heard many good things about you and I like to meet all my new NCO's. I prefer to get a first impression before the rest ruin the new guy. Did Private Rue scare you with his blind driving?"

Not the type of question I expected so my dumbfounded look answered his inquisition. "Thank you sergeant and I'm not sure what to say about the other topic?"

"He likes to pretend he's able to drive with both eyes shut. Last time he wiped out three civilian cars and a colonel's jeep."

And you let him keep driving? "I'll remember to never get in another car he's driving then."

"So how do you like the military?" he asked next. "Plan to make it a career?"

"I've liked what I've been able to see and do so far, as for a career that I'm not certain of yet."

"Well maybe we can change that here. I hope you can teach some of those guys how to cook because they stink about as bad as my feet on a hot summer's day." he joyfully laughed. "Well I'm sure you'd like to get settled in. Do you have any questions for me?"

There was only one for now "Mind if I ask what the 'A.' is for in your name?"

He was taken aback by my observation. "No I don't mind, people usually don't care enough to ask, so those who do I tell. I'm Brandon Adam Richard, First Sergeant, Bordentown, New Jersey and I'm a lifelong Phillies Phanatic."

How anyone could have this man on their hit list was beyond me but I was going to do my damnedest to see he wasn't a victim of this evil plot. We shook hands and began a long friendship, unbeknownst to either of us.

"Mr. Stein, welcome to CIA headquarters again. Are you ready for a Monday night Dallas whooping?"

"Yes it should be a good one. Are we set for our meeting?"

"They are waiting for you now. I must warn you though the Israeli is not in a good mood. He got a call earlier. His partner was killed."

"Oh how dreadful, all the killing that happens over there." bowing his head as though he actually gave a damn.

"They are in here sir. I'll see you at the game?"

"I wouldn't miss that one for the world." he smiled with an evil coldness then waited for his escort to vanish out of sight. He listened in to the conversation behind the door and you could immediately detect a strain in the relationship. "Just the leverage I need to complete my task." He knocked lightly twice before entering the brightly lit room. "Hello gentlemen, I'm the one who called this meeting. Do either of you know who I am?"

Brandon held his hand up like a school child too bashful to answer the question. Finally he answered. "You're the President's Advisor, Mr. Stein."

"That is correct. And you must be our trainee? Saif is it?" Saif's nod was enough of an admission. "I'm terribly sorry to hear about your partner. Were you close?"

"He was like a brother to me. I only wish I had been there for him when he needed me."

"Yes, I'm sure you do." Stein said with little emotion.

"Have we met before?" Saif seemed to recall something odd about this man.

"No I doubt we have." Stein replied back but the truth was much different. They had indeed met many years ago on an Israeli street. A fight had broken out in a village that Kudra and his wife were passing through on their way to see the Wailing Wall. In an attempt to seek safety, Stein had stopped the vehicle in the middle of the street and hurried his wife to follow. In her desperation to exit the vehicle, the old door handle broke and she was trapped inside as the fighting intensified. He watched as she was gunned down by the younger Israeli that now stood only meters away. He wanted to exact his revenge right there but held his cool. No, Saif Barak was going to pay the price that Stein wanted. Saif's family was already taken all that remained was him and his destiny. "Well my purpose for this visit is to evaluate how our young CIA agent Brandon here handles the task of overseeing our foreign guest. I want you Saif to submit each week at the end of the week a short summary of his job performance. Can I count on you for that and it to be fair?"

"Yes sir, I'll give you an accurate report." He was still staring at the face of Stein. "Why are you handling this and not someone inside the CIA?"

"The President doesn't want biased feedback and his relationship with your country is important for his reelection. So he has asked me to oversee this joint show of unity." Everyone in the country knew the tensions had been strained at times so this was a good ploy at pulling off his actual plan. "I would like to speak with Brandon now, alone please." he told agent Saif.

"Very well sir, I'll leave you to your business. It was nice to meet you." He offered to shake Stein's hand and as they did so, Saif noticed the healing bite mark. "That must have hurt."

"What? Oh the hand, yes it did. Enjoy your rigorous training here." he patted Saif on his back as he exited. Stein turned around in a flash to Richard and held his finger to his lips. "Shhh…" he silently went."…is he still outside the door?" he whispered into his ear.

He nodded yes, afraid to speak.

"Listen to me carefully, here is where I want you to meet me after we leave." He handed Brandon a slip of paper. "He is a double spy." Then Stein pulled back from aside the young man's head and looked at him as sincere as his fictitious face could muster. "Now go and I'll see you later."

"Cardinal Siri, it's Bishop Michael Gallagher, I have an answer to the position you have offered to appoint me. I accept to do God's work."

"That is good news, the Pope will be delighted. He likes you very much and sees you doing great things for the church."

"I have always tried to make his Excellency pleased with my work. Is he still planning a trip to the U.S. soon?" Michael was curious and hopeful to meet him some day.

"Yes, he does see a need for some guidance in America. There is much hidden strife there and if it gets worse the world will usher in the Age of Satan."

"Then now is the time for all good men to act and seek God's wisdom and navigation."

"Your words are always so true and honest Michael. May the Lord be by your side in your new calling."

Yes may he be there to watch over me. "Thank you." The Bishops next coordinated move was to let General Kelley know the funding could begin and as soon as they had the same fake list he could launder the money trail. "Paul, we are ready on my end."

"I'll get the first list to you tonight. Come on over for dinner. I'll have James' brother make your favorite."

"How can I resist a meal from a chemist chef?" They both laughed at his joke.

"On no, not again!" Eljer started feeling incompetent in his efforts to recall the exact compounds to the formula. "Damn it!"

"Keep trying later brother, the general just called and we are having the Bishop over for dinner and he has asked that you make his favorite. That chicken dish you hate because of the time."

"Do you mean the Roasted Lemon Rosemary Chicken?"

"Yes I do recall that was it."

In a split moment Eljer kissed his brother and exclaimed "You're a god send, now I remember what I was doing wrong!"

"Just because we are having chicken for dinner?" James asked while following his brother.

After finally settling in to my new room, I decided to head over to the mess hall with Rudy. I had skipped breakfast so my appetite was strong for lunch. "Any idea what's for lunch?" I asked him.

"Hopefully something better than yesterday's, it looked like a cross between breakfast and dinner from the night before."

"That's pretty bad. Let's not tell them who I am just yet. They may want me to work." I tried to humor Rudy.

He was very slow at catching on to things. What I did notice was his attention to detail. As we walked to the doors we passed the menu board. "Can't anyone spell correctly?" He switched the c and k around in chicken salad. "Now that looks better. Doesn't it?" he was content with his aid.

"Do you really drive with your eyes closed?" I mimed as we walked in.

"Not any more I don't!"

The next thing I heard as I entered was the large voice of one First Sergeant Richard "There he is, our European chef, direct from the Pentagon." waving his stubby hand for me to join the crew. "I want to introduce you to your new Mess Sergeant this is Staff Sergeant Mac Gwire."

He was a splitting image of Burt Reynolds and later I found out he drove the same Trans Am with a cowboy hat on his days off. "It's nice to meet you." I greeted.

"Are you ready to work? You start in the morning." He even laughed like Burt as he said it. All that was missing was the toothpick. Then he inserted one. The look was complete. "We feed future engineers here, they train them. The women are off limits, unless I say you can have one." Again the Burt laugh sounded. "Grab some chow and I'll see you in the AM. Top, I'm out of here now that my replacement has arrived."

Private Rue still unfamiliar with the Army's lingo asked me "Who's Top?"

"That would be the big guy in the little uniform." I quietly said out of the side of my mouth. I had to ask the next question. "You don't mind being called 'Top'?"

"Hell no, it's better than what he used to call me."

I had no answer I wanted to offer, I just raised my eyebrows and waited.

"Little Enos? From Smokey and the Bandit? Don't you Pennsylvania boys watch any TV?" he mumbled as he left.

Rudy hollers as he's just about to the door. "We didn't have electricity!"

Top turned around and yells back "That's why there's no darn light on upstairs!" The place erupted in laughter and I was enjoying my new home.

"Hello? Mr. Stein are you in here? It's Brandon..."

"Over here." *You bumbling idiot!* he flicked a table lamp on. The curtains were drawn so no one could see in. *At least he can follow simple directions.* "Did anyone see you enter?"

"No sir."

"The task I am enshrouding you in is of utmost importance to your country. We need to find out who Saif is working for and with. We know some of them but not all the players. Are you the man for this mission?"

"Yes sir I can handle him. He hasn't been a cup of tea since we met. Now I'm beginning to understand why."

"Here is a packet with his background information. I want you to study it. I want you to know him better than he knows his own self. Then when the time comes and we have his connections, I want you to help me kill him." Brandon's blood chilled from the words. "Do you have any problem with doing that?"

"None." His dedication to his country was being foiled.

The master had his pupil. Now he wanted the final piece of the puzzle and only time stood in his way.

General Kelley filed through the sheets of arms orders highlighting the deceptive ones he had inserted. Half way down the small list he came upon an unexpected discrepancy that terrified his Marine stature. An order had been submitted for shipment but the most frightening was it had been sent to the Middle East by order of the President. "This can't be right?" he shallowly spoke to himself." A call had to be made. "Mildred, I need to speak with the President, now." he tried to restrain the urgency in his voice.

"Hey Rudy, I see what you meant by them not cooking very well. I have a gut ache already. I'll catch you later. I'm going to take a short siesta. Can you wake me up in about an hour or so?"

"Sure thing sergeant, are you going out tonight?"

"Not planning to but I wanted to check out the rest of the base."

"I'll give you a tour later if you'd like?" he asked with sincerity.

Remembering the talk with top earlier I smiled and replied back "We'll see Rudy. We'll see." Fortunately for me at this post, my room was on the first floor, no climbing steps. *These boxes and bags will wait until later, time to rest.* As I lay down on the barren bed, my love's cross slide up to my throat. "I should get a longer chain, maybe later." I pulled the cross up to my lips. "Sweet dream my love, the plan is beginning to take shape. I miss you, Amanda." A single tear rolled out my eye as I faded away.

"I have missed you too my love. Your work is going well and I'm proud of what the men in my life have accomplished but my father needs you now. When you wake you must call him, it is important you call him."

"Ok Amanda, I will call. Will I see you soon again?"

"Just close your eyes and I'm right there." I could feel her hand brush over my face.

"Here's a kiss to keep in your heart." I offered back.

"Sorry Sergeant Conrad but I don't think so!" sounded a terrified voice from Rudy Rue. "Are you awake now?"

"What? Who is that?" I answered.

"Private Rue, it's been over an hour. You still want that tour?" he sheepishly inquired. "Who's Amanda, your girl back home?"

Shaking off the effects of my short rest and getting to my feet, I apologized for the misconception he certainly got from my comments. "Yes, she's a special girl and I think I left something at the Pentagon. Can you run me back over?" grimacing as I spoke those words.

"Maybe you can just get a replacement here at the PX?" he suggested.

"I doubt anyone stocks a picture of my mother Rudy. Give me a few minutes and I'll meet you outside."

"Ok, I'll see you at the Jeep."

I slipped my boots back on and watched as he exited the barracks. Just around the corner from my room was a pay phone. Good thing I still had the general's number on me for emergencies. As the phone rang through I tied my boots.

"Hello General Kelley's office, how may I help you?"

"Hello Mildred, It's Sergeant Conrad, I need to speak with him please."

"Do you miss us already?" she joked. "He just went out for a bit. Should I have him call you?"

There was no number I could leave so the next best option would need to suffice. "Tell him to meet me where the cardinal met us. He'll understand." I hoped it would be taken as urgency when she gave him the message. "Are you ready to roll Private Rue?"

"I was born ready. Hold on tight." he laughed as he drove us off.

"I hope that time in that box wasn't too morbid, my son." Kudra said as he gave Rafe a fatherly hug.

"No more than Saif's will be when I put him in one, permanently. His partner should be enjoying his by now." the pair laughed.

"I have a new ally I'd like for you to meet. Brandon Richard, this is my adopted son Rafe." They shook hands. "My wife couldn't have children so we gave him a life nobody else could. Then your new Israeli field officer ended all that when he didn't stand down as he was ordered. That's when we found out he was a spy working both sides."

"He is a monster, a coward that hides behind women and children." Rafe egged on. "I hope you are better than the last fool we tried to get to eliminate him."

"I am and I'll do my best to help you end his spying."

"I know that Brandon, that's why I asked you to join us." his eyes never showing any deceit. "Rafe will need use of one of the CIA's best long range sniper rifles and a private place to train with it. You have computer access to those items, please arrange them and get back to me."

"Pardon my curiosity sir but why use a rifle? Aren't there better options?"

"After I know who he's working with, I want them all disposed of at the same time. I have a plan to gather them in one room where my marksman son gets to have target practice. And no one gets out."

"Sorry sir I didn't mean to intrude on your obviously well devised plan. I will get Rafe what he needs."

"Good man. We will see you later." They waited until he left. "The weapons are being released. Hell will hit the streets of Israel like they've never seen before and the good President will get the blame. We must wait for the right moment to strike back at the infidels."

"What distance will I need to be ready to shoot?" Rafe asked.

Without any emotion, Kudra answered. "Across a football field that may have winds, if anyone can do it, you can."

"Okay, let me see if I have this correct." Private Rue started. "First you want to get your mom's picture back and now we are going to a cemetery to have someone bring it to you there?"

"Yeah, it's something like that Rudy. Maybe someday I'll explain but not today. I do appreciate you taking me, now can we go a little slower so I do get there?" I thought my ride through Berlin was exciting, this was border edge terrifying.

"I have my eyes open see?" Rudy showed me, barely missing a bus.

I pulled my cross out to pray.

"Oh! You're Catholic too? Did you know top was a Catholic also?" he still was weaving around traffic as he spoke. "We've been working together on a new method to construct stronger buildings for like earthquake zones. It's real high tech neat stuff."

Suddenly my attention was no longer on the road but on his invention. He revealed that in his younger years, his family had gone to California for a trip to Disney. They had experienced the horrors of a small earthquake event but it was enough for him to decide he'd never live there and wanted to help someway with buildings. That is what got him into engineering. Listening to his description of how they were attempting to make the metal foundation was intriguing. Their one flaw they felt was a temperature issue. They needed a higher heat source then a quick chill to stabilize the formation.

"When you get back, tell top I'd be interested in seeing your work. I've always liked building things." My real thoughts were, if this honeycomb design could be perfected, it could have a great impact on our ship design for both weight and integrity. Familiar surroundings began to appear, I knew we were close to the cemetery. I again asked for a sign, this one was harder to believe it could just happen.

"Here we are Del. You sure you want me to go? What if your person doesn't show?"

"Then God and I will have a long time to talk. I'll be fine Rudy. Now get back and give top my message." As he drove away, I realized I was again all alone.

Chapter 35

"Thank you Mr. President for seeing me on such short notice, I knew you would want to hear what I had to say."

"General Kelley, if what you've told me is only half true, it's still very damaging to my campaign and even worse for this country. I leave the decisions in your hands. If you need anything from this office, just contact us."

With a salute he turned and headed for his driver.

"General, your secretary called while you were in your meeting and left a message." the young driver informed him while handing the note over.

"Wait for me at the jeep. I need to make a quick call." Today's news couldn't get any worse, could they? "Hello James, I need you to meet me over at Amanda's site. Something is going on. How is your brother coming along?"

"With tonight's dinner he's fine. With his uh hmm, he's ecstatic. I'll see you there sir."

Saif always had a sixth sense for the irregular. He called back to his director to update him on the American's intentions. "It just seems odd to me sir."

"Yes, I must say it feels that way to me also. I am sending over another agent to cover your tail. There's a fox in the hen house as those Americans would say and I'm not losing another good agent."

"Who Is It going to be sir?"

"Someone I'm sure you'll trust. He'll be in contact when he gets there. Your code word will be, Shira."

"Very well sir, shalom."

The dead tone signaled he was gone. "You have your opportunity for redemption, I'm sure you won't need a second chance."

"Thank you director, just make sure my wife and Shira are protected while I'm gone." Jocheved requested.

"They will be fine. All of you are in good hands."

The winds were howling as the temperature fell, it was a cool late August summer evening. My usual great sense of direction was off by nature's reaction to me being there. This made my gut hollow with belief that my fore thought wish would not come true. How could it in these conditions. I searched around for a groundskeeper while looking at the many head stones. I was the only soul brave enough to be there. Suddenly an old marker weathered by time caught my attention. Could it be by chance or just coincidence? The name on it was Conrad Adelstein. "Can't be the same person, has to be a fluke." I told myself out loud.

"What's a fluke son?" an elderly gent with a news boy's hat and holding a lawn rake appeared almost out of nowhere.

"Whoa! Where the hell did you come from?" I yelled startled by his presence.

"I was over there and saw you wondering around. I thought I'd offer you some assistance. Who are you looking for anyways?"

"I doubt you'd know her or where to find her site." I said confidently.

"Oh don't be too sure of yourself, I know all the ones buried here. I've worked here a long time and had a hand in burying most of them." he said as if I should test him.

"Ok, I'm looking for Amanda Kelley's burial site. Which way should I go?" trying not to be prudish.

"Well you were close. The young lady is one more row over." He stopped and slapped at, of all things, a bee, the item I had pictured in my vision. But in my premonition I saw a dead bee on top of her temporary marker, not flying around buzzing an old man.

"One more row over this way?" I asked pointing the way. When I looked back to verify, all I saw and heard was not what I expected.

"Who you talking to Del?" the general sounded off.

"I...I'm not sure sir? There was an old man here just moments ago telling me where to find Amanda's site but now he's gone? I must be losing my mind or the cool wind is getting me delirious."

He scanned the area as did I yet we saw no other persons around. "Don't know what to say about that son but she is just one more row over as you were saying." He headed to her marker as I followed. "Hi my sweet, daddy's here."

As I was about to make my own comment, I felt a sharp stinging sensation on my arm. "Ouch!" I swatted the bee that apparently trailed us. It landed on her marker just as I had seen in my vision. "Oh my God." I left out as I fell to my knees.

"Are you alright Del? Are you allergic to bees?"

"Not that I know of sir. I mean about the bees but I think I'm fine now that I've reached another answer."

"Answer to what son?"

"I believe I've found our Mr. Richard from the list." I smiled as I looked up at him. "She sent me here to find something, not just to meet you. Come here and take a look." We went back over to where the gravestone read Conrad Adelstein. "This is where I was talking to the man before you came. I need to find out who he is."

"Well let's do that later. James should be here soon and we are having dinner with the bishop, perhaps he can help."

As we left, I saw over to my right, the same old man who gave me directions. I waved a condolence thank you and he returned the same. If I could have read his lips, they would have said, "May the Lord be with you."

Paul looked over my way and asked "Who are you waving to?"

"The old man with the rake over ther...?" again he was gone. "It's time to leave."

"Ah, Michael, please come in. The men should be back shortly. Smell anything good?"

"As a matter of fact I do. Not to change the subject or your generous hospitality but can I speak with you since we are alone for the moment? It has to do with Del and Amanda."

"What about Michael?"

"Their love for one another, I know our lord teaches us to love one another but theirs was so sudden. Do you feel it was real or her wanting it to be real?"

"If I hadn't read her letter, I'd possibly feel the same way. No, her feelings for him were genuine. Why do you ask that?"

"A lot has taken place and it all revolves around our young Del. I'm concerned there is a dark element surrounding him, something even he may not possibly know yet."

"Should we tell him?" her solicitude showing. "He has been like the son we never had and will be the closest example of a son-in-law now that she's gone."

"No, not yet, and don't say anything to Paul either, just yet. Let's carefully watch how things progress over the next few months. Time will tell."

"Hello! We're back." the general announced. "Hello Bishop. I hope you're hungry?" he embraced the man as though they were in church rather than his own house.

"I was growing hungrier as I talked with Doreen and kept smelling that succulent dish." He appeared spooked when I came in the door with James and Eljer. "Oh, I didn't know you were here too Del. How have you been?" he asked as he gave a surprised look to the lady of the house.

"Okay except for this stinger in my arm."

"He got stung at the cemetery." The general informed both of them.

"Visiting my daughter were you?"

"Yes Doreen and I stumbled onto something. Bishop, would you happen to know who Conrad Adelstein is? His grave is close to Amanda's."

"Let me think? That name does sound... oh yes! He was a soldier in the German Army that came over to America after the war. You know, I thought I saw Mr. Stein kneel down at that stone when we buried Amanda."

"I don't recall seeing that." Paul replied.

"With tears in your eyes neither of us could see much that day." Doreen added.

"He laid something on the ground there. I watched from behind but never thought much about it until now." James finished.

"Well my chicken isn't waiting much longer for anyone so let's eat. Del, there's enough for all of us to include you. Let's see how my cooking compares to your friend Bernhard." Eljer boasted.

The table turned quiet as everyone enjoyed the feast. Paul spoke first to break the silence. "So what were you two talking about before we arrived?"

"He asked how things have been since we last spoke." Doreen quickly submitted.

"We should really be discussing our next steps now that things are progressing." Michael suggested.

"I'd have to agree sir. Eljer, if your formula is anywhere near as good as this chicken, then we have a great winner on hand." He lavishly accepted the crown I had just afforded him.

"I must say, the formula is to where it has been in the past. Now we just need to figure what more the Germans did to make theirs last as long as it does. Something is still missing." He acted discontent that his efforts hadn't produced more.

"When the time comes, the lord will show us what's missing, so fear not Eljer. How are you doing with things on your end Del?" the bishop probed.

"Well sir, I believe I now know who the last name on the list is and he's my new company sergeant. As you stated, the lord will show us when the time is right."

"Then I have the final piece of our puzzle." the general relayed. "I have secured a section close to our observation post in the Antarctica's for the building of the vessel. It is far enough away from normal shipping and won't raise any suspicions when a ship, shall we say, gets off course. The landing area is bordered by our ally's the British."

"All that remains is time and our fate. I will get with Mr. Richard to facilitate his invention and hopefully join our team." I waited for any more input. "Then this meeting is adjourned. Bishop, would you like to close with a prayer?"

"Most certainly I would. May the lord..." his thoughts were clear, precise and inspiring. "...and to all here, may you guard over us until our calling home. Amen."

"Who's taking me home?" I joyfully asked.

"And you think he's followed by evil?" Doreen whispered to Bishop Michael. "I'll take him gentlemen. James, you and your brother have enough to clean up and Paul, you have our guest to take care of, besides, I haven't been out of this house all day. Come Del, let's go."

"So you see top, here's someone who's interested in our work. Can we show him how it's to better design future buildings?" Private Rue was giddy with anticipation.

"Why would a cook be so curious about our engineering feat? Yes Rudy, This one I've got to hear. When he returns let him know we'll talk with him tomorrow after his shift."

"Great! I don't think I'll sleep tonight one wink."

"I appreciate you taking me back, Mrs. Kelley."

"Doreen, remember? And I actually wasn't passing up a chance after tonight's earlier conversation. I want you to go with me to the cemetery."

"You mean now?" a lump built in my throat.

"Yes, grab that light and those gloves. We are doing our own investigating."

She was serious so I followed her instructions, shortly thereafter we were headed back over to her daughter's resting spot. "What do you expect to find at night?" I had to ask.

"Some answers, I want to know what Kudra Stein left there. I've never like that smug face of his." She spoke not another syllable until we arrived. "Let's go young man."

Walking around graves at night reminded me of when we went roaming away from Camp Bashore when I was in Boy Scouts. The local cemetery close by was notorious for Blue Eyed Six sightings so we did it more or less as a dare than to actually spot someone. When we went, all the flashlights went dead, at the same time and I fell into a freshly dug grave. I was never the type to be claustrophobic but that night it started to rain when no rain was forecasted and only two friends stayed to help me get out of the hole. I panicked each time I slipped out of their grips and fell back into the filling grave. I honestly began to feel that hole was dug just for me. As they became more exhausted from pulling my despair turned to helpless prayer "Please God, don't let me die here." were the words I recall speaking as their final efforts turned fruitful. "I'll do anything you ask for now on. Thank you." I proclaimed. From that turning point in my life, everything I had ever done after that was for others. I helped those in need. I sacrificed my time when someone needed it and I never asked for anything in return.

"Are you okay Del? You got awfully quiet since I said this is where we were going."

"I just hope we don't run into anyone out here."

"What, at this time of night?" she laughed.

She wouldn't have if I had told her about the man with the rake. We made our way to the grave of the German soldier. Our lights focused on the headstones until we arrived at our destination. The wind had died from earlier so every sound was amplified. She began feeling with her hands the ground over the man's grave. "Too bad we don't have a metal detector or some way of looking down into the dirt." I suggested.

"Well he couldn't have placed whatever it was too deep so help me search. Feel with your hands." she almost begged.

I anticipated a hand from an unwelcomed visitor reaching up through the dirt to ward us off. Then the chill of the night kissed my neck as a hand touched my shoulder.

"Oh my God, I found something!" she shrieked.

I stumbled back on my hands and butt dropping my light. "What?" I hated to ask. My flashlight beam illuminated the object. "Is that what I think it is?"

"Yes, it's a Star of David. Why would Kudra put this here on this man's grave I wonder?"

"We better leave it. That's a religious omen in my book and I'm not messing with someone's beliefs." Near us we heard the sound of a rake being used to drag leaves together.

She released the symbol and it fell to the ground. The raking stopped. "Let's go Del, now." Her pulse ran as we exited back to the car. "You say nothing to Paul about our trip here tonight, please." she pleaded.

"I promise, unless I feel he needs to know. Is that fair?"

"Deal." she agreed.

We arrived back at my base about a half an hour later. I'm not sure which caught more attention, the car or the fact that an older lady had drove me home. Anyone outside saw us to include Rudy who had been waiting. "Well, you better get some sleep. Oh yeah, top said he'll talk with us tomorrow after your shift. What does a cook want with our idea anyways?" he beckoned.

"An out of this world type of idea Rudy, now go get some sleep yourself."

Morning always comes sooner than you want. A quick shower to refresh and off to work I went. I was greeted by Burt's look-a-like. "Let's see what you can do with these." as he handed off the day's recipe cards. Later I believed he had hoped for my failure, he hoped wrong.

I looked over the menu items, checked the store room and began to work. I needed the distraction from the previous day's endeavors. The aroma emitted from the exhaust fans quickly drew attention. The moral of the troops could be seen changing. The others inside gathered around to learn. I commanded the diligence of my peers and earned their respect fast. I had become a leader and a teacher. The lower ranking soldiers wanted my knowledge and I was eager to share it with them. My higher ranked officers reveled in my expeditious accomplishments. I had lived up to my fore drawn expectations. The day's efforts were good and rewarding. A smile could be seen on the faces as they entered but more so when they left.

"Good job today." was all I received from Sergeant Gwire. It was more than enough for me, I had passed his test.

"Hey Conrad, let me see you in my office!" yelled top. "So you are asking about our invention, why?" he asked as I walked in and sat beside Rudy.

"Before I answer that I want to know if you would trust me with your life."

"Hell no." top replied.

"I don't know about that sergeant." Rudy answered honestly.

"But you had no trouble enjoying the meal I prepared?" I shot back. They looked at each other and knew I had a point. "Every time someone cooks they could poison your food. They could do even nastier things to it also. When I work, I respect your trust in me, so now I need you to trust in my needs. Your process I feel could benefit a great project I have access to but if you can't trust my judgment then I need to look for another source."

"We've got a lot of time invested into this and want to see it put to good use, what kind of project could you be involved in that would benefit us?" top dug deeper for a solid answer.

"Is life or death a good reason?"

"Life is always better than death." Rudy blurted.

"Now you have my attention. We'll put our trust in you, what do we get for it?"

"You get a way off this death trap. You and any family you have when the time comes."

"Death trap? What death trap are you referring to?" Rudy's innocence showed.

"Our world is on a collision course with another larger planet. If we don't build a ship large enough to carry enough people off, our species will not survive."

They sat silent. "And you can prove this?" Rudy asked.

"All I need is for both of you to meet the remaining team members and swear a vow of silence. Any objections?"

Neither one objected to my demands.

"Now let's see your plans if I may?" After viewing their inventive process, I knew it was feasible for the task at hand. "And all you feel is needed is a hotter heating source?"

"Yes." Top answered quickly. "I'm sure of it."

"I need to use your phone please, top." He handed it and I dialed the general. "Sir, they are on board. When can we gather everyone to synch up?"

"Let's go for this Monday night. My 'Skins are playing the Cowboys and we'll make it a nice informal meeting at my home."

"Are either of you a Redskins or Cowboys fan." I jokingly asked. They both nodded they were. "Oh boy, let me guess, Rudy you like the 'Boys and top you're a Redskins fan?"

They smiled and said "Yup." together.

"Sir, we will see you Monday night."

"I pity the Cowboy fan." he laughed as he hung up the phone.

The following days were busy for Rafe and Brandon as they strategically planned the firing sessions. He needed precise conditions to master the distance and the weather was not being cooperative. "I need another range to practice from and more time." he shouted at the CIA pigeon.

"I'm doing the best I can. There are other officers training off these same fields and you don't want to be caught. Your father wouldn't be happy with either one of us, would he?" the young recruit fired back.

"Just do as you've been told or there will be your own hell to pay." Rafe scowled.

After he slammed the car door, Brandon thought *"I'll see to it you find hell."* He soon sensed his role was not what he had been told it was for and needed to confess to someone. The only person he felt he could trust.

"It's Monday Night Football in our nation's capital." the TV announcer commentated.

"This should be a great game." Rudy anticipated.

"Just remember, it's only a game." Sergeant Richard quipped. "Besides that we are here to conduct business."

"Men this is more than business, it's our future." The bishop inputted.

"Exactly right Michael, if their idea works with Eljer's fuel source, we are home free."

"I told you they had something sir." I managed to get in.

"Del, if my Redskins make it back to the Superbowl, you and I are going. That's my promise. Gentlemen, for the next four months we need to work our butts off and never forget we are doing this in secrecy for all mankind, not just us."

"Hey I want to go too if they win." Top pleaded. "He's the Cowboy's fan not me." he directed his finger at Rudy. We laughed.

A flash premonition occurred and I fainted. When I came through, all the men surrounded me and were asking what happened and if I was alright. The only memories I could recall was the fact that the Redskins would lose and something terrible would take place later. The whole stadium sat quiet in prayer like a vigil. "I need to speak with you two alone." I signaled the bishop and general to follow. "If the Cowboy's win, something bad is going to happen at that stadium in the future but I don't know or haven't figured it out yet."

"Are you certain?" Michael's genuine heart felt question reverberated the rest of the night.

When the game concluded and the Cowboys were victors, the only person cheering wasn't Rudy. It was Eljer.

"What are you so happy about brother?"

"I had a dream last night and in it a young lady ensured me that my formula was only one key element away. And then she told me to watch the games' end. If the local team lost, the next following announcement would hold the key. Got any antifreeze general?"

Everyone looked at the television set and wondered, could it be that simple?

Chapter 36

The dream proved proficient but the identity of the girl remained a mystery. It wasn't Amanda as we first thought. Soon we were creating more of our potent fuel source and the heat it provided rectified the problem with the fusion of materials for the pair's inspiration. A huge warehouse was secured in the manufacturing district of Hong Kong and panels were being produced around the clock. The general was beginning to close in on whoever was responsible for the acquisition of the planted false orders. The months were winding down and his beloved football team was in the midst of another crown. Life for once was appealing and the fruits of our labor were showing. One day after a long difficult teaching seminar at work, I decided to venture out on the base to unwind. It was very cold along the Potomac River area in December but the sun shone brightly and I hadn't planned to stay out long. A few days before, a lite snowfall coated the ground and the frost from it remained visible. Suddenly a young deer transpired and it's hard to say who alarmed the other more but as I struggled to catch my footing, the slickness of the ground sent me flying on my back. With the wind gushing out of me, I blacked out.

"Wake my love, soon we will be together again."

"Amanda? Where have you been? I haven't seen you for so long."

"I've been waiting for the right time to come back. You have done well with my father and the others. Now you must find the man responsible for my death. He is near and he is with others. Be careful where you go and with whom."

"Is there a sign I can look for? What more can you tell me?" I searched for more.

"When one gun sounds, another will sound too." She bowed her head. "A great General will fall." A tear fell from her eyes.

"Can I stop it from happening?"

"No. It must take place like the sun shines every day. If the sun stops shining, all life will end."

"I feel as though I've failed you."

"You have not Del. You have succeeded more than you know but will undoubtedly know soon enough. Now go and remember."

The coldness I felt more than Rudy slapping my face to revive me. "Del! Are you hurt?" My ribs ached some so I pointed to them. Too cold to talk he assisted me to my feet. "The jeep is just over that little hill. Can you walk?"

"Yes." I managed to verbalize. "How did you know where to find me?"

"We are partners buddy. I always know where you are." He smiled. "Now let me carry you as you have carried us all."

My temperature had fallen too low and shock was a factor to deal with. He wrapped a blanket around me, laid me in the back seat and drove as fast as he could to the Emergency room at the base Hospital. Had he not been there when he was, I would have died from exposure, the doctors later told me. "I guess I owe my life to him." I replied to the one specialist.

"That is your decision young man, but certainly worth his respect." was the suggestion I received back.

"Rafe my son, your skills are masterful. The regiment of training will soon pay off." Kudra commended his protégé.

"I could pick a fly off an egg at high wind and never crack the shell." he prided in his abilities. "When do I get to eliminate the infidels?"

"If all goes as I have planned, in a few weeks. It'll be risky but I want this to be remembered for all of time. No bigger playing field than another Championship game. I just know they'll be back in it again."

"Where will I be when all of this takes place?" asked Brandon.

"You will be positioned outside of my suite box. When we signal you will lock them inside. There will be no escape for them."

"And when will I get paid? I've done a lot for you and Rafe."

"I'll pay you after the game and when we've cleared the stadium, just as you have requested, one million dollars in small bills. You have the security cards arranged?" Stein asked.

"Everything is in place and ready. I just need to know which date."

With cunning in his eyes "Make them for January 8th. I've got a gift for the good general and his friends."

There had to be some way of tracking who was authorizing the orders since Paul knew they weren't coming from the President. He devised a plan and was sure it had to flush out the culprit or culprits. Earlier attempts showed some progress and he knew that multiple locations were utilized to call so no trace could be established. "Sometimes to draw the fox out of the hen house, you must empty the house. Let's see how our villains like the next order being terminated and how they respond."

The man standing next to him, patted him on his shoulder and said "I'm so glad our governments are working together to stop these criminals. And I'm fortunate to be here to help."

"Yes we are." said the other Israeli agent. "I'll be glad when I can go home again."

The general's phone chirped. "Hello?"

"General, sir Del, I mean Sergeant Conrad, has had an accident on the post. He is in the hospital."

"Is he going to be okay?"

"They are not sure. He went into shock just after I got him here. He was outside in the cold and they are concerned over his nervous system."

"I'll be right over. You tell him to hang tough and we'll help him through this."

"Will do sir, please hurry." Rudy's voice was breaking.

"Something is wrong?" the darker of the two men asked.

"Very much so, our leader is apparently not doing well. I must go to see him." It was the first time any of them had heard the higher ranking officer refer to me as their leader. This was the beginning of the turning point.

Once the general arrived and made known that he was there to see me, he was escorted to my room. I had been admitted into the ICU and was under twenty four hour observation care. My status was critical and they gave me less than a ten percent chance of coming out of my coma. The cold had severely affected my organs and nervous system. Like the father he was and the one I never had, he knelt beside my bed and prayed aloud. "Dear lord, I know you can hear me and although I have lost faith in you in the past, I ask now that you give this honorable man your loving grace and administer your healing hands upon him in his hour of need. He has fought hard for you and for his beliefs in you, please do not fail him. I do not blame you for my daughter's demise any more. I'm quite certain I know who is responsible and he will get his one way ticket back to you. Del, if you can hear me in there, I promise you here and now, if you make it…no when you make it through, we will go to the big game to see my Redskins play. Now get well because we need you. In God's name I vow, amen." He sat beside me the rest of that night. The following morning he was joined by the trio of Doreen, James and Eljer.

"How's he doing Paul?" the lady of the group asked.

With grimace in his face the general answered "Not very well. His vitals have dropped more since I came in. I fear the worst is happening again and don't want to lose another one."

"Perhaps he needs a mother's touch." Doreen soothed. In her best recollection of how mother sang an old Irish love song, she began humming the tune then sang "*The Rose of Tralee*". The gentlemen couldn't help but join in as they remembered their homeland. After they finished and dried their eyes, the doctor walked in to check on me.

"He is not to have any visitors for a while. Who are you people?" he sternly asked.

Eljer jumped first "We are his family."

"His records show he has no family."

"Everyone has a mother and father." James countered. "Those records can't be right."

"Honestly doctor I'm General Kelley Joint Chiefs. We know he has parents in Pennsylvania but he doesn't speak with them much. So we are his adoptive family here. We are only here to help. Is there anything we can do?"

"Yes! Leave as I've said!" again he showed no compassion. Then he felt a tug on his smock.

"You better be nicer to them." I informed the arrogant doctor as he wheeled back around to see I had come out of my coma.

"This is a miracle! How are you feeling? I've never seen anyone in all my years here as a doctor, come out of a coma so quickly!" he sounded astonished.

"I'm parched. May I have something to drink?"

"I'm afraid only ice for now until we've run some test but after that yes!" he was still in shock. "I'll return shortly."

"I guess that means we can stay then." broke out Eljer.

"Wow dear, that was some song you choose to wake him up with."

"I only planned to comfort him." she said modestly.

Outside the window stood Private Rudy Rue with a single tear rolling down his face, he was pleased with the end result.

"Well Del, I guess we are going to a football game when you get out of here."

"Why?" I asked still feeling the cold's effect on my system. "Did you win tickets like in my dream?"

He chuckled. "How did I win tickets?"

"Mr. Stein said he couldn't go and offered them in a raffle drawing. Anyone could win them and you win them. At least in my dream you do." Everyone stopped smiling as the room's mood changed. "Did I say something wrong?"

A few weeks had passed before I was able to regain enough strength in my legs to walk again. Sure enough, the general's Redskins were in the midst of another playoff run and the last game before the Superbowl was the upcoming weekend against the San Francisco forty-niner's. The general almost opted to not throw his name in the hat but wanted to dispel the myth of my dream. Instead he put both of our names on the same piece of paper figuring if it was meant to be, the inclusion of my name could possibly break the dreams forecast. When he heard his name called, he accepted his fate. "Well you need to get as strong as you can so we can enjoy this game." he half smiled.

"You are not as happy about going to this game as I expected. Why?" my curiosity peaked.

"I fear it was a setup but we must go through with it."

"The big General is fearful? What could make you so solicitous?"

"The outcome my son, please promise me no matter what, you take care of Doreen when I'm gone."

"Oh I think it'll be the other way around, she'll take care of both of us as she has in the past."

With a radiant smile back on his mug he replied "Yes she has hasn't she. That is what a truly good wife will do. She will never bury inside of her even her deepest darkest feelings. She will look to her companion for the support to help subdue the demons she holds. She will trust with all of her heart like she has never trusted before and then she will do the hardest thing of all." He paused. "She will watch you die before her for her honor and in God's glory."

"Ah...let's change the subject. So, is big John going to run over the golden boys?" his head still lied in my bed.

Friday was release day from the hospital. I had to walk from my wheelchair to the car waiting outside. I managed to cloak the pain and cover my grimace enough. I wanted out but more so, I wanted to see that game. Just as I was about to get in, another vehicle pulled alongside and out from it came someone I wasn't anticipating. "Del, young man, glad to see you're up and about. I hope you enjoy my box seats." Mr. Stein showed enthusiasm.

"Yes, I'm sure we will. You made a trip all the way over here just to see me?"

"But of course, I was concerned and then elated to hear you were going to the game. Besides that I'm leaving tonight for my trip."

"Sorry sir, I guess I should show more appreciation for your generosity. That was an honorable thing you did."

His reasoning for doing it was not for the kind of honor I thought it was intended for but to ensconce his plan. "Don't worry my...friend. Just sit, stay warm in the box and enjoy the view. I'm sure you'll never forget it the rest of your life." A twinkle manifested in his eye.

As he got back in the stretch limo, I saw another figure sitting inside. He tipped his hat as if to acknowledge my presence and then with the sun shining through the tinted sunroof, it illuminated his facial features ever so slightly. The face I thought I'd seen before. "Aviv?" I barely spoke.

"What Del?" James asked.

"Oh nothing bud, I just thought I saw someone from my past."

"Who?" the general inquired.

"An Israeli agent from Berlin. Silly, right? What would he be doing here?"

"I did not know the German's had Israeli agents." laughed James. "Too bad they weren't there before the great war. That would have saved some lives."

"Yes, save lives." murmured the great general. "You will be staying with us at the house Del. Doreen has prepared a nice room downstairs so you won't need to climb steps and when she says to make yourself at home...then make yourself feel better than at home." That was the first and only time I saw him smile that weekend besides one other time.

As we pulled in front of the house, something creepy feeling raised the hair on my back. Definitely something was out of place. Then as Doreen made her way out onto the steps, she pulled a cord and then I saw it. It was a "Welcome Home" banner she had constructed and it warmed her smile to see my appreciation. "Hello my son. I'll have you ready for that game in no time." she mused. "Follow me to where you'll be staying."

The great house was full of Redskins' décor in honor of their achievement yet again this year. "No superstitions here, right Doreen?" my lower lip still quivering.

"Just the good kind, the type God grants. Now stop wasting your energy and eat for strength. Paul is not going alone to that game and certainly not just with two rugby brothers to argue which game is better." My stunned look must have been all she needed to decipher it's meaning. "Yes, they are going also. Seems it's a large room and enough benefits to feed a starving African nation. I'll watch from home…with Amanda." She radiated from her own thought of a mother daughter moment happening once again.

"Thank you, Mom. You have been the best example I could have ever been gifted and in such an extraordinary way. I will always honor you and never forget how you've treated me. I love you." I realized as I said it, I had just said it more times to her than I had to my own real mother in the past six months.

With tears welling up her vision, she held me tight, possibly in remembrance of her daughter and how it felt to hold her. "I love you too Adel."

"If I hadn't have seen his face before this morning, I would've sworn it was a younger you." Rafe noted to Kudra.

"That's precisely why I wanted and needed you to view him up close. I wouldn't want you to shoot the wrong one, now would you?"

"Here are your credentials Mr. Stein." Brandon passed them over. "Everything as you requested."

Reaching into his breast pocket he pulled out an envelope and exchanged it for Brandon's. "I'm sure you'll like what you find inside." He held up a champagne glass. "Let us celebrate with an early toast." He handed a previously poured glass to each occupant so they could join him. "Prost!" he exclaimed. He watched as the pair drank their share, that same twinkle in his eye. As Rafe finished his Brandon began to display distress. "Something wrong with your drink?" he questioned.

"You bastard." were his final words. Inside the envelope was a note that simply stated *"You're dead for double crossing me."*

"I won't be sharing another toast with you after this is over." Rafe informed him.

"There won't be any need to my son. We will have the final item we need when this is finally completed. No one will dare mess with us after we have our own nuclear device." He started to exhibit a sinister laugh joined by the remaining live rear occupant.

"Would anyone care for some tea?" James asked.

"Do you have any of your Earl Grey?" I requested.

"Does a General wear stars? Why of course, I wouldn't be caught dead without any. I'll be right back."

"Del, there have been some behind the scene events happening while you were in the hospital. I didn't want to cause you any more worry or stress than you were already experiencing. So, if anything happens to me, this envelope is for you and you only. Is that understood?"

"Now you're beginning to concern me sir. What do you think might happen to you?"

"Hopefully nothing but we never ever know when the lord will call us home. Look at what happened to Amanda. She never anticipated her death, I'm sure."

"I miss her."

"So do I and there will come a day when I'll be missed."

"Here you go young man." James interrupted. "Just the way I taught you to enjoy it."

"Where's Eljer?"

"He's working on something for the game. Do you need him?"

"One of his grand stories would be excellent. Don't you agree?" I asked looking at the general's auspicious smile.

"No one tells them better." Paul agreed as he placed the letter in his top desk drawer as I watched. Behind the den door stood Doreen listening in, tears flowed from her jade green oculars.

Chapter 37

The big game day had finally arrived. After a day and a half of home nursing, my legs felt strong enough to walk but forget about running anywhere. The surprise item Eljer had been working on was moments from being revealed. The general was all outfitted in his *Theismann* jersey, James had on a borrow *Riggin's* jersey and I was wearing a young standout's jersey by the name of *Darrell Green*. As we anxiously awaited the younger brother to join us, Doreen came laughing around the corner barely breathing from her condition. "Oh my good lord, I hope we see you guys on the TV set!" she continued to break up. "Without further ado, here's Eljer!"

In one quick action, he jumped around and into our view wearing an authentic *Hogettes* outfit. "Ta Da! So what do you guys think?" By the time Doreen helped the last one of us back to our feet, he had begun laughing along with us. "I honestly like it. I saw the guys on the telly wearing this stuff."

"This should be an enjoyable and memorable game." James snickered.

"Enjoy the game dear." Mrs. Kelley gave her husband a loving tender kiss marked by a long look into his eyes. "I love you."

"I love you more." he gave back. "I'll see you when we see you." He smiled and touched her face with his hands, then gave her one more kiss for good luck he proposed.

The parking lot was packed with Redskin faithful and vendors galore. We made our way past the gates and up to the box seats Mr. Stein so graciously had awarded us. The view was magnificent and a lifelong memory in the making. Eljer had made the acquaintance of a few other *Hogettes* and was inducted as an honorary foreign liaison. The catering crew asked what we wanted to drink and told us when they would start to bring in the food.

"Thank you again Paul for including me. I hope your team wins."

Behind us came a voice we hadn't heard from in a while. "Then let us pray since I missed you two in church this morning." It was the Bishop.

"Michael, please come in and join us!" Paul was glad to see our church contact. "How did you know where to find us?"

"Your lovely wife told me where you guys would be and who is going to stop a man of the cloth from going to see a General?"

"So what news do you bring us of your trip to the Vatican?" I anxiously needed to know.

"Calm down Del and I'm glad to see you're doing much better from the news I received. I prayed for you often. Word from the Vatican is no one suspects anything and we should have enough by the end of the year to cover all our cost for the next two years. You can start to cut back on the fictitious orders Paul."

"This is turning out to be one hell...I mean grand day, sorry Michael."

"The lord knows you meant well. Let's kick some ass, isn't that how it's said?" we all chuckled from his verbal usage.

"I wish I had some binoculars or a telescope to zoom in on those, ah players." Eljer commented while obviously looking at the cheerleaders.

"I brought a pair along." the bishop informed him and handed them over.

From the sheer embarrassment, he blushed as he accepted them. "Thanks."

"No problem Eljer, just clean them off when you're done." He then winked at him because he already knew his true intentions.

"You are going to share them during the game aren't you?" I asked.

"But of course I will." He then imitated what the field cheerleaders were doing.

"God, I hope no one looks at us now with him dancing like that in our box." The general commented while covering his head.

As James returned from the souvenir stand, he promptly saw his brother acting like his old self. "Can't you wait until the game is being played or are you trying to draw attention?"

"Hey, if they see me now, they'll be looking during the game more. So either join in or cover up like him."

Before long word went out, there was another costumed Redskin nut in the box area and we were on national TV.

"Here you go gentlemen. I hope you find your box seats comfortable. If you need anything, just grab your phone and someone will assist you. Enjoy the game, it should be a great one." The usher left them alone and closed the door on his way out.

"He has no idea how many people will be talking about this game for years." Rafe said in a boasting fashion. "When should I get the equipment ready?"

"You can start after the first quarter has completed. We don't need to rush too soon. The last thing we need is unwelcomed attention at this stage of our game." They laughed together. Stein pulled out the huge binoculars from their case to view the other side of the field. His grin widened when he saw the party happening in his own private suite, courtesy of his own generosity. "They seem to be enjoying the pleasantries I have provided. Care to see?"

Rafe accepted the goggles and inspected each person's location inside the ticking tomb. "This is just too good to be true but I'll accept the gift."

"Hello, D.C. police, how can I help you?" the desk sergeant asked the caller.

"Yeah, ah, you guys have a dead body down here near the river."

"Who is this please?" he asked wondering who would be out there when such a big game was about to be played.

"Ah, my name is Duncan, sir. I'm a homeless vet, been living out on these streets for a long time. I used one of my quarters. Can I get it back and maybe a hot meal for calling?"

"Well Duncan, you tell me exactly where you are and I'll have one of our officers meet you there. Then we'll get you what you're asking for. Sound good buddy?"

"Okay officer but I can tell you I didn't have anything to do with his killin' and can prove it."

This should be interesting. "How can you prove it to me over the phone Duncan?"

"I don't have a knife. Lost mine years ago and never found another one."

"How does that prove it friend?"

"His heads been cut off and it's sitting in his lap. Now do you want the location?"

The desk sergeant dropped his half smoked cigar from out of his mouth and shouted for dispatch to get on the line.

"Welcome fans. Are you ready for a football game?" the announcer provoked. The crowd roared to life. The occupants to suite 171 began cheering on their team as they were being announced. Across from them in suite 101 the pair sat emotionless, for now.

"Hey let me see those glasses Eljer, please." I asked, patiently knowing he wasn't watching the team or the players but instead the ladies.

"Oh, all right, here." He handed them hesitantly and hoped I'd be finished with them fast.

"Man this place is packed. Great glasses Michael." I complimented our bishop. He preferred we call him by his name when we were out in a public event like this and I had no trouble accepting his request. "Are these Army issue or Marines?" I joked. "You can really zoom in on people. Isn't that right Eljer?" I only worsened his eagerness to have them back. "I guess we should have brought a pair along?" I asked my question directed at the general.

"We should have, I guess. Maybe if we have a chance to go to the *Superbowl* we'll each have our own." He stirred the thought.

"Thank you again for being the best father figure I could have ever wished for, you will always be my "Dad"." I hugged the man stronger than I had ever hugged another before and with the kind of love a son gives his father for those irreplaceable moments in life. As I pulled back, I saw the tears showing in his face for the gratitude.

"I'd do it all again and never change a thing."

As I handed the binoculars back to Eljer, I reminded him "I would like them for the half time show. I called first dibs, so they are mine." and smiled.

"Alright, Del. You did and you'll get them." He smiled back.

"Duncan, lead the way." The responding officers instructed. "So where do you live out here?" the senior one asked.

"I usually stay in a warehouse or dumpster if they're open and clean. I came down here after hearing some friends found dumped clothes and shoes around this area. I sure didn't expect to find him." as he pointed to the general spot just beyond a small knoll.

"Stay here while we check out the body."

"What about my meal?"

"You'll get that down at the precinct when we take you in for questioning."

"But I already told you guys I had nothing to do with it."

The officer could see he was telling the truth, there was no blood on his hands or on his clothes. Still they'd need to take a statement and double check his story. "I believe you and so will the others if you just stay put. Here,"… he pulled a fresh candy bar that he just bought from the vending machine from his upper pocket and tossed it over "…this should tide you over until we get there." He made the final paces over to the corpse and gasped at the sight. Whoever tossed this body here wasn't expecting it to be found so quickly and was obviously in a hurry. His hope was their carelessness also left valuable clues. He searched over the DB's body and clothing then noticed something peculiar. "Dispatch, come in."

"Go ahead."

"This is Officer Collier. We are on location for the call in on the dead body. We need the Feds down here ASAP, I believe this is one of their guys."

"And how did you come to that conclusion so fast?"

"Whoever did this, well, his ID card is stuffed in his mouth and has a note attached."

"What!?! Who would be so stupid?" the dispatch sergeant stated.

"I don't know but the note says to see an Israeli agent named Saif Kabak at Quantico."

"That marks the end of the first half with the score deadlocked at zero. Neither team has had any success at moving the ball." the TV commentator pointed to the obvious. "This is looking to be an outstanding defensive game as we suspected. At least these guys are enjoying the game." The crew flipped the scene over to the suite that contained a fully dressed *Hogette* dancing.

"There they are!" shouted Doreen to her house guest. "They are really enjoying their time together, aren't they?" her smile enlarged when she saw her husband and Del. "I suppose it's time for you to go?"

"Yes, you have helped us enough. I just hope we can help."

"I'm certain in some way you will. God speed gentlemen." and out the door they went. As she watched them from inside the warmth of her home load into the vehicles, she glanced over at the picture hanging closest to her on the wall. "Hi baby, daddy's at peace."

As soon as Saif heard the news, he knew it was time to spring into action. "Was Brandon able to leave any clues before he left?"

"The only thing we found on his computer was this." the young agent produced a printed copy of paper.

Saif read it's vital contents, dropped it to the floor and ran outside. There he loaded into the waiting transport. "Let's get this thing going!"

"It's half-time Eljer!" reminding him of his prior commitment with the binoculars.

Again he handed them over like a child having his best toy taken away. His head bowed in surrender and away to the Men's room he scurried.

"Was I that rough on him James?"

"No Del, he has always been that way with objects since we've been children. Our father once gave him a rather exceptional train one year for his birthday. In one of his drunkin' rages he smashed it under his feet because Eljer, he claimed, had left it sitting out on the floor. Fact was, I had put it up on the fireplace mantle just to avoid such a disaster. You can speculate how it ended up on the floor."

"Wow, I don't know which was worse, him getting something he wanted and then losing it or me never getting anything I asked for but rather what my father wanted to give me as a replacement offering."

"Such as...?" James questioned.

"One year I really wanted one of the new five-speed chopper styled bicycles that were popular. A friend had gotten one for his birthday, so I was hoping to maybe get one for mine and we could ride around our small town together. Instead, he went to a local farmer's auction that sold private goods every Tuesday. Wednesday that year was my birthday, so when he pulled out from the garage that old rusty heap, my heart sank. There was no banana seat. It was a hard yucky seat. The tires were huge and round yet thin not small and fat like my friends. It was hard for me to get on it so I threw it down on the ground in frustration and said I didn't like it or wanted it. I watched him cry from the window as he picked it up and brushed off the dirt. The only other time I saw him cry was when his mother died."

"Sounds like your father had tried to give you what he was able to give you Del." came from the Bishop. "Your non-acceptance of his gift broke his heart as much as he broke yours."

"Are you suggesting he made an attempt to try and fulfill my wish with what he was able to get?"

"Yes, exactly that way, when you look at it clearly."

"Money wasn't an issue for him though Michael. The next day he went out and bought a brand new car...after taking back the bike to the auction house so it could be sold the next week. I never received a replacement anything. Maybe now you can understand why I don't talk much to my parents. They only see things their way so it's like conversing with a brick wall. I'll talk to the brick wall, it will at least just stand there and listen."

Eljer had been listening outside the room when he returned. He immediately turned back around and headed off.

"You have a lot of penned up aggression I feel towards your folks." James commented.

Realizing he had a valid point, I shook my head. "Yes James, much like Eljer has had. I guess we both need to let it go."

"Del, a great leader you have become. The world has a chance of redemption with you still around." The general acknowledged while grasping my shoulder firmly. "Michael, let's say a prayer for our team, that the second half be better and more revealing."

"Look at those fools praying to their God as though he'd help them. With one shot I could end their pain. Please let me end this now so we can go home." Rafe urged.

"Have patience my son. There would be mass hysteria and we don't want that until the end. That will provide us the cover we'll need. Besides, they are not going anywhere as soon as that door gets locked." Stein's cold eyes never blinked.

"Who is going to do that?"

"Someone they would never suspect." For once his deep hatred and glazing ogle turned to look at Rafe. "Always use every angle you can when devising your best laid plan and the answers will follow." There came a knock at their suite door. "That should be them now." Stein's grin broadened.

"I wonder where that brother of mine went besides the loo? He's probably chasing down some derriere."

"No I wasn't! I went for this, for Del." Eljer, after having heard my story, returned with a brand new pair of binoculars from the vending stand. "Here Del, these are better than that pair and although they can't replace the bike you never got, maybe they will create a new memory, one that will help you to put behind you the pain from the past."

As I stood staring at his generosity, my mind drifted back to that day when my father drove up with his shiny new car. He had attempted to cover his preplanned farce by buying me a used bike rather than give up his desire for the newer item. His own son's want in life meant nothing over his but here was a man who I barely knew that was giving me a gift even I hadn't realized I had asked for. "Thank you Eljer." the subtle tear showing as I brushed it away. "You are like a brother to me also. I hope you and James someday have the chance to reconcile with your father."

"We are counting on it Del and I believe you may have just started us on our way." He looked back at his brother and nodded. James returned the nod as his show of gratitude and agreement.

"Well Del, this has turned out to be a great day so far. Now if we can get our team to play ball a little better, it may just end up being your most memorable ever." Bishop Michael smiled from his own suggestive thought.

Again the knock at the door beckoned. "I believe I'll let you answer that Rafe." He waited. "Son, go answer it, please." still Stein grinned.

As Rafe repositioned his assembled sniper's rifle against the wall and covered it with the team towel, he instinctively knew his father knew more than he was revealing. "As you wish sir." he said with the slightest disgust detected in his voice.

"You'll thank me when the blood recirculates to your legs."

Where else would it go, to my brain? "Hold on I'm coming." As he opened the door, the marvel of the vision that was waiting on the other side sent him to his knees. He hugged and held tight the usher that waited to come in so as not to draw suspicion from his reaction.

"Rafe let me come in please. Hello again Kudra." the usher acknowledged his presence as the door closed while Rafe still clinged like a lost child that had been rejoined to his parents.

"Hello my dear. Are you enjoying the game as much as we are?"

As the usher looked down into Rafe's eyes her reply said it all "Now I am." The woman lowered her head and kissed Rafe's. "I have missed you."

"These glasses are awesome Eljer! I can see right into the other side's boxes as though they were next to us!" Peering over with a thankful smile, he was too busy watching the ladies perform their cheering act. His attempts to imitate their moves made us all laugh with joy. I returned to scanning the other side. "Hey! There's the President's box with all his security aides." I waived over like a giddy child. They apparently had already known who we were from the General's status and possibly Eljer's antics. The next box contained the owner and his guest. Next to them were more dignitaries and "butt kissers" as I put it. The next two boxes were darkened out but I could detect movement in the one. "Can you believe someone isn't in that boxed area?" I directed my question at the general.

"Well think about it Del, this one would possibly be dark too if we hadn't have been fortunate enough to get picked."

"Yeah you're right. Hey wait. I can see someone in the other dark spot next to that one. Someone's hugging? Maybe that's why it's dark over there?" I said smiling at the thought I may have interrupted someone's privacy. "Hey Eljer, maybe you can zoom in on them making out?" I toyed with him.

"Where? Which one are they in?"

"The fifth one to the left of the president's box."

"Oh I see...they are really going at it. Talk about a half time show. Turn the lights on brother so we can see!" he yelled but it only fell on our ears. "Sorry Bishop, been awhile for me. Oh hell who am I kidding when I say that to you, you've never been with a woman."

"There is more than one way to love a woman Eljer, it doesn't always need to be physical. In fact, if you can love another and show it without the need for touch, it can be stronger than any man's attempt to break that bond. True love is not confined to just physical feelings. It goes much deeper than that."

"Well maybe you should go tell them because they are like all physical."

"How long have you been here?" Rafe asked.

"I brought her over just after we discovered Brandon had turned on us. I needed someone reliable to complete his part of the plan. I knew if you found out before today who it was, you'd be next to worthless at fulfilling your task. Don't prove me right now son. Besides that, your wife is watching you, so make her proud."

"Oh I have missed you terribly. How is Avivah? Who is taking care of her? Is she here with you?" Rafe babbled on.

"Calm down my love, she is with your mother and they are safely tucked away. I have missed you also and as soon as we are done here, we can go home." Geva assured her husband. She grasped him by his neck sides and looked deep into his loving gaze. "You must compose yourself and remember the mission and why you're here. Do not let my presence diminish the preparations you have sacrificed so much time away from me for." Her words hit their intended mark and she saw her husband's demeanor return to where it was before she opened the door.

Stein watched without remorse as she carried out her control over the man in her arms. She had turned him into putty with a few simple words. Women could easily do that he noticed early on in his own marriage. They had a God given way of manipulating men's emotions yet man remained in control only because he made the woman submit to his needs. Once women discovered a way to draw away from men's control, then the end would be near, for women would take control of the Earth and make man submit to their desires. "Are you okay now my son? Or has she gotten control over you?" Stein irked his adopted son's ardor.

"No one controls me father except Allah himself. I work to do his bidding." He was offended by his father's remark.

"Good, glad to see you are still in control. Now I'll give you until the beginning of the next quarter to release your penned up aggression next door. But keep the lights off so no one sees you! Geva, come here!" Stein barked out another order.

"Yes?"

"Ease his tensions as a good wife would do. I need him to shoot straight." He winked as he released her hand. He stood to give her a kiss on her cheek and send them on their way.

"Brother, are you still watching them?" James moaned.

"Hel...I mean heck yeah. They are not brother and sister or mother and son. And now she's kissing the old guy. Boy how would you like to be over there?" Eljer tapped my shoulder as I watched the ending of the half time show.

"I thought you liked cheerleaders?" I attempted to change his choice of viewing direction.

"I do but I don't see two of them kissing on the field."

The whole room gave out an "EWE!!!!" from his provocative thought.

"Ok let me see those glasses please Del." the general asked. I handed them to him not quite sure where he was going with it. He began scanning the far side until he found the room. It still remained dark inside with just a small glimmer of light coming from the stadium lighting. He caught the door opening as he focused and for a moment his face turned puzzled. He pulled the glasses away and rubbed his eyes before going back to continue his surveillance. "That's odd." he said softly. "I thought I saw someone in that room that should be out of the states."

"Let me look." my curiosity peaking now. As I focused in on the room, the door to the adjacent room opened allowing the well lite hallway lighting to filter in and illuminate it and the pair of lover's standing in the opening. They had resumed their passion from the other room and anyone looking on could see it was heating up.

"You go buddy boy!" Eljer cheered on the man of the couple.

"Eljer!" I reprimanded. "Watch the game!" yet I was engulfed into the couple locked into my binoculars. Not because of what they were doing, because of whom they seemed to be. While they were lost in their own fiery fervor, someone had unwittingly hit the light switch momentarily. In that instance I saw both faces and recognized each but couldn't understand the full meaning of this vision. As the man reached to turn off the lights, I saw a distinguishing mark on his hand, that's when the lights went out as I passed out with them.

"Adel you must awake. My father needs you."

"Amanda? Why are you here now? Is something wrong? I haven't seen you for so long."

"There's no time to answer all your questions. Do not believe everything you see for deception can misguide. God will only show you what you need to see, you must figure out the rest. Pray for the dove to provide shelter."

"Why does your father need me? To do what?"

"Catch our killers." and she faded away.

"Wow! That was some tumble you took." Michael held my shoulders as the others helped me back to my feet.

"What happened? Ouch! My head is throbbing." as I reached back and felt a rising lump.

"You were mumbling something about an old friend being here at the game and the girl he was with just before you fainted." James filled me in.

I looked at the general and asked "Are they still in that room?"

"Which room Del?"

"The second blacked out one." I answered while trying to regain my footing. "My glasses, where are the binoculars?"

"Here they are but I'm afraid they aren't as good as they were, you broke one lens when you fell." Eljer looked upset.

"Sorry El, I didn't mean to break them. I'll still use them." Trying to refocus with one side onto the room, I could see it was now dark again. "How long was I out?"

"Almost the whole quarter, we called for medical assistance and they are on their way. Just sit down until they arrive." the general requested.

Noticing the movement in the other darkened room I asked "What's the score?" never leaving my strained focal point in the other room.

"We've taken a commanding lead. We are up 21-0." Eljer gloated.

Releasing my attention, I looked over at him as the knock at the door signaled the presumed waiting medical staff. "I'm afraid that won't last long, they'll tie things up."

"Hogwash!" James blurted as he opened the door. "How could you say such a thing?" He stepped back to allow the staff through.

I turned to whisper into Eljer's ear quickly just before the person entered. His dumbfounded look changed when the woman walked in. He appeared flushed like he had seen a ghost.

"Hello gentlemen, who here needs my medical attention?" as she analyzed the rooms occupants. "Oh I see someone."

Eljer had raised his hand sheepishly, volunteering to submit to her astute medical training.

"Okay there Mr. pig person, come with me. Have a seat in this wheelchair."

Eljer whispered back into my ear before leaving with her. As we watched her push him out the door and then stop to close our door, he gave us a thumb up and to me a wink followed by the lip-synced words "We win!"

Chapter 38

"I am so grateful for you bringing Geva here to watch me make both her and you proud father."

His modest look back was just a sampling of his egotistical ways. "She has done well so far. As you can see, one is soon to be out of the way leaving very few for you to finish off. I hope she doesn't show you up?" he provoked more heated waves from Rafe.

"Why do you insist on pushing my hatred higher father?"

"Because I know that's when you are at your very best and your better than very best is what is being summoned upon you now. Do you understand what is at stake here?"

"Yes, I do."

"Do you?" Stein still didn't believe Rafe was grasping the complete picture. He was correct but was soon to be inspiring his follower to new heights and perceptiveness. "Your beloved homeland has been war torn for far too many years and we have the power to end all of that today. A nation's future is literally in your hands right now, no actually your eye and fingertip to be precise. One wrong miss and like dominos, it will all topple." He left his words sink in before continuing. "I have chosen you for your skills but more so for the honor at redemption. The general you see over there through your scope, he ordered the assault the day your mother was killed, so he is responsible for her death."

The fury built in Rafe's face as he picked up the assault rifle to take aim on his unsuspecting prey. When the scope's crosshairs fell perfectly on the general's head, he squeezed the trigger ever so lightly until the hammer fell sounding the metallic click. No shot rang out, this time, but it was a good practice run that would have resulted in a fatal hit. "I will not miss." he spoke while slowly exhaling before taking aim on his next target.

"What did you say to Eljer that chilled his bones?" asked Michael.

Everyone remaining in the room waited to hear the answer. "The lady that came in...she was the same one we saw over in the darkened rooms. He confirmed my suspicion with his reactions."

"But what did my brother say to you before he left with her?"

"He asked if she was the same one from my dream."

"Was she?" Michael asked.

"Yes. She is the unknown person from my dream. She is the deliverer of death."

"What made you come to that determination Del?" Michael questioned.

"In my dream she was flanked by the image of a tall skeletal figure carrying a scythe. That could only depict Death as we have modernized it's symbolism."

Agreeing with my interpretation, Michael asked the hardest question next. "Is it one of us here now that you feel she has singled out?"

"Yes but it couldn't be Eljer."

"And how do you know this?" James scrutinized.

"Because I have already shared with him this dream and he was the only one that knew anything. He too recognized her after my stirring of his memory. He has the upper hand over her and can stop her but he cannot stop death from coming. That has already been preordained. Someone in this room must die in order for the rest of us to complete our mission." A chill of death itself filled the air as all inside our cubicle accepted the fate of our outcome.

"Do you know when it will occur from your dream?" Paul requested.

"Unfortunately the only thing I know is from your daughter's message. When one gun sounds, another will sound."

"Then it seems we have one last quarter to wait, unless they tie things up and we go into sudden death is it?" James pointed out. Suddenly the opposing team had scored twice leaving the deficit down to one touchdown. Just as I had previously predicted, they would soon tie the game and the winds of time would begin to echo their call for a sacrifice.

"So where are you taking me honey?" Eljer tried to disrupt her intentions with his own small talk.

"I am taking you downstairs where we'll see an awaiting physician to check out your vitals. How are you doing?" Geva asked with a frown on her face. She pushed faster hoping to end her commitment to Stein and wanting to rejoin her husband. She had no true concern for her soon to be captured victim. She thought to herself *"Don't let the white nurse's outfit fool you for I am a black widow in waiting."*

"I'm still feeling dizzy and my heart is beginning to ache. Does that mean anything to you?"

Again her thoughts stayed hidden. *Sounds like you need me to end your misery.* "Well that's for the doctor to evaluate." The elevator doors opened to the bottom levels where security officials combed the area for suspicious activity during such a high level event. "Hello officer, I have a patron to go to the medical area. He fell ill while watching the game." Geva notified the first person she saw.

"Well I hope it wasn't from them losing their lead. The Forty-niner's just tied the game I'm afraid to tell you sir."

"Then she better move faster or my heart will give out."

"Ma'am, it's just down that corridor then the second wing past the locker rooms. Good luck fella'." he said as they proceeded.

"Lucky for me it's near the lockers I suppose." Eljer commented.

"And why's that?"

"Maybe I can get an autograph?"

I highly doubt that unless they are going to hell with you. "Let's get you to the doctor first." Geva mumbled as she searched for the prepared syringe in her uniform's pocket.

Eljer sensed and felt the irregular motion of the chair as it moved closer to the entrance door. "Something wrong back there sweety?" but he was already well aware of her planned intentions. She offered no reply just a swift movement towards his neck with the needle. He lunged forward out of the now stopped chair just as it pierced the fleshy feeling skin. She pushed hard on the plunger to send the fluid running on it's way.

"Nothing's wrong now for me but for you it soon will be." She temporarily laughed as he staggered back towards the chair.

"You bitch! What did you inject me with?"

"Just a small potent cocktail that should start working about now." she replied looking at her watch. Only thing though was Eljer wasn't hitting the ground quite the way she thought he should be.

He reached out and grabbed her arm with his hand. His grasp was stronger than it should have been for a man that was just injected with the lethal dose she administered. "Is something wrong honey? Oh, that's right, you missed, BITCH!" He tugged at his false costumed face and pulled it away from his real mug. The stain on his shirt from her injection showed he was truthful in his statement. She in fact had totally missed. The rubberized mask had protected him from her attempt due to a small added feature he included after a conversation with Del one night. Wrapped carefully around his neck were layers of a new compound material whose strength was as remarkable as was the thickness. Although it was paper thin, the composite was impenetrable yet flexible.

Geva looked down at the spent vial and immediately noticed the bent tip. "No! This cannot be!" She reached inside her other pocket for the second syringe. Eljer had not planned for this and jumped to halt her retrievable of the deadly amalgamate. They struggled to suspend the others effort just as the infirmary doors opened.

James' face told more than he let on. "Don't worry, he'll be alright." I tried to console him.

"I hope you're right Del." He looked at his watch like an impatient mother waiting for her child to come home from school or work. "He's been gone for a long time now and we haven't heard anything back."

We all sensed the gloom. The team had spiraled out of controlling the game and precious time remained. "No news is good news, right Del?" Bishop Michael joined me in my efforts to comfort James' worry.

Just then, our phone chimed and James dashed to answer it. "Hello? Eljer?"

"She should have called us by now don't you think father?"

Trying not to show his displeasure with Rafe's accurate comment, he stood. "I believe we may need to go to plan B my son. Prepare to do so while I make a call." He dialed an extension number and waited for the answerer while watching Rafe.

"Hey stop that you two!" the security guard yelled at Eljer and Geva. As he attempted to separate the pair, another man broke through the commotion.

"Drop it Geva!" Saif ordered with the cocking of his gun completing the directive. "I won't hesitate to use it! Now drop it!"

She had no choice but to follow his command. As she loosened her grip on the syringe, Eljer released her hands. It was all she needed to break free from him and grab the guard. She moved like a coiled viper, her quickness caught Saif off guard. Before he had time to drop the hammer and end her rebellion she had the needle positioned against the inexperienced weekend guard's neck. "Now you drop it or he dies!" Her declaration was futile as she knew Saif would not let her leave here but she still needed to try.

"Lady, I'll count to three..." he began as he aimed point blank at her. He never intended to finish as he pulled the trigger. The flash from the barrel of his trusted pistol temporarily blinded the other hall occupants as Geva fell backwards from the blast. The needle never penetrated the would-be victim and he slumped downward against the hallways wall. "Are you okay?" Saif asked.

"Scared as all hell but yes, I'm okay."

"Good, Eljer, call up to let them know we got her."

"I will do that Saif."

After the Secret Service officer answered with his name, Stein began plan B. "Hello, this is Stein. Get the President out of here now! I was just informed there may be a bomb on site."

"Mr. Stein, I thought you were out of the country for the week?" the guard queried.

"I am. Now let's move it or I'll make certain you lose your job." The muffled sound from the receiver let Kudra know they were doing their job.

"We need verification Mr. Stein. Today's call word is?" he waited for the correct answer.

"Today's words are 'Star Wars', now hesitate any longer and I'll have you removed."

"You are correct sir." He ordered the other SS guards "Move the president out now. We have a verified possible situation. Thank you for your help sir. We'll see you when you get back." Again he waited for a response but his time he heard noisy commotion in the background.

One of the remaining guards saw his puzzled look. "Is there something wrong?"

Holding a finger up to halt his query temporarily, he detected more confusion and then the announcer in the background commentating. "Sir, are you watching the game?"

Stein realizing he didn't have the phone completely covered thought quickly. "Yes, I'm watching it on TV. You know how big a fan I am of the Redskins."

"Yes sir we do. I hope that some miracle happens and they still win this one. Goodbye and enjoy the game." He hung up the phone and joined the other members in moving the President to safety.

"That was too close." Stein remarked. "We will need to wait a few minutes before moving." He peered out the crack of the door's opening and watched as the President was shuffled into the elevator for the ride to the waiting limousine downstairs. His well laid plan was beginning to come unraveled. For the first time in months, sweat was rolling down his face and he wasn't the only one that noticed this.

"Who was on the phone James?" Paul asked as James' stunned look searched for an answer.

"I have no clue who it was. They just said help is nearby." The phone rang a second time. James was still closest so he picked it up. "Hello?"

"Oh dear brother, thank god you are okay. We have caught her but I'm afraid I may have bad news. She had a key on her. Check your door."

James walked over to the closed door and discovered it was locked. "It's locked Eljer."

"We are on our way. I'll see you soon brother." and the phone went dead.

"Now who was that?" I asked.

"It was Eljer, he is okay but our door was locked by the woman apparently. He is on his way with her key."

"Why would she have done such a thing?" Michael questioned. Then the announcer proclaimed that the home team was on the move. Like a bolt of lightning it hit him. "It's a trap! We are trapped in here!"

"Quickly set up before they score the winning field goal." Stein ordered Rafe.

As he prepared the sniper rifle again, it dawned on him what his father had just said. "How do you know they'll score and score a winning field goal?"

"Don't question me now. I'll explain everything after we are done here. Now hurry, time is running out."

"The President is secured and on the move." the head SS man signaled over his microphone. "We are going back up to that room to double check something. You two come with me."

"What's wrong?" the younger of the two asked.

"Something that was said by Stein doesn't add up. It provoked my senses and that's not a good thing." They broke out in a gallop back up the stairs.

"Saif take this key and go. You can move faster without me. I'll catch up."

"Good job Eljer. We'll catch them, trust me."

"Trust is not the issue, getting there in time is. Now go!"

Saif tucked the key in his pocket and continued to assail the stairwell like a cheetah bounding and taking three steps at a time.

"Del, check those darkened rooms again. See if you can find anyone in there still."

Grabbing the better pair, I scanned over and focused in on the darkness. "I don't see anything sir." Panning the row of rooms, I noticed another empty but well lite one. "Looks like the President left early. Maybe he is going to congratulate the team in the locker room." Still scanning I heard the stadium erupt with cheers and looked down at the field. With less than a minute left, the kicker was accurate for the go ahead score. "We are back on top!" I rejoiced and was joined by two others. Paul sat back down in his chair to await the final click.

"Hit the lights!" Rafe yelled back as he entered the room. "Damn it, they already scored."

"Don't worry, just set up." Stein calmed his own nerves with a deep breath. Then lay his hand on Rafe's shoulder. "You can do this." he said so convincingly. "Just remember when to shoot. Okay?"

"Yes, I'm fine now." Rafe reassured his master as he lined the cross hairs on his first target. "Just say the word."

Saif was running out of steam as he began the ascent of the last segment of stairs. Trying to hurry he went from three down to two steps but stumbled and cracked his knee on the steel steps. The pain shot throughout his leg but the determination took over as he fought to get back up and on his way. "Stupid fool!" he yelled at himself.

Eljer was still following up the stairs but had a distance to cover. He could hear Saif yell out. "Are you okay?"

Saif had no time to give a long drawn out answer. As he reached the door, he hollered down the echoing stairwell. "I'm okay, keep coming." and through the passageway he went. Seeing an usher nearby, he wobbled over to her. "Show me where box suite 1/1 is fast!"

"And who are you? Secret Service too?" she quibbled.

"I'm C.I.A. now, move it!"

"Get ready Rafe." Stein watched the clock tick off the last few seconds of the game. "Ten, nine, eight,"

Over on the other side of the field we were doing the same thing as our hearts raced. "Seven, six, five,"

"Four, three, two, now." Stein spoke calmly as Rafe squeezed off the first round.

"Two, one..." the blast blew out the window sending shards of glass flying over everyone. Temporarily confused by the shot happening sooner than we had all planned, our own devised scheme was thwarted. Outside the door we could hear a key trying desperately to unlock the confines of our holding cell.

"Look out!" someone yelled as the anticipation of yet more shots to come began.

Rafe found the second target in his cross hairs and squeezed the curved trigger. Just as he began, out of his sight were the releasing of white winged warriors as though sent by God as his angels to fight evil. They crossed in line with his deliverer of death. The projectile ricocheted off one daring messenger of peace to send it just off course enough to pass by the General.

As Stein watched in his own powerful binoculars, he was astonished by the dove's sacrifice. "Reload Rafe quickly!" he ordered.

Rafe was already in the motion as he too had seen the result in his scope. As the next bullet chambered, he saw the door to their room open.

"Hurry men! This way!" Saif yelled through the commotion.

On the other side of the stadium the Secret Service men had received notification that gunshots were being fired from around their location. "We will go room to room." the senior agent ordered. As patrons were rushed out of their suites, they discovered the first darkened room and checked it carefully. Unaware to their own knowledge, they had alerted the room's previous occupants to their intrusion.

"We have company nearby. Make this shot count." *Or it may be your last.* Stein attempted to rectify Rafe's unfortunate luck with encouragement.

As the general and I stood to run for the doorway, a sense of eyes watching fell over me and I hit the deck while trying to pull Paul down with me.

Rafe's aim was unobstructed this time as he fired off his last round.

The general launched forward from the impact almost landing in Saif's outstretched arms. His body lay motionless as Saif returned back behind the door for cover.

"It's a hit! Let's go Rafe." his father slapping him on his back. Pulling open slightly the door, he saw the agents leaving the first room and head for the next in line. "Get ready to move out."

Eljer came crashing through the stairwell door after hearing people speaking of someone turning the place into a firing range. He saw Saif standing outside the suite. "Are they still in there?" he shouted.

Saif nodded.

"We must get them out!" he yelled as Saif tried to halt his advance still not knowing if it was safe to head back into the room. Eljer's adrenaline took over as he pushed Saif aside. Throwing caution to the wind he barreled in and saw the general's body still not moving. The first movement that caught his eye was the bishop heading over to me. Then near the fallen fichus tree he saw his brother. "James, are you okay?" he asked. He got no response and his heart began to tremble. He dropped to his knees and turned his brother over and discovered the gaping wound to his neck. Eljer grabbed anything he could to try to stop the flow of blood from the wound. As tears filled his eyes, he felt a slight moving from his sibling's hand. "James, can you speak?"

His eyes opened to see Eljer holding him in his arms and the tears kissing his cheeks as they fell. Even though the second bullet had ruptured his jugular vein, he still tried to speak. "I'm so very proud of you. Dad would be too."

The younger brother wailed in pain and the sound could be heard throughout the stadium like a ghost echoing for revenge.

"It's time to go son." Kudra led the way and kept watching back for the agents to resurface from the other dark room as the reverberating cry from Eljer caught up to them.

"Mission accomplished." Rafe gloated. Just then he saw a figure appear from one of the stairs.

"Tah'ana!" belted out the big man. "Stop I said!" as he drew his gun.

The yelling prompted the SS agents to join the hall. Upon seeing the gun, the senior member shouted "Drop your weapon!"

Jocheved raised his hands over his head and calmly advised them back "I am MOSSAD and I'm here to apprehend that terrorist." Then he laid down his pistol and stepped back into the doorway.

As the agents reacted and went in Jocheved's direction, Rafe snickered. "You lose again fool."

"My ID is in my back pocket. Please check it quickly."

They searched and produced his credentials. "Why are you not here with someone?"

"Who said I wasn't. Now join me in capturing those two men before they can escape."

"Oh dear lord no." Michael caressed Eljer's shoulder. "I'll try to get him help."

"Don't bother, he's gone." Eljer sobbed uncontrollably now. As he looked upwards to the heavens, he made one request. "Father, come take him home."

I had made my way over to the general with Saif and we turned him over. The exit wound was large from the large caliber bullet yet he lived. His pulse was weak and he was still unresponsive. As the young female usher looked in, Saif yelled at her. "Get help now!"

Down the steep steps the culprits ran. They could hear the multiple footsteps in pursuit behind them. "Good thing we left that rifle behind. I'd hate to be carrying it right now." Rafe commented. "Plus it would be like a beacon."

"Stop your talking. They'll hear us for sure you idiot." Instead of continuing down, they exited near one of the large terminal gates where they flowed into the crowd. Stein dug for the car keys in his pocket.

"Stay here with him Del. I've got work to do." Saif ordered. As he left, the wounded dove landed carelessly on the jagged window sill and keeled over. It's divine duty was complete.

"Hold on Paul. Help is coming." I looked over at Michael who had his head lowered in prayer. As he raised it from completing his request to the lord, his grave look confirmed my worsening fear Paul was not going to make it. "Paul, I know you can hear me, you need to follow the dove to find Amanda and she'll lead you home." His hand, although frail, found the strength to somehow squeeze in response to my instructions. "Don't worry I'll stay here with you, the rest of the way." His grip released slowly as he drifted off again.

As Stein and Rafe speeded up in their gait towards the car, another spectator asked "Can you believe we won that game and then the chaos afterwards? Do you have any idea what happened?"

Rafe answered before his father could. "Some crazed Israeli with a vendetta is what I overheard."

The burly bearded gentleman looked at the pair and began walking in another direction.

Stein was not pleased with his students comment or the fans reaction. "We must hurry before he alerts police to our location."

"Why? What did I say?" Rafe questioned.

"I don't believe it was so much as what you said as it was the smell of gunpowder on you." Like an overabundance of cologne, the burnt smell lingered more than either had realized and to a trained nose it was very detectable. "My guess is he is some sort of cop and is going to search for an on duty one. We may only have a few minutes to disappear from sight."

"How much further is it to the car?"

"It's not how far that worries me. It's getting out of this parking lot that concerns me. We may need to take a different route." Stein updated Rafe to another unplanned flaw in his scheme.

"Officer! Are you guys looking for two suspicious men about six feet tall, one looks like Middle Eastern the other maybe German?" the same patron that spoke with Rafe asked.

Jocheved broke through the barrier of assembled agents and security men. "Yes! Which way were they headed?"

Directing with a pointed finger, he shown the direction he had just come from and the pairs suspected route.

"Thank you, sir. Let's keep moving they are close."

Saif's knee was swollen with pain yet he concentrated on filtering out the affliction and was closing in on the transport that brought him to the stadium. The man seated saw him and asked as he got closer "Are you shot?"

"No but we need to get to the other side as quickly as possible. I believe an extra set of eyes can help in finding our culprits." he yelled as he entered. They were gone in moments after he secured his own seating. Alongside him sat a sniper's rifle equipped with scope and a full clip. He grabbed it, checked the clip then loaded the first round into the chamber. "It's time to go hunting." Saif finished.

"There's the car." Stein pointed to the black Lincoln Continental. "Here, you drive." He said to Rafe as he passed him the keys.

"Which way are we going?"

"The opposite way everyone else is headed. There's a back entrance for all the stadium deliveries. We'll make a run for it." As they started to enter the car, the posse had caught up to their location.

"Halt! Stop now or we'll open fire!"

"Gun it Rafe!" and the car came to life and jumped as he slammed the accelerator to the floor. They shot like a rocket through the few remaining cars on the lot.

"Fire!" Jocheved hollered and the onslaught of slugs began.

As the spent shells dropped to the ground, Stein laughed with his sinister trademark evilness. "The car is bulletproof thanks to your government, you fools!" The Lincoln extended it's distance as the firing halted. As the pair smiled at their accomplishment, a huge black military Suburban blasted into their back quarter panel sending them sideways and into a spin.

As Rafe grappled with the steering wheel, another smash shot from the beast of metal crushed the back driver's side door sealing that side. They tried to retreat from this barrage and raced to gain speed again over the much larger vehicle. "Where should I go?" Rafe begged for an answer.

"To our right, over there is another exit." Stein directed.

"But it's full of cars!"

"Then go through the guard's shanty! We'll fit."

Again Rafe punched the pedal to the floor to gather as much speed as they could. The underpaid parking attendant waved for them to halt but his effort was futile. They were not stopping for anything. He dove at the last second as the fortified battering ram blasted through the tiny thin building sending debris in all directions. Showers of glass and wood pelted off the trailing black menace that was staying in close proximity.

"Which way are they headed now?" Saif requested an update.

"They just plowed through Gate F and are heading for Twenty second street." the informer over the radio broadcasted. "Can you intercept? I have another agent in pursuit in a black Suburban. Also be advised they seem to have armored protection."

"We are heading to close off their exit route now. Can you contact your man and let him know?"

"I can try but I think his radio is down. He is not answering."

"Roger that, we copy. Your voice sounds familiar, do I know you?" Saif inquired.

"I believe you may, Saif, happy hunting."

Saif sat stunned by the comment for a second then grabbed a map. Showing where he proposed to catch the pair, he pointed with his rifle end. "Let's get in front of them here." His words were acknowledged with a head nod and a severe banking turn.

"He is still on our tail father! Try to shoot his tire or something!" Rafe urged as he weaved in and out of traffic at a high speed. Kudra Stein was no marksman but was an accomplished shooter from his own training at the range. He pulled the semi-automatic from his shoulder holster and lowered his window. Repositioning himself for a better angle, he leaned out the open passageway to fire. Just as he was about to intersect with the Suburban's path a blast from above hit the back window shattering it and sending another message.

As Saif reloaded after his disappointing miss, he yelled to the helicopter pilot "Keep it as steady as you can." He aimed carefully again waiting for the right moment for the passenger to emerge.

"Damn! Where did that come from?" Rafe screamed.

"They have eyes in the sky, head for the bridge!" Stein demanded.

"They are circling back around the stadium." Saif told the pilot. "Where could they be headed?"

"It looks to me like they are attempting to get across the bridge. If they do that, they could go any direction they'd choose and possibly lose us."

"Then let's not let that happen. Get in front of them and down on that bridge."

Medical help arrived as the generals pulse slowed more. They began with an IV of fluids to try and replenish what vital blood he had lost already. The second paramedic was joined by one of the in house doctors and together they started addressing the terrible wound. "Please tell me he will be alright." I almost demanded them to perform a miracle.

"We will do what we can, now please give us room to work." the doctor ordered us. The first medic after completing the IV began attaching the electrodes for monitoring Paul's heart rate and other vitals. After relaying their results he waited for further instructions.

"There is barely anything sir, should I prepare an adrenaline shot?" the second medic asked.

"Yes and also the paddles, get them charged up. He's beginning to go into defib."

Michael reached over and put his arm around me as we watched. His way of being fatherly was comforting as we knew there was nothing we could do but watch. Eljer still held his brother in his arms, talking about the old days and things they did together that drove their father nuts. Every so often he'd add in another "I love you brother." The somber moment was broken by the gasp behind us.

Chapter 39

"Paul! No!" cried out Doreen.

I halted her path to him so the medical staff could continue working. "How did you get here so fast?" I had to ask.

"I came because I got worried."

"What could have gotten you worried?"

"A visit from your friend perhaps?" she replied.

"What friend of mine would come to visit you and make you so worried?"

"An old friend?" she provided as her answer.

"Who?" I pondered as I left to head for an outside view to see if I could catch anything happening.

"The chopper has left. Try to stop that damn truck!" Rafe ranted again.

This time without the annoyance of a buzzing bird, he reached out with his pistol as the vehicles changed positions. He took aim on the front tire as they crossed over. In a flash the occupant of the Suburban had pointed his own pistol and fired. It hit Stein's upper shoulder making him release the gun from his hand and sending it crashing to the ground and under the pursuer's wheels. As he fell back into his seat now bloodied, his look of despair signaled to Rafe things had just gone from terrible to seriously bad. They were now entering the beginning section of the bridge. "A little further father and we're clear." He tried to reassure himself more than Stein.

I could see multiple flashing lights headed back around the stadium like a Fourth of July parade in superfast motion. Out in the distance, the silhouette of a black police helicopter began to make it's decent. Everything seemed to be converging on one area. *The binoculars go get the binoculars.* I instinctively told myself. I rushed back to the room. The crew of workers still tried to revive Paul from his present state. In the chaos of the gunfire, all the beautiful flower arrangements had been knocked over, their contents strewn around the floor. I found a still unblemished rose, as I looked around the room, near where the general lay. As I grabbed the glasses with one hand and swung them around my neck, I reached down to retrieve the rose. For a moment I thought I saw Paul's eyes open and a smirk crease his face, and then the paddles hit him with another jolt of juice. "Here Doreen, please take this rose and keep praying. Don't stop praying." I brushed her face with my hand and for a second it returned me to the night I had left Amanda. "Michael, pray with her." And back out the door I ran.

As the black Suburban decreased the distance, Stein knew they were not going to make it. "Rafe we must plan to evacuate from the vehicle."

"We will when we get across. I'll find us another car or truck." Then the terror from above was back and setting it's body directly in his path only a few sections further blocking their exit route. Rafe speeded up more as though his game of chicken could be won.

Saif quickly exited the side door and grabbed the sniper rifle. This time he changed magazines and reloaded with fresh ammo. His skills had blossomed from the vigorous training at CIA headquarters just as his old partners had developed. He lowered the cross-hairs onto the driver's side of the window. A gentle squeeze and the only warning shot was away.

The blast tore through the windshield's armoring and into the seat between the men. "He's shooting armor piercing bullets!" Rafe screamed as he watched through the now spider webbed window, Saif reloading. Intuitively he locked the brakes and spun the car around. From his reaction, the black emblem of death that trailed screeched to a halt and waited for the next move. Both vehicles now faced each other and from the sound, more were on the way. "What should we do?" he asked in a now quiet unbelieving tone. They were trapped.

"Get out and fight like a man!" Stein scolded. "You stopped the car in the middle of this bridge instead of continuing on like you should have; now fight to get us out of here." His words infuriated Rafe as he tried to exit.

"My door's jammed! I can't get out."

Stein opened his and slumped down alongside the car. His cover was good for the moment and the door provided protection from the other direction. "Let's hope he isn't using the same bullets as the one in the chopper. Pop the trunk open." Rafe pushed the button to release the trunk lid. Stein scooted back and reached in to fish for another weapon as he waited for his son.

"Oh no you don't." Saif said as he watched. He fired another round that hit the brace for the trunk splitting it in two. The lid crashed down onto Stein's outstretched hand. The shrill scream could almost be heard all the way back to the stadium. "Ooo...that must have hurt." Saif humored himself.

Stein's throbbing hand slowly retracted from the closed lid as he urged Rafe to join him outside the car. "Hurry son, I need you." He moved back to the door position and looked in to see what was taking him so long.

Rafe wrestled with the seat belt buckle but it had gotten jammed also. He looked over towards the murky pest as it's door opened. A figure evolved from the confines and moved to the rear of the vehicle. Rafe worked feverously to free himself from the webbing.

"Cut the belt!" Stein suggested.

Rafe dug into his pocket for the blade Stein had just given him at Christmas time. It started to do it's job as the hidden figure reappeared from the back.

This time the man carried a large bazooka like weapon. He was close enough for them to hear his voice. "This is for Shoshanna you bastard!"

"Aviv?" Rafe was confused. He had stopped cutting to focus on the person talking. As the man lowered the weapon, he saw his face, again. His blood sent chills up and down his spine and he moved faster to cut free from his captivity. Stein heard his son's word and looked.

The vision of the deadly device the man held and the name of the man was enough to send Kudra Stein into another survival mode. "Good luck son. May Allah bless you in the afterlife." were his parting words as he watched the hull rise on Aviv's shoulder.

Saif watched in amazed disbelief through his scope. "That can't be?" he softly whispered.

"Goodbye, brother!" Aviv yelled out as he unleashed the rocket. Rafe had just cut the final piece as he watched his life coming to an end just as Aviv had to hear his wife's end from the cry of his friend.

Stein barely made it to the side of the bridge as the projectile burst into the Lincoln. The blast sent him flying and downward to the river below.

From the stadium, I could see a huge ball of fire erupt on the bridge. A stiff breeze blew over me at the same moment as to signifying a calming end. "The general!" I ran back to the room.

As metal shards ceased raining down, Aviv ran over to inspect what remained of his demolition. He watched as another tall figure ran closer. As the man got closer, he extended his hand and waited for a long overdue meeting. "Hello my old friend."

Saif said nothing and grabbed Aviv with a huge embrace. His hold was as tight as anyone who has ever welcomed home their brother. "I never wanted to believe you were gone. Somehow I just knew it." They smiled at each other then walked over to the side of the bridge where they saw Stein go soaring from. Looking down and judging the distance, Saif commented "I guess they'll be dragging a body out of there. There's no way he survived that fall or the cold water." They could only look at each other in hopes he was correct in his presumption.

I could hear the flat line tone of the monitor as I got closer to the room. Still running, I slide inside to a halt just inches from where Doreen, Eljer and Michael stood watching. She still held the rose I had given her. "What happened?"

"They lost him Del." Doreen cried. "You promised me he'd be alright."

I turned and looked at the others as they bowed their heads in prayer. "Hit him again!" I shouted at the doctor.

"It won't help him now. He's gone I'm afraid to say."

I reached down and hit the button they had been reloading the paddles with and demanded "Hit him again!!!"

The medic stood to confirm the doctor's prognosis. "Like he said, it won't help him now, he's gone. We're sorry."

Unaccepting of their assessment, I reached out to grab the paddles. "If you won't do it, I will!" My hands knocked loose the grip of the medic and dislodged the instruments sending them downward. As they hit the floor, the paddles landed on their activation buttons sending the discharge outward. The extreme voltage surged into the ponding of water I had been standing in sending the shockwave through my body. Doreen screamed from the sight and dropped her rose. As the last of the discharge raced through my internal organs overloading them with an unnecessary current, my mind caught the rose as both my body and the flower hit the floor at the same time. Everything went black after that.

"Hello? Can you hear me Adel?" a familiar voice asked.

I tried to respond but my mouth couldn't move. I attempted to open my eyes. The light was extremely bright. It reminded me of when I was that kid in the backyard of my parents place. Where was I? The hospital? How were the general and Doreen and all the others? So many questions I couldn't ask. My neck felt numb and my hands and feet tingled. Who was calling me Adel, I hated that name.

"His eyes are opening. I have some pupil dilation. He seems responsive doctor."

So I am in a hospital. Why don't I hear anyone I know?

"Get his wife. She'll want to try to speak with him."

Get my what!? I'm not married you fool! Get me Eljer or Doreen.

After a brief moment, a soothing voice from the past spoke. "Del honey. I'm here for you. Can you feel my hand?" she asked as she held my hand with hers.

What little touch I could feel paled in comparison to hearing Amanda's sweet vocals. Like hearing angels singing in heaven I thought. Now I wanted to open my eyes more to see her beauty. I forced them as far as they could comfortably go and after a few blinding seconds, the vision began to return. There she sat next to me and a smile ensued. *Hi beautiful. Want to go for a second date?*

"My God it's a miracle! He's beginning to respond. Get the big man here now! He is going to want to see his work. You rest easy Adel. We got you back now and we are going to keep you."

As I transferred my focus from Amanda to the other voice, another familiar face uncloaked. *Why is Aviv here? Did I die too? That sort of makes sense because he and Amanda are both here. But why would I be in a hospital and not heaven or some other worse place?*

"He's on his way up here now." a second familiar voice informed everyone. "Has he done anything else?"

"Yes, he just moved his head!" Aviv said cheerfully.

"That is terrific news! He has regained some motion. Have you tested his reflex responses to touch yet?"

"No not yet. Why don't you do that and I'll watch for facial disparity."

"Ok, starting with his left foot, now his right. Anything?" the second voice inquired.

"No, I'm afraid not. Try his hands."

The other doctor walked alongside the bed to my upper area. He glanced down at my still open eyes. "Hello Adel." His breath reeked of garlic. "I am glad to see you are awake."

As he took my hand, I could almost feel him holding Amanda's hand too. He rubbed an object against my hand and I wanted to pull it back but found no strength. He tried the other hand and got the same result.

"Something happened, his face grimaced?" Aviv wasn't sure how to discern the expression.

"He felt something but isn't quite certain what it was. Not yet at least. We will need to let the healing process continue. Time is all he needs now." came a voice I hadn't recognized. As the man leaned over my face, his warming smile and pleasant breath introduced himself. "Hello Del, I'm your doctor." He righted himself and asked "Has anyone told him anything about why he's here or where?"

"No sir we haven't yet."

The good doctor checked my monitors and vitals and found them to be improving. "Then let's update him while he's still somewhat coherent shall we. Del, these two men are my assistants, ah Doctors Kabak and Maciar, or you may recognize them as Saif and Aviv. They have been with you since your accident. About a year and a half ago, you were celebrating your fortieth birthday with some old Army friends. You went skydiving and your parachute didn't open fully. Your neck was broken in the fall and subsequently left you paralyzed from the neck down. You've been in a comatose state since then. That's where I came in. I have been doing research on regenerative stem cell work particularly with military soldiers wounded in battle. Your wife, knowing you had very little chance of living long with your injury, permitted us to try a new technique. It appears we may have found some success. I want to give you a day or two to see where things progress from here, after that, we'll get you off this ventilator and see if you can speak. If this sounds good to you, please blink once for yes and twice for no."

My mind searched frantically for answers. Was someone playing a bad joke? Who are you really, I wanted to ask. *Get these tubes and things out of me!* I blinked once for yes.

"Good, good! Here's your lovely wife Janelle back. We'll give you a moment alone with her and then back to resting. I'll see you in the morning."

Wait! Janelle? Who? As the woman I recalled as Amanda peered deep into my blue eyes, I watched as her hand left Saif's hold. He leaned towards her and whispered into her ear something. She tried to hold the giggle back.

"Hi honey, I have missed you and so has your children." She planted a soft kiss on my forehead.

Hey that's my signature thing. What children? Oh I bet you missed me while I was out. What am I saying, you're Amanda, I think?

"Maybe later I can test the other extremities the doctors didn't." she whispered softly into my ear sending chills and an ache in my groin. "I love you dear, now get some rest." She exited to where the doctors had convened looking back just once before she left.

The only doctor to return was Aviv. "I drew first watch Del. I know this has been a lot to digest. I have a small sedative to help you sleep." As the fluid entered my IV, I could only hope for a fast recovery and faster answers.

The late morning shift found me alone with my unfamiliar self-proclaimed lead doctor. I watched as he checked over the charts. He turned around as though he knew I was surveying things. "Good morning Del. Your overnight progress has been remarkable. Nothing short of what I'd call a miracle. Can you squeeze my finger for me?" He placed his finger in my palm. The sensation was deeper than the night before. I tried as hard as I could to do what he asked. My hand slowly closed around his digit. "Excellent!" he exclaimed making me move some. The monitor signaled the doctor. "Would you like that tube out?" My head acknowledged I would. "Okay, I'm going to spray some liquid into your throat to help numb and lubricate it so the tubes don't agitate you." He pulled the tape away and sprayed, the taste was awful! Slowly he removed the tubing. Finally I could begin breathing again on my own. "Swallow what I sprayed and it'll make your throat less irritable."

"It's awful." I said as best I could.

"I know. My wife use to spray it in my mouth when I snored. It made me stop real fast. Well you can speak still, at least a little."

"Were you serious about what you told me?"

"Everything Del, from the accident until today." He knew I had more to ask. "Now just relax a moment and let me fill in the rest. Do you remember anything of your life before the accident? Like right before it happened?" I nodded yes. "You were having some marital issues and another issue?"

"Marital issues?"

"Not everything in life is as we think it is. One day everything is grand and wonderful and then the next it can all be taken away in a flash." He felt my outer throat area. "It will still hurt for about a day."

"Thank you doctor...?"

"That's right... you still don't know who I am." He went over to the door to look outside, saw no one and locked the door. When he came back he sat down beside me on the bed. "Let's start from your beginning. I know you just had an episode with a very bad man who wanted to do the worst thing anyone could do to a person, he wanted you dead!"

I scooted back in my sheets.

"You have also been visited by a group of fellow workers some of who didn't make it out alive." His words were haunting.

"How...?"

"How do I know? Now you're beginning to open your mind and ask the right kind of questions. Actually I've known you for a very long time. And I know the man who is trying to kill you and why he wants you dead. More importantly you should wonder why I wanted to save you or even how I was able to save you from the clutches of death. A miracle? Yes, but for all the right reasons. You have that power in you too."

"Me? Perform miracles?"

"Do you doubt it? You have always wanted to make a difference."

"But I'm not God or Jesus or even some Saint. How could I possibly perform a miracle?" my throat began to feel amazingly better.

"See that stuff works wonders on healing the throat."

"What was it?"

"Holy water, pure holy water." He laughed. "You were saying?"

"Okay now you really have me curious. How do you know me?"

"I know your mother and father."

"Jon and Bea, how do you know them?"

"Bea yes but not Jon. And I know her because she is your father's chosen one."

"Wait you are confusing me now. What exactly are you trying to say?"

"Jon is not your father."

Stunned by his words, I asked "Then who is?"

"You should ask your mother that, she'll be here later today to see you."

"You talked to her? Ugh, that's not who I really wanted to see today."

"Why not, she is your mother."

"Yes, an overly protective mother. Why did you tell her anything?"

"I didn't tell her."

"Wait a minute you keep stalling on a key question. Who are you?"

"Now you're finally figuring things out and using your mind." With a glimmer in his eye like Santa Claus, he said "My name is…"

To be concluded…

www.ingramcontent.com/pod-product-compliance
Lightning Source LLC
Chambersburg PA
CBHW081550040426
42448CB00016B/3277